Disability and Social Policy in Ireland

Social policy in Ireland

Other titles published by UCD Press:

Contemporary Irish Social Policy
edited by SUZANNE QUIN, PATRICIA KENNEDY
ANNE O'DONNELL AND GABRIEL KIELY

Irish Social Policy in Context
edited by GABRIEL KIELY, ANNE O'DONNELL,
PATRICIA KENNEDY AND SUZANNE QUIN

Disability and
Social Policy
in Ireland

edited by
Suzanne Quin and
Bairbre Redmond

University College Dublin Press
Preas Choláiste Ollscoile
Bhaile Átha Cliath

First published 2003
by University College Dublin Press
Newman House
86 St Stephen's Green
Dublin 2
Ireland

www.ucdpress.ie

ISBN 1 900621 93 2

The views expressed in this book are those of
the authors and are not necessarily those of the
organisations which they represent.

Cataloguing in Publication data
available from the British Library

Typeset in Ireland in Adobe Garamond and Trade Gothic
by Elaine Shiels, Bantry, Co. Cork
Text design by Lyn Davies
Index by Maria Pierce
Printed on acid-free paper in Ireland by Betaprint

Contents

Foreword SYLDA LANGFORD   vii

Contributors to this volume   ix

Abbreviations   xiii

Introduction

SUZANNE QUIN AND BAIRBRE REDMOND   1

1   Disability policy in Ireland

ANNE DOYLE   10

2   Education policy

PATRICK MCDONNELL   28

3   Employment policy

PAULINE CONROY   45

4   Social security and disability

ANNE MCMANUS   57

5   Access and independent living

GRÁINNE MCGETTRICK   68

6   Health services and disability

SUZANNE QUIN   83

7   Gender and disability

PATRICIA NOONAN WALSH   99

8   Ethnicity and disability

MARIA PIERCE   113

9   Ageing and disability

BAIRBRE REDMOND AND JENNIFER D'ARCY   129

10   The mixed economy of welfare and disability

ANNE GOOD   139

11   Poverty and disability: A Northern Ireland perspective

JEREMY HARBISON   155

12   An emerging rights perspective for disabled people in Ireland: an activist's view

DONAL TOOLAN   171

13   Towards free and inclusive societies for people with disabilities

GERARD QUINN WITH ANNA BRUCE   182

Notes   200

References   203

Index   226

Foreword

I am pleased to welcome this book as an important addition to the library of modern Irish social policy textbooks, not least because it is the first to specifically address some of the key policy issues in relation to disability. The book is also a timely contribution to modern Irish social policy textbooks, coming at a point of significant developments for people with disabilities in Irish society and during the European Year of People with Disabilities, 2003.

During the latter half of the twentieth century, a number of factors came together to create a rapid and fundamental transformation of Irish society. What these factors were, and the changes they gave rise to, have been explored in works such as *Contemporary Irish Social Policy* and its companion book *Irish Social Policy in Context.* Specific interest groups emerged during this time and influenced the progression of agendas dealing with issues relating to women, travellers, the unemployed and other social groups. People with disabilities and their families also emerged as a distinct grouping with its own concerns in relation to social goals.

This new awareness amongst people with disabilities and their families and carers was clearly discernible by the early 1980s. Service providers and policy makers also began at this time to recognise the changing agenda and the need to respond to the new demands that they would face as a result. Many of these changes came to fruition in the 1990s and, indeed, are continuing to do so in this first decade of the twenty-first century.

This book examines issues which impact profoundly on people who have a disability. The overview of developments, in relation to disability policy in the chapters, provides an historical map to the successes and challenges to date, as well as indicators as to where future Irish social policy on disability issues may lie. Each of the contributors is actively involved with one or more fields of disability policy and practice and brings a unique perspective to the issues explored. These include marginalisation and inclusion, barriers to inclusion and the changes and challenges that await.

An underlying theme throughout the book is that of socio-economic rights and their value in delivering adequate and equitable public services in response to citizens' needs. Modern public service delivery, particularly with the post-Second World War development internationally towards the welfare state, has been strongly influenced by directive principles based on socio-economic norms. This approach is founded on a needs/resources balance which is essentially discretionary to the state at any given time. Clearly there is a need to engage in debate and empirical examination before we contemplate any move to another model. In the meantime, there is new evidence, both at home and internationally, of an evolution towards public service delivery framed in the principles of equity, transparency and accountability. This approach offers the prospect of a new consensus approach to public service delivery.

The introduction observes that those at the receiving end of disability services during the last twenty years may have seen scant evidence of any marked change in thinking. However, the developments recorded in each of the chapters, supporting inclusion and equal participation of people with disabilities, give some grounds for confidence and optimism for the future.

This book will be particularly useful for students of social policy and social services, for practitioners in a variety of disciplines, for policy makers and for disability interest groups. The editors are to be congratulated for providing us with this timely publication which will no doubt help to advance disability policy issues.

SYLDA LANGFORD
Assistant Secretary,
Department of Justice, Equality and Law Reform,
Ireland

Contributors to this volume

ANNA BRUCE studied at the University of Lund in Sweden and she also has a postgraduate qualification in International Human Rights Law. She is member of the Disability Law and Policy Unit, National University of Ireland, Galway.

PAULINE CONROY is a social policy analyst and director of the research and design company Ralaheen Ltd. She is a guest lecturer in European social policy at University College Dublin. Dr Conroy has conducted research into the costs of disability in Ireland, on the recruitment of people with disabilities into the Irish public service and has worked with the International Labour Office on a Code of Practice for the employment of people with disabilities.

JENNIFER D'ARCY works in Bray Partnership as Education Co-ordinator. She lectures part time with the Department of Social Policy and Social Work and the Equality Studies Centre in University College Dublin. Her main areas of teaching include education policy, social gerontology and ageism.

ANNE DOYLE is a Principal Officer in the Department of Justice, Equality and Law Reform. She had a leading role in the preparation of the Employment Equality Act, 1998, the National Disability Authority Act, 1999, and in the establishment and resourcing of the Equality Authority, ODEI – the Equality Tribunal and the National Disability Authority. She has also been involved in developing and implementing equal opportunities policy at national and EU levels.

ANNE GOOD is Senior Researcher at the Irish National Disability Authority. Prior to joining the National Disability Authority in 2001, she worked as a lecturer in the Departments of Sociology and Social Studies, Trinity College, Dublin, and as Director of the Irish Council for the Status of Women. She was also a founder member and researcher with the Brussels-based Centre for Research on European Women.

JEREMY HARBISON is currently chair of the Northern Ireland Social Care Council and Senior Fellow in the Institute of Governance, Public Policy and Social Research at Queen's University Belfast. He has worked at senior levels in the Northern Ireland Departments of Health and Social Services, Social Development and Environment on policy responsibilities. Previously he had responsibility for the provision of statistics and social research across the civil service of Northern Ireland.

PATRICK MCDONNELL is a Newman Scholar and part-time Lecturer in the Equality Studies Centre at University College Dublin. He also lectures in the Department of Education at UCD and in the Centre for Deaf Studies at Trinity College, Dublin. His research interests include disability relations in Irish society and the linguistics of Irish Sign Language.

GRÁINNE MCGETTRICK is the Equality and Information Officer in Bray Partnership. She has worked in a variety of organisations within the community sector, specifically in the area of physical disability and mental health. In her research capacity she produced the 'Evaluation of the INCARE personal assistance programme' for the Centre for Independent Living. She is also involved in third-level teaching in community development.

ANNE MCMANUS is a Principal Officer in the Department of Social and Family Affairs. Most of her career in the Department has been in the area of policy development, including policy on disability payments, PRSI policy, child income support and tax/welfare integration. She has recently moved from policy development to the implementation of the Strategic Management Initiative in the Department. She previously worked in the Department of Finance and the Department of Health.

MARIA PIERCE is the Research and Teaching Fellow in the Department of Social Policy and Social Work, University College Dublin. She has recently completed research for the Equality Authority on issues of multiple identities for people with disabilities from ethnic minority communities. She has worked in the voluntary sector and has experience as a researcher in the areas of gender equality, lone parents and the delivery of social and information services at local level. Her current research interests are in the area of social gerontology

SUZANNE QUIN is a Senior Lecturer in the Department of Social Policy and Social Work, University College Dublin. She has worked as a social worker in St Vincent's Hospital, the Eastern Health Board and as Head of the Social Work Department in the National Rehabilitation Hospital. She has also lectured in social policy in Trinity College, Dublin, and in the Institute of Public Administration. Her area of research is health policy and the psychosocial effects of long-term conditions on individuals and families.

GERARD QUINN is Professor of Law and Dean of the Faculty of Law at the National University of Ireland, Galway. He served as a full member on the Commission on the Status of People with Disabilities and has worked with the European Commission on its disability policy. He has published extensively on international and comparative disability law and has co-authored a major paper on global trends in disability law to mark the tenth anniversary of the Americans with Disabilities Act. He is a member of the Human Rights Commission of Ireland.

BAIRBRE REDMOND worked as a social worker in the intellectual disability services for over ten years before moving to the Department of Social Policy and Social Work in University College Dublin as a lecturer. She has a long-standing interest in helping to develop better standards of practice between professionals and parents of disabled children. Her most recent research work in this area has been the design and evaluation of a new reflective training model for health and social service professionals. She is a founding member of the Centre for Disability Studies in UCD.

DONAL TOOLAN has worked as a broadcast journalist and advocate on Disability Rights issues for over a decade. He has been the Director of the Forum of People with Disabilities, a rights-based grouping that works strategically to achieve legal, social and cultural recognition for the rights of disabled people in Ireland. A member of the executive of the Irish Council for Civil Liberties, his documentary series *In From the Margins* on RTÉ won him the award of Broadcast Journalist of the Year in 1993.

PATRICIA NOONAN WALSH was appointed NDA Professor of Disability Studies at the National University of Ireland, Dublin in 2002. Her research interests include ageing, inclusive employment and education, and the health and quality of life of people with disabilities. She is co-editor with Tamar Heller of *Health of Women with Intellectual Disabilities* (2002), and is a Fellow of the International Association for the Scientific Study of Intellectual Disability (IASSID).

Abbreviations

ADA	Americans with Disabilities Act
AHEAD	Association for Higher Education Access and Disability
CIL	Centre for Independent Living
CSO	Central Statistics Office
DAM	Disability Awareness Movement
DART	Dublin Area Rapid Transport
DFI	Disability Federation of Ireland
DPI	Disabled Peoples' International
DRC	Disability Rights Commission
EEA	European Economic Area
ECHR	European Convention on Human Rights
ESRI	Economic and Social Research Institute
IASSID	International Association for the Scientific Study of Intellectual Disabilities
ILO	International Labour Organisation
IRC	Irish Refugee Council
LFS	Labour Force Surveys
NCCA	National Council for Curriculum and Assessment
NDA	National Disability Authority
NDP	National Development Plan
NESC	National Economic and Social Council
NESF	National Economic and Social Forum
New TSN	New Targeting Social Need Policy (Northern Ireland)
NGO	Non-government organisation
NRB	National Rehabilitation Board
OECD	Organisation for Economic Co-operation and Development
PAS	Personal Assistance Service
PPF	Programme for Prosperity and Fairness
PPRU	Policy Planning and Research Unit (Northern Ireland)
SCD	Sickle cell disorder
SERC	Special Education Review Committee
SPIRASI	Spiritan Asylum Services Initiative
UNHCR	United Nations High Commissioner for Refugees
WHO	World Health Organisation
WPA	World Programme of Action

Introduction

Suzanne Quin and Bairbre Redmond

The purpose of this book is to provide a text covering all major areas of social policy in relation to disability in contemporary Ireland. In the past decade in particular, major developments have occurred in all of the areas included in this book, which have had direct and/or indirect impact on policies for people with disabilities. These have been accompanied by changing approaches to the creation and implementation of policy informed by the concepts of rights, partnership and integration. Yet until now there was no one text that drew together these developments, analysed their impact on service provision and identified new challenges posed by changes in demography, socio-economic conditions and advances in medical knowledge and technology.

The book is aimed at a number of different groups which have a shared interest in social policy and disability. It will be of interest to students of social policy, being of particular relevance to those undertaking taught postgraduate courses in disability studies, equality studies and special education. It is pertinent to a range of professional training courses for social workers, psychologists, doctors and nurses and the same professional groups employed in the areas of physical disability, intellectual disability and mental health. It has relevance for all agencies engaged in policy creation and implementation in this field including the substantial range of non-government organisations. Given that this area of policy has been considerably influenced by actual and/or potential service users, it will be of interest to a number of people with disabilities and to their families. Finally, it is likely to be appropriate for courses in comparative social policy as well as disability studies courses in other countries.

The contributors to the text reflect the major stakeholders in social policy and disability in Ireland. It incorporates chapters written by academics, researchers, policy makers/implementers and service users. Each chapter addresses a specific area of social policy and forms a complete unit in itself. Taken together, the chapters provide the reader with a readily accessible and wide-ranging overview of social policy and disability in Ireland.

The decision to embark on the publication came from the editors' experiences in teaching courses on social policy and social work in relation to disability at both undergraduate and postgraduate level. The need for a book bringing together the main areas of policy and the principal stakeholders in the area of disability was evident from the lack of a basic text to recommend to students and others interested in the field. Coming from professional backgrounds of working in the fields of intellectual and physical disability, the editors were aware of the lived experiences of people with disability and their families in trying to access services to maximise their participation in society.

This is a timely book in relation to disability in Ireland. The last decades of the twentieth century saw marked changes in thinking about disability and about the role of services in addressing the issues of people with disabilities. At the same time, those at the receiving end of services might have seen scant evidence of such changes in practice. Services for people with disabilities and their families have been characterised by the piecemeal approach of policy development in this field. In the absence of state provision, historically the role of service provider was taken by what are now termed non-government agencies stemming from three categories: religious organisations, secular phil-anthropic organisations and groups of concerned persons such as parents and relatives of people with disabilities. Over time, in some areas the state took over largely or completely while in others it developed a partnership approach in which the service remained delivered by the non-government agency with, in many cases, financial backing by the state sector. The particular contri-bution of non-government organisations in the field of disability in Ireland is documented in chapters 2, 6, 7, 8 and 10.

Marginalisation and inclusion

In spite of service developments in various fields, the position of people with disabilities in Ireland has remained marginalised in many respects. The overview to the Report of the Commission on the Status of People with Disabilities describes those with disability as 'the neglected citizens of Ireland' (Commission on Disability, 1996: 5). The concept of citizenship is an impor-tant one in relation to any group that is marginalised. Marshall (1952) described citizenship as having three essential elements: civil, political and social rights. Oliver (1996), in applying Marshall's categories to the situation of people with disabilities, claimed that while on the surface they may be seen to hold the same rights as others, when examined in more depth this is not so. Absence of basic infrastructure along with inadequate service provision may, in reality, be insurmountable obstacles to the achievement of these rights in practice. It is the area of social rights that Oliver (1996) regards as being particularly vulnerable in this respect. This is because equal participat͟ social living in its broadest sense is dependent on the extent and adequacy of each area of social policy provision to counteract economic, social and attitudinal barriers to full social inclusion.

Of central importance to the concept of rights is the legislative provision underpinning policy provision. Doyle in chapter 1 traces the evolution of public policy and provision from a primarily medical and specialised approach to disability issues to the development of mainstream mechanisms for service delivery, underpinned by equal opportunities legislation. She examines the effects of landmark court judgements on national policy and practice and considers the impact of the EU and of other international influences on national policy formulation.

In recent years, legislative changes have impacted on a number of policy areas relating to disability. In chapter 13, Quinn (with Bruce) argues that human rights should be the basis for any legislation in relation to people with disabilities. The importance of considering both legislation specifically concerning people with disabilities as well as general legislation that is of significance for them in one or more areas of policy is emphasised. The chapter charts the evolution of human rights in the context of disability. The variety of ways in which the United Nations has made a particular contribution to this area is examined in some depth. Specific mention is made of Ireland's role in the ongoing process of creating a UN treaty on the rights of persons with disabilities. Reports from a total of 19 different states on disability issues in relation to the International Covenant on Economic, Social and Cultural Rights are analysed in this chapter which provides an international perspective on disability rights and legislation.

The importance of considering specific as well as general legislation is reflected in a number of the chapters concerned with specialist policy areas. McDonnell, for example, examines in chapter 2 the Education Act (1998), the Employment Equality Act (1998) and the Equal Status Act (2000) in relation to education. Following on from that into the area of employment, Conroy, in chapter 3, examines in some detail the provisions and limitations of the Employment Equality Act (1998). Both Conroy and Harbison (chapter 11) also comment on Article 13 of the Amsterdam Treaty of 1997, which, among other things, will issue a non-discrimination Directive in 2003 that will pressurise employers in Ireland to begin making obligatory workplace modification in order to accommodate workers with disability. However, general EU legislation still lags behind the powerful equality legislation evident in America from the Disability Act of 1990.

The goal of full citizenship for people with disability is undermined by factors such as unemployment and its relationship to poverty and deprivation (Commission on the Status of People with Disability, 1996). A number of authors in the book have suggested that the ability of disabled people to achieve economic participation in society is severely limited by a range of factors, with educational disadvantage identified as a significant early determinant. McDonnell's chapter on education policy reveals that, in spite of a move towards mainstream educational settings, there were over 4,000 pupils with disabilities enrolled in mainstream education in Ireland in 1993 who were not receiving any specialist support beyond that provided by the class teachers, with smaller schools being particularly disadvantaged in this regard. McDonnell also highlights that – in the participation in Irish education policy making and planning – the ethos of 'expertism' still exists where users of the special education are rarely consulted in the policy making process. Exclusionary practices also exist in curriculum development, in the structures of examinations and in education research. McDonnell uses the example of how linguistic deficits have been emphasised in educational policy-making for deaf children without an appreciation of the broader cultural and linguistic perspectives of the deaf community.

Failures in the educational system to adequately respond to the needs of those with disability are also identified by Conroy (chapter 3) as an important factor in the lack of participation by disabled people in the labour market. She notes that almost two thirds of people of working age in Ireland who have a moderate degree of disability did not complete second level education or did not complete any form of vocational training. Conroy argues that such a lack of educational and training opportunities goes some way to explaining the stark figures that, in 1996, 67 per cent of people of working age without a disability participated in the labour market in comparison to only 32.9 per cent of those with a disability. She looks at contemporary employment policies and explores the differences between more established schemes such as the three per cent quota system in civil and public service employment and sheltered employment policies. She also looks at newer employment initiatives for those with disability such as supported employment, rehabilitative employment and the impact of the Employment Equality Act, 1998 on the employment opportunities for disabled workers.

Although Conroy notes that people with disability in Northern Ireland tended to have somewhat higher level of education and training than their counterparts in the south, Harbison (chapter 11), taking a Northern Irish perspective, confirms that those with disability in the North also leave school earlier and with fewer qualifications than their non-disabled peers. However, Harbison argues that educational disadvantage is not the sole reason why unemployment levels remain so high. Both Conroy and Harbison examine international and EU data which indicate that people with disability are less likely to be in employment and, if they do have a job, they are more likely to be under-employed relative to their level of qualification. The employment opportunities for people with disability are also more likely to be in low-paid jobs with poor prospects and their level of pension provision is unlikely to adequately protect them against poverty in their old age.

The Report on the Status of People with Disabilities (1996) acknowledged the clear links between disability and poverty, a connection that is aggravated by high levels of unemployment. Harbison identifies the issue of the additional costs of disability and also discusses the marginalisaton or exclusion from services and community activities experienced by many disabled people owing to lack of transport, access, opportunity, by negative attitudes towards disability and by discrimination in the workplace. Harbison outlines the UK's Sanction Plan and the specific response of the Northern Ireland Executive to tackling social exclusion through the New Targeting Social Need Policy (New TSN). New TSN focuses on improving employment and the employability of people with disability. It also looks at areas of inequality such as housing, health and education and it addresses issues of social exclusion and marginalisation.

In chapter 4, on social security and disability, McManus also looks at specific social security responses to disabled people on low income in the Republic of Ireland. The Commission on the Status of People with Disabilities (1996: 123–31) had noted that at a national level there was no coherent policy of income support for people with disabilities. The Commission's recommendation was for a unified payment scheme called a Disability Pension that would replace the existing complex schemes. They also recommended a variable Costs of Disability Payment scheme. McManus reports that under the Programme for Prosperity and Fairness (2000) a number of working groups were set up, one to 'examine the range of complex issues associated with the benchmarking and indexation of social welfare payments' and another to examine the feasibility of introducing a Cost of Disability Payment. Disappointingly the former group failed to achieve consensus and, at the time of writing, the second group has yet to make a report. McManus also notes that the unified Disability Pension proposed by the Commission has been considered as problematic by the Department of Social and Family Affairs, but that the underlying problems which the pension was designed to address have been recognised and simplification and rationalisation of the existing income support schemes are under way.

Barriers to inclusion

At the most basic level, access to the built and external environment is critical. It is, as stated in the report of the Commission on the Status of People with Disabilities (1996: 153), 'a prerequisite condition necessary to enable their access and participation in any or all of the other aspects of social and civil society'. This echoes an earlier comment by Lonsdale (1990: 148) that 'one of the greatest forms of discrimination which many people with disabilities face is having lack of access to buildings and functions'. McGettrick, in chapter 5, addresses this issue by looking at the concept of barrier-free design in the built environment. Her chapter incorporates an in-depth analysis of a key instrument governing environmental access for people with disabilities in Ireland namely Part M of the Building Regulations 1991 and their subsequent revisions in 1997 and, most recently, in 2000.

Another area of basic provision that impacts profoundly on the lives of people with disabilities is that of transport. Good (chapter 10) draws on Drake's (1999) typology for understanding state welfare policy in the area of disability. Applying this typology to Irish disability policy, she argues that it is piecemeal but aspiring towards a hybrid model. Her chapter offers a comprehensive overview of one policy area, that of transport policy, and demonstrates how deficiencies in access to transport can hamper the effects of policy initiatives for people with disabilities in education, training and employment. 'Without accessible, affordable and appropriate transport', she points out, 'people with disabilities are ipso facto excluded from mainstream economic and social life'.

Attitudinal barriers are also recognised by a number of authors as being significant in limiting progress for those with disability. McDonnell (chapter 2) identifies the psycho-medical model of disability, which locates the problem of disability within the individual and 'defines disability as a form of individual pathology'. Quin, in chapter 6, also highlights the failure of the medical model of disability to take into account the social context in which the disability occurs and the perception of disability as a 'personal tragedy' for individuals and their families. Toolan, taking an activist's perspective in chapter 12, looks at how the development of a rights-based response to disability challenges traditional, 'charity-focused' approaches to people with disabilities. He examines the social, economic and cultural factors that have limited the recognition of the rights of disabled people.

Changes and challenges

Changes in Irish society also have been explored by a number of authors in the book in terms of their implications for policy and for service provision. As we move into the twenty-first century, the profile of those with disability in the country is changing. Redmond and D'Arcy note that, in broad terms, the proportion of older people in the Irish population is increasing but not at the levels of other EU countries. However, they also note that the Irish Intellectual Disability Database and the early data emerging from new National Physical and Sensory Disability Database both point to a significant impending increase in the number of people with a lifelong disability, now in their middle years, who will live into old age. In chapter 7, Walsh refers to this as an age-quake and she highlights specific issues such as the prevalence of Alzheimer's disease amongst people with Down's Syndrome. Redmond and D'Arcy (chapter 9) look at the implications of this 'greying' of the disabled population and of the policy challenges in terms of the housing, health and inclusion that face this important older group in future policy planning. They recommend an appreciation of 'the subtle yet essential difference between older disabled people and those who have become disabled as part of the ageing process' and the development of a range of services that support healthy ageing.

In the same vein, Pierce, in chapter 8 on ethnicity and disability, reflects another change in Irish society. Until very recently, Travellers formed the only substantive ethnic minority group in the population so that policy and services were formulated for what was regarded essentially as a mono-ethnic population. Hence, providing for a more diverse ethnic and cultural population of people with disabilities presents new challenges for service development. Pierce focuses on the difficulty of identifying the specific needs of disabled persons who live within marginalised ethnic groups – the principle of 'recognition and respect for identity'. She highlights the problems of specific groups – migrant workers who have a higher level of disability because of engaging in relatively hazardous occupations; and asylum seekers who have mental health needs resulting from trauma and torture. As Pierce notes, there is a challenge for organisations of and for people with disabilities to become not only aware of diversity within their own organisations but to work towards full inclusion of people with overlapping identities at every decision-making level.

There is an increasing social emphasis on what Martz (2001: 161) describes as the notion of human perfection that is often judged unidimensionally on physicality. Quin, in chapter 6, explores some of the implications of new developments in health care on disability issues. She comments on the problems caused by scientific advancement which suggest that disability might be eliminated or cured by means of technology or avoided through reproductive medicine or genetic engineering. Quin discusses the danger of undue focus on the eradication of disability in that resources might be devoted to its elimination rather than addressing the social barriers to participation in society.

Double jeopardy

An interesting dimension raised in more than one of the chapters is that of simultaneous membership of different marginalised groups. Thus the combination of being a women, an older person, or a member of an ethnic minority (or even all three) as well as having a disability can result in what has been termed double jeopardy, triple oppression or simultaneous disadvantage. Pierce, for example, points out in chapter 8 that ethnic minority people with disabilities 'far from being exempt from racial discrimination, may be even more vulnerable to racial discrimination'. Similarly, women who have disabilities may have to deal with discriminative practices stemming from both gender and disability stereotyping.

The particular experiences of women with disabilities in the field of health care are cited as examples of double jeopardy by both Walsh and Quin in chapters 7 and 6 respectively. Despite making up just over 50 per cent of the total population, women formed another group whose policy issues were traditionally ignored or marginalised. It is only in recent decades that the particular issues for women in society have gained recognition. Women with disabilities have experiences and difficulties, some of which are common to both genders and others that are uniquely about being female. Similarly, some are transnational, while others relate to the particular circumstances of women with disability in Irish society.

While acknowledging the hazards of simultaneous disadvantage, Redmond and D'Arcy also point to some potential positives in the experience of double jeopardy. This relates to the possibility of transferred learning in which effective ways of coping are adapted to meet new challenges. They draw a comparison between people who move into old age after having a disability for all or most of their lives and those who acquire a disability through the process of ageing. The latter, they suggest, 'will have developed life strategies . . . and may well have made plans for their old age that accommodate their disability'.

This leads to a further recurring theme: the importance of not regarding people with disabilities as a single category in policy formulation. Each of the chapters points to both similarities and differences within the population with disabilities that need to be taken into account in policy areas such as education, employment, social security, independent living and health care provision. Some of these differences arise from the variation in type and degree of disability as well as the fact that disability is but one of the many characteristics of a person. Any 'catch all' policy approach will inevitably be both simple and wrong.

While the focus on this book is on Irish social policy in relation to disability, many of the core issues raised such as access to education, employment, health services, social security as well as the public and private built environment transcend national boundaries. Each of the chapters reflects transnational issues and responses along with what is unique or different in the Irish context. Taken together, the chapters provide a wide-ranging review of the many facets of disability and social policy in Ireland early in the first decade of this century. They demonstrate the complexity and inter-relatedness of each of the policy areas included. It is clear from the content that there are many outstanding issues to be addressed. The best way to safeguard the likelihood of simplistic solutions to complex issues is to ensure that all of the stakeholders and, most importantly, people with disabilities themselves, combine in partnership in the planning and delivery of integrated services. The range of contributors to this book reflects this approach.

Chapter 1

Disability policy in Ireland

Anne Doyle

Introduction

This chapter outlines the key developments that have underlain public policy and service provision for people with disabilities over the last 20 years. The key developments described are the information basis for public policy, the mainstreaming of public service provision, equality legislation, disability specific legislation, social and economic rights and the international perspectives influencing these matters. Developments in policy and practice over the range of state sectors are dealt with in some detail in other chapters of the book and are not discussed in detail here.

For the most part, the public policy approach in relation to people with disabilities was static until the 1980s. Before then, disability policy was seen primarily as a matter for the Department of Health and its agencies. Services for people with disabilities, whether medical treatment or care, employment, education or occupational training were catered for, by and large, in that sector. The 1980s saw a gradual realisation that public policy decisions beyond the health sector, and in such diverse areas as transport, information technology and employment, impacted directly on the lives of people with disabilities and their capacity to participate in society. Policy makers and key service providers in the health sector began to recognise that other policy makers and service delivery agents were also central to the successful evolution of disability policy. The approach came to be called mainstreaming and was more fully developed in the 1990s. By the end of that decade, most of the major public bodies had accepted, or were coming to terms with, their policy formulation or service provision role to people with disabilities, thus ending an era of separate service delivery mechanisms for people with disabilities.

The 1990s saw the enactment of broadly based anti-discrimination legislation, which specifically outlawed discrimination against people on grounds of disability. Emerging issues in the new century include programmatic measures to deliver accessible mainstream public services and the question of socio-economic rights, such as rights to housing, health care and employment.

Important contributors to the direction and scope of the disability policy agenda in the period under review have been the many voluntary and umbrella organisations and interest groups that operate in the disability sector. Key influences in the change process include the National Association of Mentally Handicapped in Ireland (founded in 1961); the Irish Wheelchair Association (founded in 1960); Mental Health Ireland (founded in 1966); the Forum of People with Disabilities (founded in 1990); National Parents and Siblings Alliance (founded in 1998) and People with Disabilities in Ireland Ltd (founded in 2000).

Statistical information about people with disabilities

National data on disability
Statistical needs in relation to the prevalence of disability have been poorly served in the 20 years under review. The year 2002 saw three significant developments aimed at addressing existing information gaps: the Census of Population, the Quarterly National Household Survey and a report from the Statistics Board.

Historically, the Census of Population for the years 1841 to 1911 collected information about people with disabilities (in the long-discredited terminology of the time – deaf, dumb, blind, lunatics and idiots). Information on incapacity collected in the 1911 Census of Population is set out in Table 1. No census-based information was collected on the prevalence of incapacity among the general population between 1911 and 2002. The Census of Population (2002) sought information about disability. Data and analysis in relation to these questions are expected to be available in April 2004. The National Disability Authority (NDA) (established in 2000), in conjunction with institutional arrangements for mainstreaming, has identified the option of a post-census study of people with disabilities as an optimal approach, which if adopted in relation to the next Census of Population in 2007, would be in advance of practice internationally. The costs and benefits of such a study have yet to be evaluated.

The Central Statistics Office, in the Quarterly National Household Survey conducted during the second quarter of 2002, sought information about disability. The survey recorded a prevalence rate of disability of ten per

Table 1 **1911 Census figures: information on incapacity (total population: 4,381,951)**

	Lunatics and Idiots	Deaf and Dumb	Dumb not Deaf	Blind
Total	28,437	3,145	865	4,312

Source: Central Statistics Office, Census of Population, 1911

cent among the general public, in response to a range of questions. Table 2 sets out the relationship between age, employment and disability identified in the survey. This information is interesting in view of the link between disability and poverty evidenced in national research (Whyte, 1994; Beresford, 1996). The Central Statistics Office intends to repeat surveys of this nature periodically and to build up longitudinal data.

Table 2. **Persons aged 15 to 64, classified by International Labour Organisation economic status**

	In employment '000	Unemployed '000	Not economically active '000	Total '000	Percentage of persons in employment
Persons with a disability/ longstanding health problem	108.6	7.5	154.8	271	40.1
Age Group					
15–24 years	11.1	1.8	17.7	30.6	36.3
25–34 years	22.4	2.1	15.8	40.3	55.6
35–44 years	24.1	1.3	22.6	48.0	50.2
45–54 years	28.2	1.4	38.1	67.7	41.7
55–64 years	22.8	0.9	60.7	84.4	27.0

Source: Central Statistics Office, Quarterly National Household Survey, 2002

Limitations in the statistical information about people with disabilities in Ireland are linked to the wider question of the need for social statistics generally. The Statistics Board, in co-operation with the Department of the Taoiseach (2003), is working towards proposals relating to the collection of statistical information on each of the nine anti-discrimination grounds contained in the Employment Equality Act, 1998 and Equal Status Act, 2000. The work envisaged has a medium to long-term perspective.

Information maintained by service providers
Since the 1911 Census of Population, the main repositories of information about the numbers of people with disabilities have been disability service providers and the health boards. Information held by these institutions was clinically based and does not appear to have fed into any national database or integrated health service management information system.

Database on intellectual disability

Reliable information about people with intellectual disability is reasonably accessible owing to the high reliance of members of this group on service provision and universally applied diagnostic tools. In the early 1940s, the Hospitals' Commission, a statutory body under the aegis of the then Department of Local Government and Public Health, funded a survey to establish the number of people with intellectual disability in the country. The report, finalised in 1943, showed a high prevalence of intellectual disability (22 persons with intellectual disability per 1,000 of the population) (Robins, 1986: 194). Descriptions in the report of the difficulties encountered by the researchers in collecting their data give an insight into social attitudes of the time and the personal lives of people with intellectual disabilities. More recently, information about the prevalence of intellectual disability was collected by the Medico-Social Research Board in a Census of the Mentally Handicapped in the Republic of Ireland in 1974 and again in 1981. In 1995, a National Intellectual Disability Database was established to ensure that information would be available to the Department of Health and Children, health boards and voluntary agencies to plan and provide services to people with intellectual disabilities and their families. The Database seeks to record information for every person known to have an intellectual disability and assessed as being in receipt of, or in need of, an intellectual disability service. Information on the prevalence of intellectual disability (moderate, severe and profound) by age in each of the years 1974, 1981 and 2000 is set out in Table 3.

Table 3 **Prevalence of intellectual disability**

Age	Moderate			Severe			Profound			Total at all levels		
					Degree of Handicap							
	1974	1981	2000	1974	1981	2000	1974	1981	2000	1974	1981	2000
0–4	189	214	130	143	92	38	99	26	17	431	332	185
5–9	809	955	623	617	330	225	224	99	61	1,650	1,384	909
10–14	752	1,035	838	583	428	280	292	117	63	1,627	1,580	1,181
15–19	698	1,203	1,008	445	508	307	241	154	88	1,384	1,865	1,403
20–34	1,498	2,419	3,027	1,017	1,129	1,212	441	340	413	2,956	3,888	4,652
35–54	1,321	1,559	2,871	626	612	1,455	201	97	409	2,148	2,268	4,735
55 plus	669	715	1,115	307	248	479	84	24	82	1,060	987	1,676
Total	5,936	8,100	9,612	3,738	3,347	3,996	1,582	857	1,133	11,256	12,304	14,741

Source: Health Research Board, 2001

Other databases
The groundwork for a National Physical and Sensory Disability Database is being laid by the Health Research Board. The objective of the database is to record individuals currently receiving disability related services or who will require them within a five-year timeframe. The database is not intended to provide a complete enumeration of the total number of people with a particular type of physical or sensory disability. Nationally, no developments have taken place as regards the putting in place of a mental health database. However, information about treatment levels and bed occupancy has been available for many years in that sector.

Mainstreaming: a policy shift

The policy of mainstreaming service provision for people with disabilities has its origins in the health sector and the views of organisations that represent people with disabilities. The terminology and principles underlying the approach probably owe much to the EU-led gender mainstreaming initiatives. The approach was adopted by Government in 2000, following on from recommendations of the Commission on the Status of People with Disabilities, and is now an established principle of public service provision, across a range of services of direct importance to people with disabilities. The medical and care services provided or funded by the Department of Health and Children remain central to the lives of many people with disabilities and this will, of course, continue to be the case.

Green Paper on Services for Disabled People (1984)
A key document in the mainstreaming process was the Green Paper on Services for Disabled People (1984) published by the Department of Health. The language and aspirations of the Green Paper show a new mindset had emerged. The use of the term 'Disabled People' in the title of the document is noteworthy, instead of 'the disabled' or 'the handicapped', which was common in earlier official reports. The Green Paper spread the net beyond health and personal social services to a whole range of social and economic policy and provision. The need for access to employment, transport and public buildings as well as equality and fuller participation in social and cultural life were among the principal conclusions.

The Green Paper also considered the question of disability specific anti-discrimination and access legislation, but in line with policy development up to that point, and favoured a promotional and consensual approach rather than one of statutory obligation. It also identified the key change agents who would deliver the broad ranging agenda from within the health sector, and principally placed that responsibility with the National Rehabilitation Board (NRB).

The intention was that the NRB would drive the access and equality agenda forward, as well as undertaking a range of rehabilitation specific functions.

In the years that followed, the NRB, and other health sector change agents, had limited success in delivering the challenging brief identified in the Green Paper. The obvious separation between the lead role in driving the necessary change and line responsibility for areas of policy or service delivery was, in hindsight, a significant weakness from the start. For example, one proposal envisaged that the Department of Health 'initiate a thorough review of all aspects of transport for disabled people' (p. 93).

Needs and Abilities: A Policy for the Intellectually Disabled (1991)

The Department of Health published *Needs and Abilities: A Policy for the Intellectually Disabled* (1991) against the background of a rapidly changing approach to service provision for people with intellectual disabilities. It is clear that the Report displayed a preference for mainstream service providers, such as those funded by the Departments of Education, Industry and Commerce, Justice and Labour, taking a greater role in service provision for people with disabilities. The new direction signalled in this Report sought to transfer responsibility for key elements of disability service provision away from the health sector and towards mainstream public service providers. Consciously or otherwise, the entire document was prepared without reference to the role of the NRB, the specialist body under the aegis of the then Department of Health, charged with special responsibility in the area of disability.

Report of the Commission on the Status of People with Disabilities (1996)

The Commission on the Status of People with Disabilities was established on 29 November 1993 under the newly formed Department of Equality and Law Reform. The Commission undertook a fundamental review of the conditions necessary to allow people with a disability to participate, as fully as possible, in economic, social and cultural activities. This review can be regarded as the most comprehensive examination of the needs of people with disabilities undertaken in the history of the State and coincided with the general development, at that time, of the Department's 'equality agenda'. The Report of the Commission made 402 individual recommendations, key elements of which were implemented in the equal status and employment equality enactments and by the policy of mainstreaming service provision for people with disabilities, including the establishment of the National Disability Authority.

Mainstreaming public services

A key vision of the Commission involved expansion of service provision for people with disabilities beyond health and personal social services to encompass also mainstream public services. This vision became part of Government policy through an Action Programme for the Millennium (1997). The

Programme outlined some of the main objectives of the Fianna Fáil/ Progressive Democrat Government (1997–2002) including a commitment 'to ensuring that disability is placed where it belongs, on the agenda of every Government Department and public body' (p. 18). Implementation required a major shift in thinking and a new remit for a whole number of public service organisations. The Report *Building a Future Together* (1998) was the result of the buy-in by these organisations to mainstreaming. The Report was prepared by the Establishment Group for the National Disability Authority and Disability Support Service and presented to the Minister for Justice, Equality and Law Reform. The Report dealt with the principle of mainstreaming services for people with disabilities and made detailed proposals for the reassignment of functions, staff and premises resulting from the dissolution of the NRB. The dissolution signalled the transfer of a lead role for a wide range of disability policy from the health sector to mainstream organisations.

The Report's recommendations included:

- mainstreaming of disability information and support services to the high visibility 'Main Street' offices of the National Social Service Board and Citizens' Information Centres, which would amalgamate with a number of former NRB offices to form a new organisation called Comhairle, under the aegis of the Department of Social and Family Affairs;
- assignment of responsibilities relating to the vocational training and employment of people with disabilities to FÁS and the Department of Enterprise, Trade and Employment. Responsibility for life skills training for people in health service day care programmes was to remain with the Department of Health and Children;
- mainstreaming of the Audiology Service of the NRB into the health boards;
- mainstreaming of the Psychological Service of the NRB into the proposed National Educational Psychological Service (NEPS), under the aegis of the Department of Education and Science; and
- establishment of a National Disability Authority (NDA) under the aegis of the Department of Justice, Equality and Law Reform.

National Disability Authority

The Report of the Commission on the Status of People with Disabilities (1996) recommended the establishment of the NDA. Following the Report of the Establishment Group, the Department of Justice, Equality and Law Reform implemented the recommendation establishing the NDA as an independent statutory agency in June 2000. Its work is a key integrating influence in the new environment of mainstream service provision for people with disabilities. The principal functions of the NDA, as provided for under the National Disability Authority Act, 1999, are:

- to act as a central, national body to assist in the co-ordination and development of disability policy;
- to undertake research and develop statistical information for the planning, delivery and monitoring of disability programmes and services;
- to advise on the development of standards and codes of practice for programmes and services for people with disabilities;
- to monitor the implementation of standards and codes of practice in programmes and services for people with disabilities;
- to liaise with service providers and other bodies to support the development and the implementation of appropriate standards for programmes and services for people with disabilities.

The NDA may report on instances of inadequate or unsatisfactory programmes or service provision to the Minister for Justice, Equality and Law Reform and recommend the review, reduction or withdrawal of State funding for the programme or service in question.

Mainstreaming in practice

Participation for people with disabilities is dependent, in the first instance, on the minimisation of physical and technological barriers to access, for example, barriers of access to the built environment, public transport and information technology. An idea which came late to public policy thinking is that of adapting existing infrastructure, systems and vehicles so that they are more accessible, or, designing new public buildings, transport and information systems so that they are accessible to all, in the first instance. The concept of universal design, or design for all, is now firmly embedded among the guiding principles of public service planning and provision.

Other chapters in this book deal with public policy in relation to specific sectors such as transport, education, employment, social security and access to buildings. The breadth and depth of consideration of these issues illustrate that the policy of mainstreaming service provision has implications potentially for every service provider, whether in the public or private sector. Mainstreaming may also have major transnational dimensions, as is the case with eAccess, which is outlined here as one practical instance of mainstreaming.

eAccess and WAI
The international context of information technology requires the application of international standards of accessibility. As a result, eAccess standards initiatives have been transnational in character, although the task of implementation must also be driven at national level to ensure success.

Tim Berners-Lee, inventor of the world wide web, has stated that 'the power of the Web is in its universality. Access by everyone regardless of disability is an essential aspect'. This aspiration can only be achieved if eAccess becomes a principle of mainstream information technology applications software. The Web Content Accessibility Guidelines 1.0 (1999), published by the Web Accessibility Initiative (WAI) of the World Wide Web Consortium (W3C), have become the de facto internationally recognised standard governing disability access. Use of the Guidelines by service providers, web site designers and others who influence information technology standards is fundamental for access to information technology for people with visual impairments among others. The Guidelines ensure that dedicated aids, such as screen readers, available to present visual information in auditory form, can be effectively utilised to access computer-based knowledge.

European Union Initiatives
The first eEurope Action Plan 2000–2 was adopted by the European Council in 2000. The Plan covers a very wide brief and is concerned with excellence in all aspects of information technology and telecommunications across the European Union. The EU-led mainstream initiative saw eInclusion as an important part of its brief because of concerns that the Information Society should promote social inclusion and not contribute to further marginalisation of disadvantaged groups including people with a disability. In order to progress matters, the eEurope Action Plan established an eAccessibility (or disability access) element to its work. As a result, the WAI Guidelines are being applied by all EU-based public websites in line with the Commission Communication on: 'eEurope 2002 – Accessibility of Public Websites and their Content' (COM (2001) 529 final of 25.09.2001). A network of EU-wide national Centres of Excellence in eDesign for All has been established.

Future work includes the development of eDesign for All standards for accessibility of IT products and European curricula in eDesign for All. A Resolution on eAccessibility for People with Disabilities was adopted by the European Council in December 2002. This Resolution continues the work of highlighting the need for access to technology for people with disabilities. The European Commission has drawn up an eEurope 2005 Action Plan to succeed the eEurope Action Plan 2000–2. Initiatives of the 2005 Action Plan and those already in place under the 2002 Plan will continue to drive implementation to a further level of integration of disability access into the overall IT strategy for Europe.

eAccess in Ireland

An Action Plan for Implementing the Information Society in Ireland (1999) was published by the Department of the Taoiseach. An Interdepartmental Group was established to ensure that public service-wide guidelines and practices would be adopted in the area of eAccessibility. This Group prepared and published Recommended Web Publication Guidelines for Public Sector Organisations (1999), also based on WAI, which include recommendations on eAccessibility and the adoption of principles of Universal Design.

Stemming from the international and national initiatives outlined above, WAI accessibility standards have been adopted by Government Departments and public service bodies as the model for accessible websites. As a result, many Government Departments have made modifications to their websites and all are including compliance with WAI as a condition for new website developments. A national contact centre for eDesign for All is being funded by the Department of Justice, Equality and Law Reform. The NDA published IT Accessibility Guidelines (2002a) as part of a Government commitment to make public services accessible to people with disabilities. The Guidelines deal with disability access to websites, public access terminals, telecoms and applications software.

Equal status legislation

In 1993, the Fianna Fáil/Labour Programme for a Partnership Government (1993–7) committed itself to the preparation of legislation that would 'prohibit discrimination and will cover a wide range of grounds, including . . . handicap' (p. 34). This commitment was endorsed by each subsequent Government, and resulted in the enactment of two statutes, the Employment Equality Act, 1998 and the Equal Status Act, 2000. The acts deal with discrimination on nine distinct grounds, one of which is disability.

The Equal Status Act, 2000 outlaws discrimination in the supply of goods and services, including access to public places, banking and insurance services, entertainment, travel, transport, professional services, education, disposal of premises and provision of accommodation and private registered clubs. A service provider must do all that is reasonable to accommodate the needs of a person with a disability, unless the service provider can show that there is a cost to him or her other than a nominal cost. Positive action measures for people with disabilities are permitted.

The signal importance of equal status legislation for people with disabilities remains to be fully grasped both by service providers and by people with disabilities themselves. Further work in disseminating information about, and increasing awareness of, the protections available and the duties imposed under the legislation is a key element in the equality framework of the current partnership agreement, Sustaining Progress: Social Partnership Agreement 2003–5 (p. 60).

Reasonable accommodation

Reasonable accommodation is a central concept in regard to discrimination against people with disabilities. The Employment Equality Bill, 1996 was found by the Supreme Court, in a judgement on 15 May 1997, to be unconstitutional in light of the way the concept of reasonable accommodation subject to undue hardship was treated in that Bill. The Equal Status Bill, 1997 was the subject of a Supreme Court judgement on 19 June 1997 which stated that 'the President has referred to the Court a Bill which is known to contain provisions in similar terms in all material respects to provisions contained in a Bill referred on an earlier occasion (the Employment Equality Bill) which are now known to be repugnant to the Constitution. In the result, counsel on behalf of the Attorney General properly and unavoidably acknowledged that there were not submissions which they could advance to the Court in support of the constitutionality of . . . provisions of the Bill'.

Following the Supreme Court judgements, the reasonable accommodation provisions of the equal status legislation were reviewed, and revised legislation – the Equal Status Act, 2000 – was enacted. As with the Employment Equality Act, 1998, the concept of 'undue hardship' was replaced with that of 'nominal cost' to the service provider in this case. The 'nominal cost' provision might be seen to have left the equality enactments to some degree 'less equal' in the protections they afford to people with disabilities. However, the limits of case law in this area have yet to be explored.

Case law

The interpretation of 'nominal cost' may be one of relative, rather than absolute cost. The groundwork for such an interpretation was laid by the then Minister for Justice, Equality and Law Reform during passage of the employment equality legislation through the Oireachtas. He explained the provision, as follows, during the Committee Stage of the Bill: 'The term as used in the Bill, may be interpreted in a relative sense. In other words, what may be regarded as nominal by a large enterprise … will not be the same as that regarded as nominal by a small business'. (Seanad Éireann Debates, vol. 154, 26 February 1998). Existing case law such as Equality Officer Decisions, DEC–E/2002/001 and DEC–E/2002/4, both employment equality cases, confirm a level of success in this respect. There is no reason why similar interpretations under the Equal Status Act, 2000 will not occur in the future.

People with disabilities have been slower than some other groups to take cases under the equality enactments. Statistics available from the Equality

Tribunal show the percentage of all employment cases taken on the disability ground has been of the order of 14 per cent and much less in the case of equal status cases, of the order of five per cent. Under both Acts, people with disabilities have not taken as many cases as other groups – about 148 cases in all since the coming into force of the legislation. Table 4 sets out the position in each of the years since enactment of the legislation.

Table 4 **Complaints on disability grounds made to Office of the Director of Equality Investigations (ODEI)**

Year	Employment Equality Total	Employment Equality Disability	%	Equal Status	Equal Status Disability	%
2000	139	10	7	8	0	0
2001	260	26	10	854	18	2
2002	309	44	14	998	50	5

Source: ODEI, 2002

Disability legislation

In 1997, the incoming Government, in its Action Programme for the Millennium, made a range of policy commitments relating to people with disabilities posited on the principle of 'ensuring that people with disabilities have equal opportunities to participate fully in all aspects of society' (p. 6). Later in the same year, as part of the agreement with the Social Partners, Partnership 2000 (1996), the Government stated that a Disabilities Bill would be prepared to 'provide a legislative basis to advance and underpin participation by people with disabilities in society'.

The Disability Bill, 2001, which fell with the 28th Dáil would have given a statutory basis for a programme of investment in infrastructure (primarily public buildings, transport and telecommunications) and service provision over a four to 20 year period to assure high levels of accessibility to public buildings and services. The approach built on the principle of mainstreaming and placing statutory duties on a range of public service providers to deliver on disability accessible infrastructure and services. The legislation conferred no new individual right of civil action and instead, proposed elaboration of the existing monitoring role of the NDA to assure compliance.

The legislation also proposed a statute-based needs assessment of health care and personal social services for people with disabilities. Individual statutory means of redress were proposed in relation to the assessment process and related service provision through a disability specific complaints procedure within the health service analogous to that available in relation to social welfare benefits.

Arrangements for advocacy services, already specified in the Comhairle Act, 2000, were to be significantly extended to provide both support and training for self, peer and group advocacy and a personal advocacy service, mainly for vulnerable disabled adults or their children. Comhairle was also to be the locus for a new sign language interpretation service for deaf or hard of hearing people utilising both sign language interpreters and a new videophone service.

In addition, the Bill specified a statutory framework for the three per cent target for the employment of people with disabilities in the public service, a moratorium on the use for commercial purposes of information from genetic testing, and the establishment of a Centre of Excellence in Universal Design.

The Disability Bill, 2001, proved unacceptable for a variety of reasons to a significant number of organisations that represent people with disabilities. As a consequence, the Government undertook a further consultation process which was completed in February, 2003. The Agreed Programme for Government (2002) gives a commitment to the preparation of an amended Bill which would include provisions for rights of assessment, appeals, provision and enforcement.

Socio-economic rights

The question of rights to services for people with disabilities is an emerging issue. The Report of the Commission on the Status of People with Disabilities (1996) contained a blueprint for disability legislation (Appendix C: Outline Principles of a Disabilities Act). Primarily a proposal to address discrimination against people with disabilities, the blueprint was in large measure incorporated into law as a result of the two equality enactments, which provide a right of redress to ODEI, the Equality Tribunal, in cases where discrimination may have occurred. The Commission also called for rights-based assessment of need and service provision, coupled with grievance and redress provisions.

Since the mid-1990s in Ireland and in other countries, disability interest groups have been pressing for statute-based social, cultural and economic rights. A deal of ambiguity exists about what a rights-based approach might mean in practice. Mary Daly, Queen's University Belfast, in her paper 'Access to Social Rights in Europe' (2002), read at an Institute of European Affairs Seminar, says 'although the term "social rights" is widely used, the means and consti-tuents of a social rights approach to well-being are not immediately obvious'. Practitioners and disability interest groups tend to view rights as a means of ensuring that State resources are available to fully meet each individual's disability-related needs with high quality public services or fully funded private services within a short timeframe. Economists and legal experts, who use the language of rights, vary widely in the way they envisage such a system applying in concrete terms. Consideration of issues such as the 'progressive' application of such rights, the link between rights and resources and the meaning assigned to enforceability, gives rise to models which may not be especially useful in delivering the short-term practical benefits sought by interest groups.

Socio-economic rights, while applicable to citizens in general, are seen as having wider implications for marginalised groups, including people with disabilities. It is noteworthy that examples of Western States which have adopted a statute-based approach to the broad range of socio-economic matters are not in evidence. The Report of the Constitution Review Group (1996) rejected the idea of enshrining some specific personal socio-economic rights in the Constitution and thereby making them justiciable. However, the Report stated that there could be no objection to 'expressing the substance of these objectives as directive principles addressed to Government and Oireachtas but not justiciable in the courts' (p. 236).

The National Economic and Social Council (NESC) has also considered the question of social, economic and cultural rights in Reports No. 105 (1999) and No. 110 (2002) and, while remaining convinced of the validity of core socio-economic rights, concluded that 'in view of the complexities . . . it does not presume that they can always deliver the simplicity that is sometimes supposed to be their main advantage' (p. 109). Among the fundamental issues involved are the close connection between such rights and the appropriate locus of decision making about the distribution of exchequer resources in a democracy. Questions about whether the State might prioritise spending on health or social welfare, roads or schools are generally seen as matters for political consideration and judgement. The consequential issues include the role of elected representatives in setting and re-balancing, from time to time, the scope of such rights, having regard to their duty to formulate public policy; the basis of such rights in public consensus and in taxation policy; and the resolution of conflicts between the competing rights of different socially excluded groups.

The means of enforcing socio-economic rights is also an important question. Indeed, the way rights to services are enshrined in national law, where this occurs in other jurisdictions, varies widely. The practical value of having such a right, in terms of assuring high quality public service provision for individual citizens, is highly dependent on the code of law applicable in the state in question. In Ireland the judiciary have been slow to treat of socio-economic rights as is evidenced by recent case law (e.g. *Sinnott* v *The Minister of Education* and *T.D.* v *The Minister for Education*). The latter judgement considers the consequences 'if courts extend their powers to questions which are essentially political they will soon either fossilise developments on such issues or lose that basis in formal and technical logic and consistency, which is an essential hallmark of legal, though not necessarily of political, discourse'.

It is noteworthy that a number of quasi-judicial administrative structures have developed in recent years, some of which follow an Ombudsman-style model, including the proposed Children's Ombudsman and the Information Commissioner. The ultimate locus of reporting available to these bodies is the Oireachtas, where political decisions about allocation of resources are made and debated, rather than the Courts where legal judgements are given. Such developments may well provide a model for future consideration.

International perspectives

Council of Europe
The Council of Europe, founded in 1949, has a wide brief with a specific focus on human rights. The European Social Charter (revised) (1996) specifically requires all Council members to take measures to guide, educate and train people with disabilities in a mainstream environment, where possible, and to promote their access to employment and to social integration. The Charter and, of course, all Council of Europe human rights instruments, apply equally to all citizens, including people with disabilities.

The Council of Europe admits members to join together in a 'partial agreement' to engage in work to which only some members of the Council wish to subscribe. Co-operation between States in the area of the integration of people with disabilities exists through the Partial Agreement in the Social and Public Health Field, of which Ireland is a participating Council member. Since the mid-1980s, a significant body of detailed and informative publications have issued from this source across a range of interests from sheltered employment (1982), to accessibility of buildings (1993), employment strategies (2000), anti-discrimination (2000), cochlear implants in deaf children (2001) and the impact of new technologies on the lives of people with disabilities (2002). Council of Europe Resolutions and Recommendations have also issued under the Partial Agreement in the areas of rehabilitation (1992), the vocational assessment of people with disabilities (1995), inclusive new technologies (2001) and universal design (2001).

A meeting of Ministers in Paris, in 1991, called under the Partial Agreement, stressed the need for a coherent policy for the integration of people with disabilities. Council of Europe Recommendation No. 92(6) was adopted by the following year. A second meeting of Ministers takes place in Spain in 2003 involving a review of achievements of Council members to date, particularly in relation to the implementation of the Recommendation No. 92(6).

European Union

Following Ireland's accession to the European Economic Community in 1973, Community action, specific to disability, focused on Commission initiatives for funding national integration, training and employment schemes, under the 1st Action Programme (1983–7) and the Helios (1988–96) and Horizon (1995–9) programmes. Commission Initiatives post-2000 have adopted a policy of main-streaming funding. Under the EQUAL Initiative (2001–8), disability funding may now be drawn down for projects which promote new means of combating discrimination in the labour market, through transnational co-operation.

As a result of a European Commission Communication (COM (96) 406 final) of 30 July 1996, 'Communication of the Commission on equality of opportunity for people with disabilities', a High Level Group on Disability was established comprising representatives of the national governments and relevant interests at EU level. The Group is kept advised of new policy developments and acts in an advisory and information giving capacity to the Commission. The year 2003 has been designated European Year of People with Disabilities. The purpose of the year is to focus attention on disability and to raise awareness among the general public about the rights of people with disabilities to equal opportunities and protection against discrimination.

The Treaty of Amsterdam (1997) included, for the first time in EU law, a competence specifically in relation to disability. Article 13 of the Treaty states that: 'the Council, acting unanimously on a proposal from the Commission and after consulting the European Parliament, may take appropriate action to combat discrimination based on . . . disability'. In 2000, the Council adopted a Commission proposal for a Council Directive (2000/78/EC) of 27 November 2000, establishing a general framework for equal treatment in employment and occupation. The Directive applies to persons with disabilities among others.

United Nations

Following the establishment of the UN in 1946, the UN Commission on Human Rights set about negotiating a Universal Declaration of Human Rights. Two other international Covenants followed in 1966, one on economic, social and cultural rights and the other on civil and political rights. These instruments together are known as the International Bill of Rights and their provisions apply to people with disabilities, as well as other persons, although clearly they are not disability specific in their focus.

The UN declared 1981 to be the International Year of the Disabled Person. The Charter for the Year focused on the right of people with disabilities to equal opportunities and full participation in the life of society. The years 1981–92 were designated as the International Decade of Disabled People. In 1982, the UN adopted 'The World Programme of Action concerning Disabled Persons'. The Commission on Human Rights appointed a Special Rapporteur to examine the relationship between the human rights conventions and the rights of people with disabilities. Subsequently, the UN General Assembly adopted Standard Rules on the Equalisation of Opportunities for Persons with Disabilities (1993). The Standard Rules are non-binding, are disability specific and cover a broad range of life activities including accessibility, education, employment, income maintenance and social security, family life and personal integrity, culture, recreation and sports, and religion.

Since 1998, Ireland has tabled a biennial resolution entitled 'Human Rights of Persons with Disabilities' at the UN Commission on Human Rights. In 2000, the Office of the UN High Commissioner for Human Rights, then Mary Robinson, commissioned a study on existing UN human rights instruments and disability issues. The study, 'Human Rights and Disability: The current use and future potential of United Nations human rights instruments in the context of disability' (2002) was financed by a contribution from Ireland and found that while existing human rights mechanisms address the issue of disability, the potential of the instruments was largely untapped. The study articulated the view that a new human rights instrument would allow that potential to be explored and utilised. In 2001, Mexico proposed a resolution for an International Convention to Promote and Protect the Rights and Dignity of Persons with Disabilities. Following adoption of the resolution, the United Nations General Assembly agreed to the establishment of an Ad Hoc Committee to consider proposals for a disability specific convention (Resolution 56/168). The Ad Hoc Committee met in 2002, and work to consider the options for a disability specific UN Convention is now under way.

Summary

Unlike most other marginalised groups, the initial barriers facing people with disabilities may not be ones of prejudice or attitude, although these may be present, but a question of physical access or a need for appropriate supports to access activities and facilities, designed without specific regard for use by people with disabilities. In the last decade, public policy has tried to address the twin issues of equality and universal access through anti-discrimination legislation, with a right of redress, coupled with a mainstream approach to public service delivery.

In many cases, access is both an equality and a mainstreaming issue. For example, the financial cost of making web sites accessible, especially when eAccess is factored in at the design stage, may not be significant. There may, therefore, be scope to regard eAccess as a reasonable accommodation for the purposes of the Equal Status Act, 2000, even in light of the 'nominal cost' to the service provider limitation currently in the legislation.

Disability policy now covers a very broad agenda that is influenced by international developments. The acceptance by Irish social and economic policy makers that equality and universal access principles now guide and shape our environment will become increasingly evident as each new policy and programme is embedded in our system. Further national legislation and policy developments are in train. It is also a new agenda which poses particular challenges for public service providers, not only because of the diversity and nature of the responses required, but also because it may involve sustained infrastructural investment. In addition, it is not always easily understood that the transition to a fully disability-friendly environment requires a medium to long-term timeframe and may also involve engineering and design challenges. These factors are best illustrated where the built environment and transport are concerned, as the following examples show.

On the transport side, mainline rail cars are not, in general, wheelchair accessible and are not easily replaced, in the short term, in view of the high cost and the long life of rolling stock. Some mainline rail cars purchased in the 1960s will fall to be replaced in the first decade of this century. Similarly, railway stations pose significant financial and sometimes engineering challenges in relation to accessibility. Experience in other European countries illustrates that the time frame for implementation of plans for fully accessible mainline trains often takes place over many decades. The Dutch rail system is expected to be fully accessible by 2030, the process having commenced in the early 1990s. Access to rail travel has been actively pursued at EU level, especially in the three years up to 1999, by COST 335, an initiative which sought to build on guidelines drawn up by the European Conference of Ministers of Transport (ECMT).

Although the revised Building Regulations (2000) mark a significant development in building control, the fruits of that development will not occur immediately. It is only as time elapses and more of the national building stock complies with the standard that radical improvements in access to the built environment will become an actuality.

The Building Regulations (2000) do not apply to our streets and parks. Consequently, infrastructure such as public pathways, street parking, street furniture and signage are outside their scope. However, the Barcelona Declaration, adopted at the European Congress on 'The City and the Disabled' held in Barcelona in March 1995, aims to promote better awareness of disabled persons and is especially focused on the role of municipal authorities in determining the shape of the built environment. Local authorities in Ireland are being encouraged to sign up to the principles of the Barcelona Declaration and to implement them through a project supported by the NDA.

Chapter 2

Education policy

Patrick McDonnell

Introduction

In educational discourse 'disability' is often taken to refer to a particular individual intellectual or physical 'condition'. Here, however, I draw on a definition proposed more than 25 years ago by the Union of the Physically Impaired against Segregation (UPIAS) in the UK. UPIAS made a conceptual distinction between 'disability' and 'impairment' and defined disability as a form of discrimination in which a society 'takes little or no account of people who have . . . impairments and thus excludes them from the mainstream of social activities' (UPIAS, 1976: 3–4, cited in Oliver, 1990: 11). In this sense there are no 'categories of disability'. Rather, disability constitutes a form of exclusion not only in relation to the physical environment but also in relation to social structures such as the economy, the legal system, health services and, of course, the educational system. As Barnes (1991: 1) puts it, 'to be a disabled person . . . means to be discriminated against'.

In its report, *A Strategy for Equality*, the Commission on the Status of People with Disabilities (1996: 5) stated that in Ireland 'whether their status is looked at in terms of economics, information, education, mobility or housing, [disabled people] are treated as second-class citizens.' In submissions to the Commission and at consultative meetings throughout the country '[t]he picture that emerged was one of a society which excludes people with disabilities from almost every aspect of economic, social, political and cultural life . . . and . . . that they were being either kept at, or pushed to, the margins of society' (1996: 5). The report of the Commission identified education and training as significant areas where participation by disabled people at all levels 'is significantly below that of the population in general' (Commission on the Status of People with Disbilities, 1996: 171).

Segregation and exclusion have been the most characteristic and persistent features of educational provision for disabled pupils in Ireland since the beginning of the nineteenth century (McDonnell, 1992). As in many other western countries, the first special schools were schools for 'deaf and dumb' and 'blind' children of the poor (Census of Ireland 1851, Part 3: 33–5; Census of Ireland 1871, Report and Tables Relating to the Status of Disease: 32–3, 46–7; Winzer, 1993). These were charitable institutions 'for instructing in morality and religion as well as fitting for some useful occupation, those who would otherwise remain a burden on society' (Stoker, 1863: 458). The Census Commissioners (Census of Ireland 1851, Part 3: 49) also urged that steps should be taken 'towards the education and moral improvement of Idiots and Imbeciles, a subject which at present engages the attention of the philanthropic both on the continent and in England, where several establishments for the purpose have been erected and are supported by the State'. However, until the 1920s, the Stewart Institution for Idiotic and Imbecile Children, established in 1869 (Census of Ireland 1871, Report and Tables Relating to the Status of Disease: 84–5), remained the only educational institution for a relatively large population of children with learning difficulties. The prevailing practice was to send the so-called 'chronic and incurable classes' to a workhouse as destitute individuals or to 'a low-grade custodial asylum' (Finnane, 1981: 71) and after 1922, to county homes and mental hospitals (Commission of Inquiry on Mental Handicap, 1965: 11).

Apart from these nineteenth-century foundations, substantial expansion in special schooling did not occur until the 1950s when voluntary groups such as the Association of Parents and Friends of the Mentally Handicapped began to set up special schools in different parts of the country – an initiative which continued to grow during the 1960s (McGee, 1990). Eventually these voluntary schools were recognised by the Department of Education, effectively confirming segregated special schooling as the appropriate model of provision for pupils with learning difficulties. A somewhat different form of segregated schooling emerged from the late 1970s onwards. Gaps in provision were particularly evident in new and expanding urban areas where the perceived needs were met by establishing special classes attached to mainstream schools rather than through special schools. Most developments since the late 1970s have taken this form (Department of Education, 1993: 49), with the encouragement of the Department of Education (McGee, 1990: 52).

The Special Educational Needs sector

In 1999–2000, there were 121 special schools in Ireland with a total enrolment of 7,228 pupils, ranging in age from 3 to 21+ years and representing about 1.6 per cent of the school-going population at primary level (Department of Education and Science, 2001: 4–5, 10). A further 8,743 pupils, identified as having special needs, are enrolled in special classes in mainstream primary schools (Department of Education and Science, 2001: 4–5). The most recent detailed statistical breakdown of the 'special educational needs' sector is presented in the Special Education Review Committee (SERC) report (Department of Education, 1993) which represents an analysis of the school year 1992–3. Since then the number of pupils in special schools has remained relatively stable, while numbers in special classes have more than doubled (Department of Education and Science, 2001: 4–5, 10; see Tables 1 and 2). The types of provision and the numbers of pupils involved in the 'special educational needs' sector are summarised in Tables 1–3. The terminology in the tables is that used in the SERC report.

Table 1 **Estimated numbers of pupils with special educational needs placed in special schools**

Special Schools	Pupils	Numbers of Pupils
31	with mild mental handicap	3,300
33	with moderate mental handicap	2,000
12	with physical handicaps	570
5	with hearing impairment	550
13	with emotional disturbance	390
5	young offenders}	
5	children at risk}	350
4	children of traveller families	200
3	with specific learning difficulties	200
2	with visual impairment	120
1	with multiple handicaps	45

Source: Report of the Special Education Review Committee (Department of Education, 1993), chapter 2.

The SERC report (1993: 52, 20) estimated that attached to mainstream schools there were 155 special classes at primary and 48 at post-primary level for pupils with 'mild mental handicap', as well as 160 special classes for Traveller pupils. These provisions accounted for the great majority of just over 4,000 pupils with special educational needs enrolled in special classes. Estimated numbers of pupils with special educational needs placed in special classes are summarised in Table 2.

The SERC report (1993: 261) found that approximately 8,000 pupils 'with specific disabilities'—1.57 per cent of the total number of pupils—were enrolled in ordinary classes in mainstream primary school. It also found that 4,453 'pupils with disabilities' were availing themselves of support services, such as those of a remedial, resource, visiting or other specialist teacher (p. 266: Table 23). Thus almost half of the 8,000 pupils 'with specific disabilities' were not receiving any additional or specialist support beyond that which could be

Table 2 **Estimated numbers of pupils with special educational needs placed in special classes**

Special Classes	Pupils	Numbers of Pupils
160	Traveller pupils	1,900
155	with mild mental handicap (primary level)	1,860
48	with mild mental handicap (post-primary level)	600
20[1]	with moderate mental handicap	180
9	with specific speech / language disorders	72
8	with hearing impairment	50
1	with physical impairments	5

Source: Report of the Special Education Review Committee (Department of Education, 1993), chapters 2: 52; 3: 94; 4: 107; 5: 120, 125; 6: 155–6.

1   Includes 11 special classes attached to four special schools for pupils with mild learning impairments, with a total enrolment of 99.

provided by the class teacher or otherwise from within the resources of the school. While the report estimated that about 77 per cent of primary school pupils were enrolled in schools having a remedial service (pp. 51–2), smaller schools were particularly disadvantaged. Almost half of the pupils who did not have any additional support were enrolled in schools with less than 100 pupils (p. 267). Where learning support for pupils with special needs was available in ordinary classes in primary schools it was provided by the class-teacher or by remedial, visiting or other specialist teachers (Lynch, 1995: 64–5).

The SERC report estimates for pupils 'with specific disabilities' placed in mainstream classes are summarised in Table 3.

In addition to deficiencies in provision for disabled pupils at second and third levels (Department of Education, 1993: 58–66, 128–31), the SERC report also noted that 17 teachers had been appointed to a pilot scheme involving only 207 out of an estimated 2,000 pupils 'with severe or profound mental handicap'. It expressed concern 'that the pilot status of the scheme still continues, even after seven full years of implementation' (Department of Education, 1993: 130). In a survey conducted in 1995, the Irish National Teachers Organisation found that the scheme had been expanded to a total of 37 teachers distributed over 33 special classes – 16 located in schools for pupils 'with moderate mental handicap', 12 in day care centres and five in residential centres (INTO, 1996: 73–5).

Table 3 **Estimated numbers of pupils with special
educational needs placed in mainstream classes**

Pupils	Number of Pupils	% of Total
with behavioural problems	2,091	0.41
with specific learning disability	1,744	0.34
with specific speech and language disorder	1,087	0.21
with borderline mental handicap	1,012	0.20
emotional disturbance	989	0.19
physical disability	842	0.16
mild mental handicap	699	0.14
hearing impairment	527	0.10
visual impairment	301	0.06
moderate mental handicap	101	0.02
other	264	0.05
Total Number of Pupils	7,999[1]	1.57

Source: Report of the Special Education Review Committee (Department of Education, 1993), Appendix II, Table 17).

1   Some pupils were reported 'as having more than one disability' which gives a total number of disabilities larger than the total number of pupils.

The European context

Before moving on to discuss current educational policy in relation to disability in Ireland it may be useful to describe briefly the general context in which the education of disabled pupils has developed in western Europe. A detailed cross-national analysis is not possible within the limits of this chapter. However, recent comparative studies are available in Mittler, Brouillette and Harris (1993), Meijer, Pijl and Hegarty (1994), O'Hanlon (1995), Booth and Ainscow (1998), Ballard (1999), Daniels and Garner (1999), Armstrong, Armstrong and Barton (2000). Over the past decade, international studies carried out by the Organisation for European Co-operation and Development (1994, 1995, 1997a, 1997b, 1999, and 2000) have also tracked in some detail educational developments with regard to disability. The distinctive political, economic and social circumstances associated with the emergence of national systems of education create major difficulties for making cross-national comparisons between them. Attempts to compare policies and practices in special education are even more problematic: special education encompasses different pupil populations in different countries; the scope and pace of administrative intervention and institutional development varies considerably. Even within countries substantial regional differences can occur. Among the countries of the OECD, in terms of disability 'the educational experiences of similar students would be vastly different in different countries' (OECD, 2000: 73). The picture is further complicated by the presence of three broad levels in the educational system itself. With regard to disability, most policy development as well as initiatives in practice have focused on primary education. The prevailing pattern is that opportunities for disabled pupils to receive education in integrated settings become much more limited or are non-existent after primary level (Department of Education, 1993, section 2.3.2. See also Buzzi, 1995; Randoll, 1995; Tetler, 1995; OECD, 1997b and Armstrong, Belmont and Verillon, 2000, for some cross-national perspectives.) Thus, issues of policy and practice at second and third levels are only now beginning to be addressed (Hurst, 1998: 1).

For general comparative purposes in a Western European context, three broad phases of policy making can be identified. The first phase, based on a model of segregated provision, lasted from the end of the eighteenth century until well into the post-Second World War period. During this period special schooling constituted one element in a more general process involving the regulation and institutionalisation of 'anomalous' populations in society, especially populations of the poor (see, for example, Foucault, 2002; Scull, 1993). The second phase was associated with new orientations in general social policy, especially in movements towards de-institutionalisation and 'normalisation', typically associated with developments in the social services in Scandinavia (Reinach, 1987) and with the work of Wolfensberger (1972). In special education these movements were articulated in what came to be known as integration or mainstreaming and lasted roughly from the 1960s until the early 1990s (Rispens, 1994). The most recent phase, inclusive education, has developed out of a critique of policies and practices in integration. It has been increasingly reflected in the political struggles of disabled people to contest the representation of disability in terms of an individual 'condition' and of responses to disability in terms of 'care' and 'need', and to base this challenge on demands for human rights, social justice and equality in an inclusive society (Dyson and Millward, 1997; Armstrong, Armstrong and Barton, 2000; McDonnell, 2000; Riddell, 2000).

In spite of a considerable volume of educational legislation designed to reduce exclusion, reports from many European countries indicate that segregated schooling still retains a strong presence in their educational systems. In The Netherlands, for example, between 1972 and 1997 the proportion of primary-age pupils in segregated special schooling rose from 2.2 to 4.3 per cent (Pijl and Meijer, 1999: 82). In England, Swann (1985: 3; 1991: 1, cited in Lunt and Evans, 1994: 44) observed that while increasing numbers of disabled pupils were attending mainstream schools there was a contrary movement towards segregated provision for pupils perceived to be 'maladjusted' or to have 'specific learning difficulties'. A similar trend has occurred in Ireland where the most recent special schools are for 'children having specific reading difficulties' and 'specific language impairment' (McGee, 1990: 57–8). The existence of a highly developed system of separate special schools, as in Germany, can itself create a kind of institutional inertia (Daunt, 1993: 91; OECD, 1999: 156–7) and slow down movement towards inclusion.

There is also evidence from several countries suggesting that exclusionary practices have re-emerged, in spite of legislation designed to promote more integrated systems. In Spain, for example, educational legislation has been largely aspirational and has not incorporated mechanisms to ensure that practices followed on from policies (Parrilla, 1999: 109–10). The abolition of older forms of segregation does not necessarily mean that segregation disappears completely. Legislation in Italy in the 1970s, for example, led to the closure of all special schools but disabled pupils who were subsequently enrolled in mainstream schools were not necessarily integrated into mainstream classes within those schools (Buzzi, 1995). Resistance from mainstream schools and teachers in Greece (Vlachou-Balafouti and Zoniou-Sideris, 2000: 37–9), the lack of adequate resources and support services in Ireland (Finlay *et al.*, 1994) and the tendency to regard integration as a form of sponsored mobility for some disabled pupils in France (Armstrong, Belmont and Verillon, 2000: 70–1), are all factors which continue to bolster exclusion in these and in other European countries. More recently, too, the impact of market ideologies has created a more favourable environment for segregation even in countries such as Sweden and Denmark with relatively well established integration policies and where special education has been regarded as a function of mainstream schooling (OECD, 1999; Persson, 2000). On the other hand, pressures of the market place seem to have had little effect so far on the strongly pro-integration policies and practices of the Norwegian system (Mordal and Strømstad, 1998: 117).

Perhaps the most prominent feature of educational policy and practice in relation to disability in the EU and Western Europe generally is its national and regional diversity. In spite of this diversity, however, we can identify a number of shared cross-national features (O'Hanlon, 1995; Booth and Ainscow, 1999; Daniels and Gartner, 1999; Armstrong, Armstrong and Barton, 2000). One common policy feature has been the attempt to legislate for greater degrees of educational integration. Following on from this there has been a widespread perception that considerable gaps persist between the aspirations contained in the legislation and the practical implementation of integration policies. Gaps between policy and practice imply a capacity in mainstream schools and their teachers to resist change or to welcome 'some students, previously excluded . . . in through the front door while others are ushered out at the back' (Booth and Ainscow, 1998: 3). There has also been general agreement that inclusive policies cannot be implemented without adequate resources and support services. Another widespread perception is that inclusive education represents an option in the 'special needs' continuum rather than a fundamental renegotiation of the relationship between special and mainstream sectors. This view is most starkly articulated in the report of the Special Education Review Committee (Department of Education, 1993: 22) which advocated 'as much integration as is appropriate and . . . as little segregation as is necessary'.

These perceptions raise the most fundamental questions for policy making. How is disability conceptualised? How are 'special needs' interpreted? What criteria are used to determine pupil placement? Who decides on these criteria? If there is a conflict of interests, whose interest will prevail? Where does the main effort and responsibility for change fall – on the 'integrated' pupil, on the mainstream class, or on the mainstream teacher? In the event of a breach of the legislation, can sanctions be invoked? Whose 'rights' will be protected? Are there strategies for identifying and dealing with resistance? What is the role of disabled people in policy making and planning? In attempting to respond to these questions it is necessary to look at theories and assumptions that underlying current policy making and practice in the educational system, especially those pertaining to disability (Skrtic, 1995: 80).

Deep structures in educational systems

In analysing the relationship between educational policy and disability we can think of educational systems as working at two different structural levels – a deep structure of theories, concepts, assumptions and beliefs, and a surface structure of day to day practices in the organisation and operation of schools (Drudy and Lynch, 1993; Skrtic, 1995; McDonnell, 2000, 2001). Inevitably, surface structures receive the most attention with regard to debate, research and policy making since they reflect the more visible features of schooling – the content of the curriculum, the allocation of pupils to particular programmes, the methodologies of teaching, the distribution of resources, and so on. Surface structures, however, are related to, and shaped by conceptual frameworks that are often taken for granted and subject to far less scrutiny (Drudy and Lynch, 1993: ch. 3).

In Ireland, the past decade has been a particularly active period for the production of documents with policy implications for disability and education. Since 1992 five major reports relevant to our discussion have appeared, four dealing with education and one with disability: *Education for a Changing World*, a Green Paper on Education (Department of Education, 1992); Report of the Special Education Review Committee (Department of Education, 1993); Report on the National Education Convention (Coolahan, 1994); *Charting Our Education Future*, a White Paper on Education (Department of Education, 1995); *A Strategy for Equality* (Report of the Commission on the Status of People with Disabilities, 1996). These policy-making efforts preceded an Education Act (Government of Ireland, 1998). Several further discussion papers and reports dealing with 'special educational needs' have followed on from these initiatives. These included a discussion paper on the curriculum at second level (National Council for Curriculum and Assessment, 1999) and a discussion paper and report on arrangements for the assessment of students 'with special needs' in public examinations (Department of Education and Science, 1999, 2000). Even a brief analysis of these documents will help to identify the major underlying conceptual frameworks or 'deep structures' which inform policy making and indicate the principal mediators and gate-keepers in policy implementation.

Participation and exclusion in policy making

A good example of how deep structures inform surface practices can be seen in the workings of the Special Education Review Committee, established in August 1991. The report prepared by the committee (1993) was the first in the history of the Irish state to deal specifically with special education and as such it constituted an important review of past practice and provision as well as being a signpost towards policy development and planning for the future. The production of this report involved assumptions which in the context of special needs were taken to be unexceptional, but which in the context of other aspects of the educational system, such as gender for example, would have been considered untenable.

At an early stage in its deliberations, membership of the review committee was increased from 15 to 23 to make it representative of a wider range of interests in the educational system (Department of Education, 1993: 17). By and large, membership represented administration, management and teachers – those interests responsible for organising and delivering special and mainstream educational services. However, those who were receiving or had received special education in the past were not directly represented at all. It is hard to think of any other circumstances in the last decade of the twentieth century in which an officially appointed body, engaged in the examination of a public service, would completely exclude representatives of groups who actually received the service. The exclusion of people who actually experienced special education was not regarded as remarkable, even though membership of the committee was increased when it was felt that a more representative body was necessary.

The composition of the committee reveals the existence of a set of deeply embedded assumptions and beliefs about special education and the individuals who are placed in special educational settings. It assumed an identity of interests between the pupils and the professionals who plan, administer and operate special educational provision. It conceded to professionals an exclusive right to define problems and formulate solutions. Clearly it was assumed that the knowledge and experience of pupils and past pupils of the special education sector had little to add to the knowledge and experience of teaching, managerial and administrative professionals. The work of the committee was grounded in the belief that the experts in the field could speak with sole authority on what was in 'the best interests' of disabled pupils and without the need for any 'insider' perspective.

Exclusionary practices are also prevalent in educational research and commentary. Disability occupies a very marginal place in general studies of the Irish educational system. Major texts on policy (O'Buachalla, 1988; Mulcahy and O'Sullivan, 1989) rarely, if ever, refer to special education or disability as issues for discussion. A major review of work in the sociology of education (Drudy, 1991) shows that disability has not been an issue for research either. When disability is mentioned in educational discourse it is usually confined to a context of levels of provision, welfare advances or enlightened reform (Coolahan, 1981, 1989). Disability is absent even in studies which focus on equality and disadvantage as issues in education (Greaney and Kellaghan, 1984; Clancy, 1990; Kellaghan *et al.*, 1995; Conference of Religious of Ireland, 1998).

These patterns of participation and exclusion are inextricably linked firstly, with a particular psycho-medical model of disability and secondly, with a discourse of professional 'expertism' that underwrites this model. For almost two decades disability researchers have argued that the marginalisation and exclusion experienced by disabled people are products of a 'deficit' conceptual framework based mainly on individualised psychological and medical definitions of disability (Borsay, 1986; Abberley, 1987; Oliver, 1990; Barnes, 1991; Morris, 1991). In education, a psycho-medical model of disability locates the 'problem' within the pupil and defines disability as a form of individual pathology. In this process the socio-political relationships between pupils and their educational environments are obscured (Swain *et al.*, 1993; Phtiaka, 1997; Vlachou, 1997; Persson, 1998; Allan, 1999; McDonnell, 2000) and the search for solutions focuses on individual 'deficits', rather than on inequitable social structures (Drudy and Lynch, 1993: 59).

A psycho-medical model of disability is grounded in a discourse of professional expertise. Rose (1996: 86) defines professional expertise as 'a particular kind of social *authority*, characteristically deployed around *problems*, exercising a certain *diagnostic* gaze, grounded in a claim to *truth*, asserting technical *efficiency,* and avowing *humane* ethical virtues' (italics in original). In such a discourse of expertise, professionals claim that only they can legitimately interpret the true nature of the 'problem' or 'need', that only they can speak with authority about what is in the individual's best interests, and that they carry out these responsibilities in a context of care. It is these claims to truth, authority and care that give 'expert' practices their paternalistic character and justify the exclusion of disabled people from policy making.

Disability and policy in education

A conspicuous example of the dangers of paternalist assumptions appeared in the SERC report in its discussion of deafness and deaf students. The report noted:

> Research has shown that severe deafness can disrupt almost every aspect of normal socio-psychological development . . . All pupils with more than a mild hearing loss will experience a significant degree of difficulty in the development of language and speech (Department of Education, 1993: 106).

No sources were given to substantiate these claims about psychological and linguistic development in relation to deaf pupils. Language was equated with spoken language and no reference was made to at least thirty years of research on deaf communities and sign languages, information which would constitute an essential point of departure for the development of educational programmes for deaf pupils. No reference was made to a deaf community perspective which regarded deafness is a matter of culture and language rather than a matter for medicine and audiology, or to the possibility that low levels of school achievement among 'normally' intelligent deaf pupils might have more to do with the lack of linguistic access to an appropriate curriculum and pedagogy than to a personal deficit (Dant and Gregory, 1991; Lane, 1993; McDonnell, 1993, 1997). No indication was given that deafness implied anything other than a sensory deficit.

It is this definition of disability as a personal 'condition' that has been enshrined in recent Irish legislation – in the Education Act (1998a), the Employment Equality Act (1998b), and the Equal Status Act (2000b). According to the Education Act disability means:

(a) the total or partial loss of a person's bodily or mental functions, including the loss of a part of the person's body, or
(b) the presence in the body of organisms causing, or likely to cause, chronic disease or illness, or

(c)   the malfunction, malformation or disfigurement of a part of a person's body, or

(d)   a condition or malfunction which results in a person learning differently from a person without the condition or malfunction, or

(e)   a condition, illness or disease which affects a person's thought processes, perception of reality, emotions or judgement or which results in disturbed behaviour

(Department of Education and Science, 1998, section 2).

This psycho-medical model of disability, combined with a discourse of expertism, has dominated recent policy making and planning in education in Ireland. Proposals to change examination arrangements for 'candidates with special needs' constitute a case in point (McDonnell, forthcoming). In 1999, an expert advisory group published a discussion paper which was followed by a report on the issue a year later. In its discussion paper, the expert group acknowledged that for certain students the Leaving Certificate Examination (which marks the end of second level schooling in Ireland)

> does not adequately represent the achievements that it purports to measure. This arises partly from the fact that the scope of the present examination is fairly limited. Although there is provision for other kinds of assessment (e.g., oral and practical competencies), the examination relies heavily on performance on written papers which are administered under controlled conditions in a limited time frame at the end of students' secondary school careers. Furthermore unlike the experience in other countries the Examination does not involve any element of continuous assessment by a student's own teachers. Assessment either in written, oral or aural format is by external examiners . . . Some candidates experience difficulty, or may even find it impossible, to communicate what they know in this situation.' (Department of Education and Science, 1999: 1)

It is clear then, that the format of the examination presents barriers to some students, and from this perspective the disability stems from a particular organisational format that excludes certain students. In spite of this, the expert group defines disability as an 'individual human condition' (Department of Education and Science, 1999: 1) and thus reduces the problems that disabled people face 'to their own personal inadequacies or functional limitations' (Oliver, 1990: 7). At no point in its deliberations did the expert group display an awareness of disability as a contested concept; it merely assumed that there is a consensus about how it should be understood. This conceptual position then shapes the discussion that follows, setting out the key principles and issues, defining the problems and determining how these are to be addressed.

The expert gaze falls with far more intensity on pupils than on the structure and format of the examinations.

A similar approach has shaped developments 'regarding curriculum and syllabuses for students with a disability or other special educational needs' (National Council for Curriculum and Assessment, 1999: v). Under the terms of the Education Act, the National Council for Curriculum and Assessment (NCCA) was charged with advising the Minister for Education and Science in this regard and, as part of its brief, declared that it was 'anxious to meet this challenge in consultation and co-operation with the widest possible range of interests' (NCCA, 1999: v). The earlier White Paper on Education (Department of Education, 1995) had set out a number of guiding principles that were to inform policy-making in education, among them 'pluralism', 'partnership', and 'accountability'. The NCCA's discussion paper, *Special Educational Needs: Curriculum Issues* (1999: 1) described its target audience as 'all the partners in education'.

The discussion paper was prepared by a special education steering committee and three working groups under the auspices of the NCCA. As with the advisory group on certificate examinations, the NCCA steering committee and working groups were 'expert' groups. Membership of the steering committee represented the interests of administration, management, teachers and parents while the working groups consisted mainly of teachers. However, the educational partner with arguably the most direct interest, consisting of those who are receiving or who had received special education in the past, were not represented at all.

The Report of the Commission on the Status of People with Disabilities (1996) provides ample evidence that disabled people have views about their educational experiences and that they both desire and demand opportunities to express these views (see, for example, Preface and chapters I and II; see also, Irish Deaf Society, 1993, 1997). The failure of the expert bodies under discussion to include disabled representatives or to provide a suitable forum for expressing those views contradicts the whole notion of inclusion and partnership advocated in the White Paper (Department of Education, 1995: 6–8) and the Education Act (Department of Education and Science, 1998: 5). The point here is not that 'insider' perspectives have any monopoly on 'the truth'; rather, the issue is one of failure in recognition and representation (Young, 1990; Fraser, 1995; Kwiotek, 1999). Furthermore, the 'objectivity' or 'neutrality' of expert groups in policy development can never be taken for granted, particularly in relation to disability (King and Hansen: 1999).

Members of officially appointed bodies and other 'expert' groups monopolise policy making spaces and exercise significant gate-keeping functions. In the case of the expert advisory group on examinations, for example, one of the major issues involved the nature of the examination system itself. The expert group, however, merely acknowledged that while this merited serious consideration, it raised issues 'that go well beyond the terms of reference' (Department of Education and Science, 2000: 6) and referred no further to the matter. Thus, with regard to disability in education, the social relations of policy making are similar to the social relations of research production; not only are disabled people excluded from strategic roles in these activities, they are regarded as being passive and dependent recipients of outcomes that are decided by others (Barton, 1988; Oliver, 1992, 1993, 1996; Rioux and Bach, 1994; Clough and Barton, 1995; Moore, Beazley and Maelzer, 1998). In summing up the central criticisms, Moore, Beazley and Maelzer (1998: 12) argue that most 'investigations of disability matters . . . undermine disabled people's own agendas . . . [and] . . . inevitably recycle individual-blaming images of disabled people'.

'Expert' perspectives exert a profound influence on social and cultural responses to disability and constitute a powerful counter-resistance to a disability rights discourse. Tensions between the dominant psycho-medical model and an emerging disability critique is evident in the considerable uncertainty and instability that surrounds the terminology of special education (Kirk, Gallagher and Anastasiou, 1997: 11). Shifts in terminology, however, refer to changes in surface features rather than to changes in underlying power structures or relations. In the policy documents we have been considering, 'disability' has been deprived of its meaning as a socio-political indicator of inequality and discrimination and functions as a substitute term for 'handicap'. Another current and widely used term, 'special needs', directs the professional gaze towards the pupil rather than towards professional practices or organisational structures. In other words, psycho-medical discourse has absorbed and de-politicised the language of the disability critique. The terminology of the psycho-medical model has changed but the focus of attention remains fixed on the particularities of some individual 'condition' rather than on the marginalising and exclusionary practices and structures of society.

Disability, education and social justice

In the European Union, the amount of legislation surrounding issues of integration and inclusive education suggests the emergence of a social justice discourse in relation to disability (see, for example Association for Higher Education Access and Disability (AHEAD), 1995). There are, however, different ways in which social justice might be expressed through policies and practices in education. In an interesting analysis of social justice in relation to special educational needs, Troyna and Vincent (1996) argue that the formulation of social justice with regard to special needs has been very different from its formulation with regard to racial equality, for example. For ethnic minorities, the social justice argument invokes the language of entitlements and rights in a context of discrimination; for pupils with special needs, social justice is articulated as the distribution of scarce resources in a context of needs and deficiencies.

Troyna and Vincent (1996) point out that the rights of special needs pupils are subordinate to a discourse of expertise: educational services are provided for these pupils, not on the basis of independent rights and entitlements, but on the basis of professional authority to determine what is in the 'best interests' of the pupil. While the SERC report (Department of Education, 1993) adopted the principle that 'children with special educational needs have a right to an appropriate education' (p. 19), it also maintained that the interpretation of what was 'appropriate' was primarily a matter for the experts (p. 20). In the report, 'the goodwill of the authorities concerned' was taken to be a sufficient guarantee that the rights and entitlements of people with disabilities in education would be respected (p. 59).

A similar situation is evident when we compare responses to gender on the one hand and to disability on the other (Department of Education, 1992, 1993, 1995). In an extensive discussion on gender and equity, the Green Paper on education (Department of Education, 1992: 9–10, 67–71) acknowledged the existence of gender bias in the educational system and responded with a detailed programme of action to address this problem. The Green Paper also acknowledged that disability was an equity issue. However, since no *structural* biases were assumed in relation to disability, no equivalent action plan was deemed to be necessary. Similarly, the SERC report (Department of Education, 1993) discusses the rights and entitlements of disabled pupils in terms of individuals with 'conditions', but not in terms of individuals experiencing discrimination (O'Hanlon, 1994).

Conclusion

Despite recent discussion on policies of integration and inclusion, the orientation to segregated schooling in Ireland remains strong and a large proportion of disabled students, half to two thirds of the total at primary level, continue to attend special schools and classes (Commission on the Status of People with Disabilities, 1996: 171). Lynch's assessment that '[a]lmost all pupils with sensory and physical disabilities are fully integrated into mainstream education' seems overly optimistic (1995: 62). Furthermore, the White Paper in Education envisaged the creation of so-called 'designated schools' at first and second levels, that is, ordinary schools designated 'as centres where students with particular disabilities may be educated' (Department of

Education, 1995: 25, 54). It is not difficult to see how this organisational framework could become a 'more acceptable' form of segregated schooling. Exclusion continues to be a major problem in second and third level education (Department of Education, 1993: 59–66) and for a significant number of pupils with learning difficulties at primary level (Irish National Teachers' Organisation, 1996). Structures, curricula and support services remain relatively underdeveloped in post-primary schools while disabled students account for only a half to one percent of overall student numbers in higher and further education (AHEAD, 1994: 13; Commission on the Status of People with Disabilities, 1996: 171). In 1998–9 they amounted to 0.8 per cent of the student population at third level – some 800 out of about 100,000 students (Department of Education and Science, 2001: 64).

Two of the most striking aspects of policy making and policy implementation are firstly, the dominance of perspectives which define disability in individualised psycho-medical terms, and secondly, the privileged and controlling roles assigned to professional experts, especially those from the fields of medicine, psychology and education. Evidence from current policy-making initiatives indicates that these perspectives continue to dominate theory and practice in the education of disabled pupils.

In spite of these difficulties, inclusion has become a factor in policy-making and planning in education (Department of Education, 1992, 1993, 1995; Commission on the Status of People with Disabilities, 1996; Coolahan, 1994) and more recently, it has become important both as a matter for legislation (Department of Education, 1998) and as a theoretical concept (McDonnell, 2000). There is also a growing body of evidence that exclusionary practices and individualising models of disability are being resisted. Recent court cases have demonstrated the existence of considerable degrees of anger and frustration at the extent of educational discrimination experienced by disabled pupils (*O'Donoghue* v *Minister for Health*, 1993; *Sinnott* v *Minister for Education and Science*, 2001). Work in the field of disability studies, especially among disabled researchers, based on a conception of disability as an equality issue, has challenged such 'intolerable conditions' and 'oppressive social barriers' (Duffy, 1993, Dalton, 1996; Commission on the Status of People with Disabilities, 1996: 5; Kwiotek 1999). Significant new initiatives have also emerged. The establishment of a Centre for Deaf Studies in Trinity College, Dublin, for example, acknowledges that deafness is a cultural and linguistic issue rather than a 'condition'. Similarly the establishment of a Chair of Disability Studies in University College Dublin has potential for the development of a more extensive social and political response to disability.

Education is entering a critical transition period in which new policies in relation to disability are being developed and guidelines for new practices are being established. As these new responses take shape, from the point of view of disabled pupils and students it is important that both 'deep' and 'surface' structures of the educational system are transformed and that what emerges is not merely a reformulation of old policies and practices. One of the real dangers in the current transition period is that while some surface changes may occur, existing deep structures will remain in place. Moreover, if the deep structures of special education – those issues that underlie relations of power, control, dominance and subordination – are not identified and transformed, exclusion and marginalisation will be reproduced even under the best intentioned and well supported of reform programmes.

Chapter 3

Employment policy

Pauline Conroy

Introduction

Employment is increasingly the gateway to exercising citizenship. Paid
employment provides independent income, opportunities to interact with
friends and colleagues, to travel outside the home, and to acquire skills. In
Ireland, having a regular paid job is the road to taking out loans from a bank,
owning a home, establishing a family and saving for the future. Paying taxes
and contributing in solidarity to others, as well as to the growth of the economy,
are part and parcel of economic activity. This chapter discusses the perplexing
exclusion of people with disabilities from the labour market and opportunities
to contribute to their own economic self-sufficiency. The conflicting spectrum
of policy directions for the integration of people with disabilities into employment is explored in the context of European and international developments.

The negative heritage

Throughout the twentieth century, policy makers assumed people with
disabilities were unfit for employment on the open labour market alongside
everybody else. A very carefully organised form of disability apartheid
functioned, which separated and segregated people with disabilities into
separate schools, separate training programmes, institutions, residential
centres and a few segregated employment outlets. The approach was widely
endorsed or endured by public bodies, voluntary education and social service
providers, professionals and many families. It had the appearance of being
natural and normal. This is crucial, since the definers of 'normality' define, by
default, what is deviant or abnormal (Drake, 1999).

The so-called normality of segregation lay in the break-up of the Poor Law
(Burke, 1987) in the nineteenth century, in which non-able-bodied categories
were separated off into specialised institutions. Ireland was especially good
at this. The establishment of the Central Mental Hospital in 1850 in County
Dublin, the first 'criminal lunatic asylum', had predated Broadmoor in

England by ten years. St Patrick's Psychiatric Hospital had already led the field as the first asylum of its type in 1757. The opening of Stewart's Hospital for children in Palmerstown in 1869 was a leading example of one of the early closed institutions.

The closing down and opening up of some of the larger institutions in Ireland in the 1960s was supported by the work of American analysts such as Erving Goffman (1961). The supposedly enlightened approach, of closing down some high-walled institutions and transferring people with disabilities to the isolation of family homes, displaced their segregation from one location to another (Oliver, 1990). Segregation created the conditions for constructing a physical and social working environment crushingly unsuited, even hostile, to people with disabilities. Those who had acquired a disability fared little better than those who had always had an impairment. The chronic health status of those who contracted tuberculosis in the 1940s, the epidemic of polio-myelitis in the 1950s or the consequences of the use of the drug Thalidomide, banned in 1961, altered little the general negative discrimination policy towards people with disabilities.

The labour market today

Today in the twenty-first century, people with disabilities of all kinds and levels of severity have little opportunity to be disadvantaged on the labour market. They are generally so far removed from the labour market as to be outside its orbit and influence. The few who persist, obtain access and insist on equal treatment, often experience their status as that of outsider or intruder.

Looking at the entire population aged 15 years and over, some three per cent describe themselves as unable to work owing to permanent sickness or disability. This is illustrated in Table 1. The actual population with disabilities is much larger, however, since many are to be found inside the categories of student, retired, at work, unemployed and others.

The 75,000 people who described themselves as permanently sick or disabled in 2002 might include many who would like to have an economic activity but do not have the opportunity to do so. A special survey undertaken by the Central Statistics Office (2002) revealed that ten per cent of persons (271,000) aged 15 to 64 indicated that they had a long-standing health problem or disability. Slightly more men than women reported such a health problem or disability.

People without a disability are four times more likely to be in employment than those with a severe disability and twice as likely as those with a moderate disability (Eurostat, 2001). The gap is very wide for men compared with women. A man without a disability is five times more likely to be in employment than a man with a severe disability.

Table 1 **Population of working age in Ireland, including those unable to work because of disabilities**

Population aged 15 years and over classified by Principal Economic Status	March to May 2001 (thousands)	December to February 2002 (thousands)
At work	1,647.2	1,669.1
Unemployed	99.5	121.1
Student	379.1	380.6
Home duties	551.3	551.4
Retired	256.0	257.3
Unable to work owing to permanent illness or disability	72.9	75.6
Other	11.3	16.0
Total	3,017.3	3,071.1

Source: Central Statistics Office (2001–2) Quarterly National Household Surveys. Dublin.

Note: Classification based on respondent's own subjective assessment. Results are subject to sampling errors and other survey errors, which are greater in respect of smaller estimates of change.

Some estimates of the labour force participation rates of people with disabilities are provided by European analyses and are illustrated in Table 2. The data sets are from the 1996 European Community Household Panel and the Labour Force Survey. These surveys do not automatically include people living in residential centres and institutions, therefore the rates are likely to be an overestimation of the labour force participation rates of people with disabilities. The data suggests that there would need to be a doubling of the labour force participation rates of people with disabilities to achieve an outcome of policy parity.

Table 2 **Estimate of labour force participation rates of people with and without disabilities aged 16–64 years, 1996, and 2002, Ireland**

Labour force participation	1996 %	2002 %
Persons with a disability	32.9	42.8
Persons without a disability	67.9	67.8
Participation rate difference	35.0	25

Source: Malo and Garcia-Serrano (2001) An analysis of the employment status of the disabled persons using ECHP Data. Working Paper. Brussels: European Commission, p. 28. EIM Business and Policy Research (2001) The Employment Situation of People with Disabilities in the European Union, Brussels: European Commission, p. 40. Central Statistics Office (2002) Disability in the Labour Force, p. 6, (persons aged 15 to 64).

A part of this extraordinary gap in life chances may be explained by the failure of the education system to provide a minimum of the education opportunities and entitlements available, free, to all children. Some 62 per cent of persons with a moderate disability and of an age to work did not complete second-level education (Eurostat, 2001). They have no certificates, skills or qualifications, no Leaving Certificate, no Junior Certificate. In Northern Ireland, 43 per cent of people with a disability have no qualifications such as a GSE A level or GCSE grade A–C (Equality Commission for Northern Ireland, 2001).

The consequences are stark. While 95 per cent of people with a disability living in Irish households have an income, it is not an earned income; that is, it does not come from employment (Eurostat, 2001). It originates in social welfare payments, or family money (Conroy, 1994).

A further consequence of the education system for weakened labour market access has been the difficulties for many people with disabilities in obtaining high-level vocational training. Those forms of vocational training which are based on completion of secondary education are out of the reach of the majority of people with disabilities. Between 1973 and 1994, the European Union invested €615 m. in vocational training for people with disabilities in Ireland. Most of the training was outside workplaces or worksites, was at the most elementary skill level and was provided by social rather than employment-oriented agencies (European Social Fund, 1996). The investment failed to structurally connect people with disabilities with the open labour market.

Contemporary employment policies

Over a 25-year period from the mid-1970s to the present day, policy towards the employment of people with disabilities has been contradictory and incoherent. A piecemeal approach of five types of intervention based on three widely differing policy principles has combined to confuse employers, trade unions, vocational trainers and people with disabilities themselves. These interventions are illustrated in Table 3.

Table 3 reveals that three different employment policies are operating on the labour market. A non-discrimination law, together with forms of positive action and target/quota systems, function side by side on the same small labour market. The principles and legal rationale for each are different. A single employer – a local authority, for example – may attempt to advance all three principles:

- obligatory non-discrimination and actions to reasonably accommodate,
- voluntary positive or specific actions in favour of people with disabilities,

Table 3 **Employment policies relating to people with disabilities**

Nature of employment intervention	Types of employment policy for people with disabilities	
	Responsible department	*Nature of action*
Civil and public service employment three per cent target for the employment of people with disabilities. This originates in a quota system.	Department of Finance with a three per cent Monitoring Committee	Established by Ministerial Order in 1977 as a voluntary quota.
Sheltered employment in special workshops or centres – a form of positive action	Department of Health and Children and Health Boards	7,900 people work in 215 sheltered workshops.
Supported employment – a form of positive action	Department of Enterprise and Trade and FÁS	Employment supports to gain or retain employment on open market. In 1999, 1000 persons took part in the scheme.
Rehabilitative employment – a form of positive action	Department of Social and Family Affairs	An authorisation for persons in receipt of Disability Allowance to undertake approved work for payment. In 2001, 1,459 took part in the scheme.
Open market employment with adaptations to accommodate workers with disabilities under the Employment Equality Act, 1998.	Department of Justice Equality and Law Reform and Equality Authority	Employers are obliged since 1998, to make adjustments up to nominal cost, to accommodate employees with disabilities.

Source: Compiled by the author from Department of Social and Family Affairs, Longford, FÁS, Department of Health and Children, *A Health System for You*, 2001.

- voluntary target/quota systems of employing three per cent workers with disabilities

The Commission on the Status of People with Disabilities (1996: 135–43) devoted just nine of its 340-page report to training and employment issues. It did not distinguish clearly between labour market access and job retention and promotion for those in employment, nor did it address the significant impact of structural segregation in education and training for future labour market and employment policy.

Since 2000, responsibility for labour market training, advice and supported employment has been transferred to the Department of Enterprise, Trade and Employment and FÁS, the training authority. These important structural changes were intended to increase access to job opportunities for people with disabilities and increase their employment rate.

The longest-standing policy is the three per cent employment target for people with disabilities in the civil and public service. Established by a Ministerial Order, rather than a legislative enactment, in 1977, this policy was never debated in the Oireachtas. It has received renewed and widespread endorsement from employers and trade unions in the various social partnership agreements since the 1980s (Conroy and Fanagan, 2001a). It has been operated by all government departments, state agencies, local authorities and health boards. Although now renamed a 'target', its intention and implementation fall into the category of disability policies called quota systems. Many European countries operate quota systems, under which a fixed percentage of jobs are reserved, or are intended to be filled, by people with disabilities. In Ireland that percentage is three and has not been achieved by all departments. A voluntary target resembles a form of positive action, but may, in effect, be implemented or understood as a quota.

The three per cent target is intended to stimulate employers in the public sector to recruit people with disabilities who have achieved the same merit and qualification as other non-disabled persons. Reporting of the implementation of the target measure of three per cent depends on employees consenting to being categorised as 'disabled', a feature which can, perversely, undermine the employment mainstreaming intention of the policy. In some countries, quota systems have been found to be advantageous to the least disabled job applicants, when employers 'cream' applicants with the least severe disabilities (Samorodov, 1996).

Sheltered work is 'work' undertaken by people with disabilities in workshops specifically established for that purpose. Those who undertake 'work' are not employees in terms of employee protection legislation. The Irish Congress of Trade Unions has shown considerable interest in this group of workers under the Programme for Prosperity and Fairness (1999).

Supported work or employment is a process of supporting individuals with disabilities in their work with job coaches or similar support staff at their work site. This programme is supported by FÁS. A new strategy for sheltered workshops and supported employment was devised in 1997 (National Advisory Committee on Training and Employment, 1997). This involves converting sheltered workshops and protected employment into labour market-connected employment. The establishment of wage rates, terms and conditions of employment, contracts and planning figure among the recommendations of the new strategy which is to be in place by 2004. The sheltered workshops and supported employment are positive or specific actions undertaken to promote or accelerate the labour market or economic integration of people with disabilities.

Rehabilitative employment is a scheme which authorises people in receipt of payments, such as Disability Allowance from the Department of Social and Family Affairs, to take up part-time employment in certain parts of the economy without a loss of entitlement to their payments. The scheme is particularly useful for persons with intermittent disabling conditions or with chronic illnesses who experience remission. Examples of persons for whom the scheme is helpful are those who suffer, recurrently and periodically, from periods of psychiatric illness. The scheme can be administratively complicated for employers who face uncertainty as to whether the beneficiary is an employee or non-employee in terms of employment law. Nevertheless, it is an interesting example of encouraging regularised labour market attachment among population groups who are unlikely or unable to seek permanent employment.

The Employment Equality Act, 1998

In 1998, an Employment Equality Act was finally adopted. Its introduction had been delayed by a constitutional challenge to one of its clauses which had the effect of obliging employers to accommodate workers with disabilities at their own cost. This clause was changed. For the first time, employees, vocational trainees, job seekers and workers with a disability had a right not to be discriminated against, when compared with workers without a disability. Employers had an obligation to reasonably accommodate workers with a disability, subject to a nominal cost.

The 1998 Act is based on the principle of equal treatment between persons with and persons without a disability. It takes account of obligatory workplace adjustments so that workers with and without a disability perform or compete on an equal footing. These adjustments vary from job to job and worker to worker. It could involve a wheelchair ramp into a canteen, a special parking space or talking software for a computer. The concept of workplace adjustment is not new in Ireland. An analogous adjustment/accommodation system had been in place in Ireland in relation to the employment and protection of pregnant and breastfeeding women workers under a 1992 European Framework Directive on Health and Safety (European Council of Ministers, 1992). However, the workplace adjustments which accompanied pregnancy and maternity protection were rarely if ever used as examples in the 1990s debate on disability equality.

The Employment Equality Act, 1998, does not refer exactly to 'reasonable accommodation' but rather to the obligation on employers (Section 16(3) (b)) to 'do all that is reasonable to accommodate'. The nature of the accommodation is unknown except that it is made up of 'special treatment or facilities' (Section 16 (3)(a)).

The 1998 Employment Equality Act sets some economic rights in law. It shifted attention away from individual impairments to disabling environments. It conveys a message that discrimination is not tolerated. The Act has been used by a small number of people with disabilities (Office of Director of Equality Investigations, 2002). Table 4 gives the grounds under which cases related to disability were handled by the Equality Authority in 2001.

The 1998 Act can be criticised on a number of grounds. In the absence of any legal definition principle or challenge between 1999, when the Act came into force, and 2002, it is not known what constitutes a 'nominal cost' or how it is to be computed. The definition of disability used in the Act is a wide-ranging medical definition based on absence of capacity or missing body parts. This medicalised definition sits uneasily in a labour market governed by social and economic principles and functioning. The Act does not apply the disability non-discrimination ground to a number of employments, such as the Defence Forces. However, the definition of disability is so wide ranging, that quite immaterial impairments could justify exclusion from recruitment to the Defence Forces.

The Employment Equality Act makes no reference to targets or quotas for workers with disabilities. This is logical. An employer or workplace which is adjusted, such that all workers have an equal chance of being interviewed for jobs, recruited, assigned, retained and promoted and are equally treated in workplace opportunities, conditions and benefits, has no need of targets, reserved jobs or set-aside occupations.

The need for such a non-discrimination law is well illustrated by the situation which arose in the defence forces. During the period 1998–9, several thousand soldiers in the defence forces took individual court cases against the army seeking compensation for deafness. Over the years, the soldiers had been engaged in military exercises involving the discharge of firearms without the use of safety prevention earmuffs. Gradually, many became hearing impaired. This was a breach of health and safety of workers, causing an irreversible

Table 4 **Cases handled by Equality Authority in 2001 in relation to the Employment Equality Act, 1998**

Employment Equality Act, 1998
(Casework activity–Disability)

Sphere of dispute	Number of cases
Access to employment	24
Access to promotion	2
Access to training	2
Working conditions	15
Harassment	2
Dismissal	18
Equal Pay	1
Sexual harassment	0
Victimisation	0
Advertising	1
Total of cases	65

Source: Equality Authority (2002) *Annual Report 2001*, Dublin, p. 27.

industrial injury. The soldiers sought compensation for their injuries, with the support of their association PDFORRA (PDFORRA, 1998). The costs of paying compensation attracted considerable spectacular publicity in the Oireachtas and in the media). Referred to often in a derogatory tone as the 'Army deafness claims', the cases can be more accurately described as hearing impairments arising from mass scale industrial injuries (Dáil Éireann, 1998).

The costs of employment

There can be additional costs for employees with specific impairments in taking or holding a job. Taking a cab or taxi to work arises in the absence or adaptation of public transport. Replacement of shoes or wheelchair tyres are examples of essential recurring expenses for some employees. These are known as 'the costs of disability'. Working can cost more to a taxpaying worker with a disability compared with a worker without a disability. Such a relatively disadvantageous cost could be addressed by fiscal policy. The formulation of a tax credit for a proportion of identifiable, essential and recurring expenses of taking up-paid employment could be a form of reasonable accommodation in the tax system (Conroy and Fanagan, 2001b).

Globalisation and influences on disability policy in Ireland

Disability policy in Ireland shows the huge significance of international thinking on the disability rights movement, while the thinking of the public authorities remained often locked in earlier eras. The United Nations Standard Rules on the Equalisation of Opportunities for People with Disabilities was immensely important in influencing the concept of rights among social movements and associations of people with disabilities in Ireland (United Nations, 1994). The rules lay down a minimum voluntary code for governments in establishing a wide range of rights. These were influential in forming what is now called 'the rights-based approach to disability'.

This influence was much underestimated by public authorities, legislators and policy thinkers who looked to the European Union – to Berlin rather than Boston – for inspiration. In the event, the European Union waited for the adoption of the Standard Rules before proceeding forward itself (European Commission, 2000a). Certainly the Council of Ministers adopted a number of resolutions between 1990 and 1996, but restrained itself from passing any legally binding decisions. The European Union has been forced forward on the topic of disability. Strongly attached to the type of quota systems in operation in Germany and France, it was with a considerable reluctance that the governments of Europe agreed among themselves to the Treaty of Amsterdam which amended the preceding European Treaties with Article 13. The ratification of Amsterdam was finally adopted in 1997.

Article 13 is a non-discrimination clause which allows the Council, when acting unanimously, to take action to combat discrimination on a number of grounds including disability. In 1998, the first Member State national employment action plans included guidelines on actions to promote employment of people with disabilities. The first legal action under Article 13 of interest to people with disabilities was a Directive adopted in 2000 (European Council of Ministers, 2000). This non-discrimination Directive will come into force in Ireland in mid-2003. The Directive refers to 'reasonable accommodation' for persons with a disability and makes no reference to nominal costs. On the contrary, referring to the many national disability policies, the Directive considers that reasonable accommodation should not be considered a disproportionate burden (Waddington and Bell, 2001).

The Directive will place Europe on a quasi-equal footing with the United States Congress which had adopted non-discrimination legislation a full ten years earlier (US Congress, 1990). The Americans with Disabilities Act, 1990 (ADA), is based on a long-standing American tradition of civil rights and disability-specific legislation. The Civil Rights Act of 1964 and the Rehabilitation Act of 1973 provided America with a full 25 years of non-discrimination legislation in practice prior to the introduction of the

Americans with Disabilities Act. The new European Directive on non-discrimination appears to borrow heavily from the ADA in relation to disability. In so doing, it also will import some of the American restrictions from coverage of disability protection into Europe. In relation to disability, European employers will not be obliged to undertake employment accommodations which place a 'disproportionate burden' on them (European Council of Ministers, 2000). This is similar to the 'undue hardship' clause of the ADA.

Ireland has ratified two Conventions of the International Labour Organisation (ILO) in relation to disability and employment. Convention Number III on non-discrimination in employment and occupation of 1958 was ignored by Ireland for thirty years. It was finally ratified by Ireland in 1998, after it had adopted the Employment Equality Act, in 1998. ILO Convention no. 159 of 1983 on vocational rehabilitation and employment for disabled persons, was ratified by Ireland in a short period in 1986. Much of the content of Convention 159 was equally ignored and rehabilitation has been one of the several underfunded areas of disability services in Ireland. The ILO Conventions, and their accompanying recommendations and codes of practice, are useful in setting global standards for the employment of people with disabilities. They provide opportunities for confederations of trade unions, employers and civil servants to exchange views on how to proceed or change a policy direction.

Such international exchanges are of paramount importance in ensuring that an ever larger Europe sets policy standards and enforcement that place people with disabilities on an equal footing with all other citizens with regard to free moment, right to take up employment with equal rights in every country and the right to avail themselves of social protection across Europe. These rights are far from evident and are the subject of intense discussion among forums of disability organisations at European level as well as among members of different political groups in the European Parliament (European Parliament, 2002).

Challenges for the future

Policy for the future of disability and employment policy needs quantitative information on the labour market status of people with disabilities over time. For such a small labour market as that of Ireland, this is not an insurmountable issue. The decision to include a special question on the topic in the European labour force surveys will go some way towards starting the process. This will be supplemented by analysis of responses to the first ever questions on disability in the Census 2002.

Deciding on coherent policies will be much needed to avoid causing intractable confusion among employers. The uncertainty among employers as to whether they should be adapting their workplaces, how and for whom, continues to confound even forward-thinking employers (Conroy and Fanagan, 2001a). When this is accompanied by exhortations to 'target resources' (National Economic and Social Forum, 2002: 39), it becomes even more confusing. Targeting of resources can imply a group or collective category of persons with a disability, while the Employment Equality Act prohibits discrimination against individuals, rather than groups. A single employer action, when directed at an individual worker, can be classed as a reasonable accommodation, when directed at a group, becomes a voluntary positive action. This is confusing.

Workers with sensory impairments, such as in hearing or sight, often need only the slightest adjustment in work practice or computer software to function with a competence equal to any in a modern workplace. Yet these slight modifications and adjustments are frequently unavailable. Indeed, many persons with hearing impairment decline to describe themselves as 'disabled' – regarding themselves as speaking a different language rather than having a disabling impairment. Thanks to the advent of mobile phone text messaging, communications for young hearing-impaired persons has been improved without any state intervention.

There is a need for a centralised technical resource for employers to obtain technical information on accommodation, adjustments and procedures to be put in place to achieve workplaces accessible and equitable for all. Such a technical resource does not at present fall within the remit of any statutory body.

To date, only a handful of cases have been decided by the Office of the Director of Equality Investigations in relation to enforcement of the Employment Equality Act, 1998 on the disability ground. The reluctance of workers, job applicants and vocational trainees to bring forward a larger number of cases is part of the negative policy inheritance of the past.

A cultural revolution on the part of the working population so that they may accustom themselves to accepting people with disabilities into the workforce and into economic activity in the widest sense, will be the greatest challenge of the future.

Chapter 4

Social Security and disability

Anne McManus

Introduction and context

The social security system for people with disabilities does not operate in isolation. It is part of a wide ranging social security system covering a range of contingencies: unemployment, pensions, child benefit and so on. The system developed piecemeal over the years – sometimes through changes aimed at specific groups, but often by measures which covered more than one group. Thus, many features of the system as it applies to people with disabilities were not specifically designed for people with disabilities, but evolved as part of the overall system of income support. Social security for people with disabilities therefore needs to be understood in the context of Ireland's overall social security system.

Broadly, the Irish social welfare system comprises three types of payments:

- social insurance payments, financed in part[1] by contributions from employees, employers and the self-employed; entitlement to these payments is based on meeting particular contingencies (e.g. old age, invalidity) and from having paid sufficient social insurance contributions (known as PRSI contributions);
- social assistance payments, which are means tested, and are also generally linked to specific contingencies;
- a universal child benefit.

There is also a separate scheme of benefits for occupational injuries.

The underlying aim of the overall system is the provision of alternative income for people who cannot take part in paid employment, whether through age, unemployment, disability or illness. In line with this, the philosophy underlying entitlement to payments such as Invalidity Pension or Disability Allowance is not based on the concept of 'disability' *per se*, but rather on the concept of inability to work. So a person with a disability who is in full-time work might not qualify for any social welfare payment. The concept of inability to work is based on a medical model of disability, that is, a person's ability or inability to work is based on medical criteria, rather than an assessment of the employment or training opportunities that might be available to meet the person's needs.

The payments for people with disabilities mirror those for other social welfare contingencies in many ways. For example, the PRSI contribution conditions and payment rate for (short-term) Disability Benefit are broadly similar to those for Unemployment Benefit, while the level of (means-tested) Disability Allowance is similar to other means-tested, long-term payments such as Unemployment Assistance or the personal rate of One-Parent Family Payment. These inter-linkages recognise that people move from one payment to another as different contingencies arise in their lives.

It might be noted that unlike a number of other countries, health care is not part of the social insurance system in Ireland and is therefore not covered in this chapter.

Historical overview

The social insurance and social assistance systems, though currently admin-istered by a single department, had very different historical origins. The earliest form of formal social welfare in Ireland was the system of institutional relief for the sick and destitute poor which was provided for under the Poor Relief (Ireland) Act of 1838; the system was commonly known as the 'poor law'. The First Report of the Department of Social Welfare, 1947–9 (1950), in a historical overview of the Department's schemes, noted that 'recourse to the poor law was abhorred by the majority of people and was availed of only under the most bitter economic compulsion'.

Disabled people who had never worked had to rely on the Poor Law and its successor – Public Assistance – until the Health Act 1953, which introduced a means-tested Disabled Person's Maintenance Allowance (DPMA) for dis-abled people over 16 who were unable to provide for their own maintenance. This payment continued to be paid by the Health Boards until 1996, when responsibility for its administration was transferred to the then Department of Social Welfare. The payment was renamed Disability Allowance and integrated into the existing system of social insurance and social assistance benefits. A number of improvements, including changes to the means testing arrangements, were introduced. Since its takeover by the Department of Social and Family Affairs, the number of people taking part in the scheme has increased from 34,500 in October 1996 to 61,000 by August 2002 – an increase of three quarters.

Means-tested Blind Pensions were introduced in 1920. These were paid to blind people over the age of 50, based on similar conditions to the means-tested old-age pension (which had been introduced in January 1909). A separate scheme of Blind Pensions exists to this day – the only situation in which a social welfare payment is linked to a specific form of disability.

Payments based on social insurance evolved separately to the above means-tested schemes. Compulsory social insurance for workers during illness was first introduced in the National Insurance Act passed by the British Parliament in 1911. Under the Act, employees and their employers were required to pay contributions to approved societies, who administered cash benefits in respect of sickness and disablement. In 1933 these societies (then 65) were amalgamated into a single unified society – the National Health Insurance Society.

The Department of Social Welfare was established in 1947, and in 1949 it published a White Paper proposing the amalgamation of the scheme of social insurance for illness/disability with the two other social insurance schemes which then existed – widows and unemployment benefits. This was effected in 1952. At the same time, the two separate cash benefits for sickness and disablement were merged into a single Disability Benefit.

In 1970 a separate Invalidity Pension, modelled on Disability Benefit, was introduced, and over the years it has been adjusted to give a higher payment rate and additional non-cash benefits.

More recent changes to the overall social insurance system, such as its extension to part-time workers and to new public servants have increased the potential claim-load for social insurance payments in respect of invalidity.

Description of principal social security schemes for people with disabilities

The different social security schemes for which people with disabilities may qualify are set out in general terms below. The descriptions are intended for general readers; those seeking more details (particularly with a view to individual claims) should consult the Department's detailed booklets or its website (www.welfare.ie).

Disability Benefit: The title is somewhat of a misnomer, as the payment caters mainly for people who are ill, as distinct from people with disabilities. It is available to people who are unfit for work, due to either illness or disability and who satisfy certain PRSI contribution conditions. The payment can continue indefinitely, provided the client has sufficient PRSI contributions and continues to be unfit for work.

Invalidity Pension: This can be paid instead of Disability Benefit to people who are regarded as permanently incapable of work and who satisfy the PRSI contributions. This is paid at a slightly higher rate than Disability Benefit, recognising its long-term nature. It also attracts entitlement to a range of non-cash benefits, such as free travel and, depending on the individual's household circumstances, free fuel, free electricity and similar benefits.

Disability Allowance: This is a weekly means-tested allowance paid to people between 16 and 66 years of age with a disability and whose income falls below certain limits. The disability must have lasted, or be expected to last, for at least a year and arising from this disability the person's employment capacity is substantially restricted.

Occupational Injuries Benefits: These are paid to people who have been injured at work or are affected by occupational diseases. Although the person must have been at work in insurable employment to qualify, there are no additional PRSI qualification conditions. The principal payments are:

- Injury benefit, which is a weekly payment for up to 26 weeks to a person who is unable to work because of an occupational accident or illness;
- Disablement Benefit, which is paid in respect of loss of physical or mental faculty as a result of an occupational injury/illness. This may be paid even if the person is still at work. The payment depends on the degree of disablement, as medically assessed. It is paid as a lump sum if disablement is assessed at less than 20 per cent; for assessments above 20 per cent, a Disablement Pension is paid.

There is also provision within the occupational injuries scheme for medical care expenses and for pensions for dependants in the event of death from an occupational accident.

None of the above payments makes any distinction between different forms of disability (i.e. physical, intellectual or mental). In practice, of course, some people who have been disabled from birth might not be in a position to take up employment covered by social insurance, and therefore would not build up entitlement to contributory payments; they would be more likely to depend more on means-tested payments. In contrast, people who become disabled later in life might have built up sufficient contributions to qualify for social insurance payments.

Additional payments are available to carers:

Carer's Allowance: Introduced in 1990. It is a means-tested payment for people who provide full-time care and attention to someone with whom they live. This can be paid indefinitely.

Carer's Benefit: Introduced in October 2000 and is paid to people who leave the workforce to provide full-time care and attention to another person. It is not subject to a means test, but it is subject to PRSI contribution requirements. Carer's benefit is limited to a maximum of 65 weeks.

Domiciliary Care Allowance: Parents of disabled children may qualify for this benefit from their regional health board.

I might point out that, while the above social welfare schemes are particularly relevant to people with disabilities, there are other schemes as well available to them. For example, given the increased incidence of disability in old age, some pensioners might be regarded as 'disabled', but would generally be in receipt of a Retirement or Old Age Pension, rather than a disability-related payment.

The number of people in receipt of the various disability-related payments is set out in Table 1.

Table 1 **People in receipt of long-term illness/disability payments in September 2002**

	Male	*Female*	*Total*
Disability Benefit (for 1 year or more)[1]	9,000	18,000	27,000
Invalidity Pension	28,000	24,000	52,000
Disability Allowance	37,000	25,000	62,000
Disablement Pension	9,000	2,000	11,000

Source: Department of Social and Family Affairs

1   A further 28,000 people are in receipt of Disability Benefit for less than a year, in many cases in relation to illnesses of short-term duration.

Key policy issues

Some of the key current policy concerns relating to social welfare for people with disabilities are:

- Poverty amongst people with disabilities
- Meeting the additional costs of disability
- The overall complexity of the system
- Payments to people in residential care
- Access to employment opportunities for people with disabilities

Poverty amongst people with disabilities

The Review of the National Anti-Poverty Strategy (Department of Social and Family Affairs, 2002) recognied people with disabilities as a vulnerable group. Because of data deficiencies[2] the strategy set few specific targets for people with disabilities, but it set the objective of developing appropriate data in the first place.

Until such time the as alternative indicators are developed, the annual 'Living in Ireland' Surveys carried out by the ESRI remain the best indicator available of poverty trends for this group, although their limitations are acknowledged. The results of the 2000 Survey in Nolan *et al.* (2002) found that:

- The risk of consistent poverty[3] for people in households where the labour force status of the household reference person was 'ill/disabled' fell from 36.2 per cent in 1994 to 11 per cent in 2002.
- The risk of poverty for these households is twice the average for all households.
- People living in households where the reference person is 'ill/disabled' represent almost eight per cent of people in consistent poverty.
- Looking particularly at people in households which are in consistent poverty and who are receiving social welfare payments, between 1994 and 2002 there was a significant increase in the proportion of people whose payment related to illness/disability.

Levels of payment

Social welfare weekly payment rates are not linked either to prior earnings or to degree of disability.[4] Instead, payments are flat-rate, with additions for 'qualified adults' – a dependent spouse or partner – and for children. Benefit levels are up-rated each year, usually in January.

The maximum rate for a single person on either Disability Benefit or Disability Allowance is currently (i.e. in 2003) €124.80 per week; for a person with a dependent spouse and two children it is €241.20. Invalidity Pension is slightly higher at €130.30.

The Commission on the Status of People with Disabilities recommended, *inter alia*, the achievement as a matter of priority of the rates of payment recommended by the Commission on Social Welfare (1986) in relation to all income replacement payments. This was achieved for all rates in 1999.

Following the achievement of the Commission on Social Welfare (1986) rates, the Programme for Prosperity and Fairness contained a commitment to set up a working group to 'examine the range of complex issues associated with the benchmarking and indexation of social welfare payments'. The Group reported in September 2001, but did not reach agreement on the key question of whether there should be a formal benchmark for social welfare payments, or whether it should be left to the discretion of the Government to determine the level of welfare increases from year to year, having regard to the circumstances prevailing each year. The majority of the Group, while recognising that the exact rate was a matter for Government, nonetheless considered that a target of 27 per cent of gross average industrial earnings was not an unreasonable policy objective.

Although the Working Group did not achieve a consensus, in the Review of the National Anti-Poverty Strategy (Department of Social and Family Affairs, 2002) the Government set a target of achieving a rate of €150 per week (in 2002 terms) for the lowest rates of social welfare, to be met by 2007.

Costs of disability

Illness and disability can add significantly to the daily cost of living. For example, it can give rise to extra costs such as care and assistance, laundry, clothing, heating and telephone. In addition, people who are ill or have a disability can have accessibility and mobility problems which can increase in the ordinary costs of living.

Basic social welfare payment rates for people with disabilities do not take account of these costs: payment rates are set at similar levels to payments for able-bodied people. There are, however, a number of payments and benefits-in-kind which go some way towards alleviating the additional costs involved. These include free electricity, gas and telephone rental allowance schemes administered by the Department of Social and Family Affairs, as well as exceptional needs payments administered by health boards under the Supplementary Welfare Allowance scheme. People getting Invalidity Pension or Disability Allowance are entitled to free travel on public transport, but some of those who qualify may not be able to use it. Health boards provide some assistance with travel costs, including a monthly, means-tested Mobility Allowance and also the Motorised Transport Grant scheme for the conversion or purchase of adapted cars. The Commission on the Status of People with Disabilities (1996) noted that these benefits go some way towards meeting the additional costs of disability, but stated that 'These benefits are not comprehensive and in many cases are paid on a discretionary basis.'

The Commission on Social Welfare (1986: 352) commented that: 'While the disabled may have additional needs these should not necessarily be provided for through higher, across-the-board, income maintenance payments.' Neither did the Commission favour an additional payment related to the degree of disabilities, pointing to the problems of definition which would arise.

The Commission on the Status of People with Disabilities shared the view that the costs of disability should not be met through general income maintenance payments and proposed instead that there should be a Costs of Disability payment, which would vary with individual needs, and which would be available to all people with disabilities irrespective of their age and employment status. The Commission envisaged this being linked to a nation-wide assessment procedure based on needs.

Under the Programme for Prosperity and Fairness (2000), a Working Group, chaired by the Department of Health and Children, was set up to consult with the social partners to examine the feasibility of introducing a Cost of Disability Payment. At the time of writing, this Group is still under way.

Complexity of the system

The Commission on the Status of People with Disabilities commented on the complexity of the range of income supports available to people with disabilities. The Commission (1996: 125) took the view that 'the system of payments is neither coherent nor comprehensive'.

The Commission's proposed solution was a Disability Pension, to be paid to all disabled people who were unable to work or who were unable to work to full capacity. This would be paid on a non-means-tested basis. Effectively the Disability Pension would be a universal pension for people with disabilities.

The Department took the view that the payment of a universal Disability Pension would be problematic. The reasons are set out in some detail in the official *Progress Report on the Implementation of the Recommendations of the Commission* (Department of Justice, Equality and Law Reform, 1999a: 56–60). The main problems identified were as follows. Firstly, it would be very difficult to operate a universal payment for one specific contingency, within the context of an overall social welfare system which is based on social insurance and social assistance; the social welfare system is an integrated one, with inter-linkages between different payments in recognition of the fact that people move from one payment to another as their circumstances change over their lifetime. A general move away from a social insurance/social assistance mix and towards universal payments has been examined in the past and rejected. Secondly, the group which the Commission proposed should qualify – people working below their full potential – was difficult to define, given that large numbers of people (with and without any disability) work for below average earnings. Other technical issues, such as residency and payment abroad, would also need to be addressed.

Although the Department has identified problems with the Commission's proposal for a universal Disability Pension, the underlying problem which it was intended to address – the complexity of the system – is recognised. There has been some simplification since the Commission reported. In particular, the transfer of DPMA (now Disability Allowance) to the Department of Social and Family Affairs has given one clear point of contact for income maintenance needs.

Currently, as part of the Government's Expenditure Review Process, the Department is carrying out a review of the various income maintenance schemes for people who are ill and people with disabilities. The review is looking at a wide range of issues, including the possibility of some rationalisation of the schemes.

People in full-time residential or institutional care

People who qualify for contributory benefits (i.e. Disability Benefit or Invalidity Pension) can receive their payment whether they are living in the community or in full time residential/institutional care. However, people in residential/institutional care who do not qualify for contributory payments may be excluded from Disability Allowance. This has been the subject of some adverse comment: for example, the Commission on the Status of People with Disabilities (1996: 126), in setting out the weaknesses of the current system, included 'the non-payment of allowances to people in residential care, which creates unacceptable levels of dependency'.

The reasons for this disqualification are largely historical, and in recent years a number of measures have been introduced to ease the restriction. For example, the 1997 Social Welfare Act extended entitlement to partial Disability Allowance to people who were resident part time in institutional care. Since August 1999, people getting Disability Allowance who are admitted to residential care can retain their payment. However, a number of people remain (estimated to be in the region of 5,000), who entered residential or institutional care before August 1999 and who therefore cannot benefit under these arrangements. The situation remains under review.

Social welfare payments and employment

While the Department of Social and Family Affairs does not itself operate employment and training programmes, it aims through its range of supports to encourage and assist some people who are sick and people with disabilities who are in receipt of social welfare payments to identify and take up available

employment, training and other self-development opportunities, where appropriate. This is achieved through a range of measures, including:

- exemptions from the 'Rules of Behaviour'[5] which apply to the contributory illness and disability payments;
- income disregards in the case of means-tested payments, for those engaging
  in rehabilitative employment or self-employment and rehabilitative training;
- participation on the Back to Work Scheme, in which people on long-term
  illness and disability payments can retain those payments on a sliding scale
  for three years (four years where engaged in self-employment);
- the Back to Education scheme, which enables people on long-term illness
  and disability payments to attend second or third level education;
- the Job Facilitator network, which assists people to return to work, training
  and education by advising them of the options available, encouraging them
  to take up these options and providing supports, where necessary; and
- exemptions from liability for employer and employee PRSI contributions,
  in certain instances.

However, these measures operate in the context of the underlying conditions
for entitlement to any of the schemes. As currently structured, the income
maintenance system requires people in this situation to be classified as being
permanently incapable of work in order to qualify for benefit. On the other
hand, the same system recognises the employment potential of these people
by providing a range of employment supports to encourage them to re-train
or re-enter the workforce. The Working Group undertaking the Expenditure
Review of the Department's Illness/Disability payments has identified this
issue as one of the key areas to be addressed. To date, some of the particular
problems identified by the Working Group are:

- Difficulties involved in reconciling the underlying qualifying criteria,
  which require claimants to be incapable of work, with the fact that they
  may have some employment potential. Schemes define people as being
  'capable' or 'incapable' of work, whereas in reality people may be partially
  capable of work, or capable of rehabilitation, training etc.
- Poverty traps and/or work disincentives faced by people getting social
  welfare payments and, in particular, getting additional benefits such as
  medical cards which might be lost on taking up employment.
- The lack of any structure for identification of people on social welfare
  payments who would benefit from rehabilitation or employment supports,
  and their referral to suitable options.

There are no easy solutions to these problems; in particular there may be no
one solution for all cases, but the Working Group is examining a range of
ways of addressing these.

Challenges for the future

The agenda for the future will need to address the policy challenges set out above. First and foremost is the challenge of adapting the system to accommodate the expectations of people with disabilities that they should be able to work to the best of their abilities. There is no simple solution to this: a combination of measures may be needed, reflecting people's diverse needs and abilities. Possible measures would include better identification of people's work potential and referral to appropriate services, as well as recognition that some people may have some capacity for work, but may never achieve full-time employment.

Secondly, an emerging area is the question of long-term care and its financing. This affects both people with disabilities in need of care and also our elderly population which will grow substantially in the medium to longer term.

As to the overall range of social welfare payments, it is envisaged that for the foreseeable future the mix of social insurance and social assistance will be continued. Within this, there is scope for some rationalisation of the range of payments, to achieve a simpler overall structure. As more people take up employment covered by PRSI, social insurance payments are likely to take a larger role. However, within the social insurance structure, increased take-up of 'atypical' forms of employment brings into focus the gaps in the social insurance system. A particular case is the lack of any social insurance cover for illness or disability for self-employed people. The National Pensions Board (1998) in examining options for the extension of social insurance to the self-employed, recommended that initially cover for long-term illness or invalidity be provided on a means-tested basis, with the possibility of a social insurance payment to be reviewed at a later stage in the light of experience. Invalidity Pension (or some similar payment) for self-employed PRSI contributors is therefore likely to be on the policy agenda in the future.

In recent years, much of the social policy agenda has been driven by the various national partnership agreements, most recently the Programme for Prosperity and Fairness. At time of writing, the PPF is due to expire and negotiations on a possible new Programme are scheduled to begin before the end of 2002. It remains to be seen what additional measures in relation to social security for people with disabilities will emerge from this process.

Acknowledgement: This chapter draws on research undertaken by my colleague Enda Flynn in the Department of Social and Family Affairs. Thanks are also due to Phil Cox, also from the Department, who provided comments on an earlier draft. Any errors or omissions are of course the responsibility of the author.

Chapter 5

Access and independent living

Gráinne McGettrick

Introduction and overview

The concept and practice of independent living has a relatively short history in the field of disability. Born primarily out of disability activism in the 1970s, the ability and capacity of disabled people to achieve independent living require the existence and availability of a number of essential prerequisites including accessible housing, community care supports, such as personal assistance, accessible transport, assistive technology and peer support. Furthermore, independent living requires the recognition of an individual's civil and human rights, the empowerment of disabled people to exercise choice and control over their own lives as well as their engagement in the decision-making process.

'Access' is one of the core elements essential to the achievement of independent living. However, access has many different elements. In the broadest sense, disabled people need access to the political, economic and social structures to enable them to participate actively and to achieve independent living. The environment within which disabled people operate, specifically the built and external environment, plays a fundamental role and is a pre-condition for permitting this broader access. Disabled people's ability to perform even the most routine of daily tasks is severely diminished because of a predominately inaccessible environment (Barnes, 1991: 180).

The built environment forms the focus of this chapter. The discussion pertains primarily to people with physical and sensory disability, as they are one of the primary stakeholders in terms of the creation of a barrier-free environment. The chapter is concerned with creating an understanding of what independent living is, placing access and the external environment within the independent living framework and discussing the current access provisions in the context of contemporary Irish social policy.

Brief historical overview

The history of disability is in general characterised by marginalisation, segregation and institutionalisation. By examining the history of disability, it becomes clear why disabled people continue to remain on the margins of society. Because of their status, disabled people have historically played little or no role in how society was constructed. Driedgner (1989: 2) points to the impact that such exclusion has had in relation to accessible environments. The 'warehousing' of disabled people in institutions and the 'shutting away' in family homes have meant that they have had no input into the design of the built environment, with far-reaching implications:

> If mobility impaired people could not enter buildings, they could not attend university, hold down a job or find a place to live outside an institution. Without education and income, disabled people could not become independent and enter the mainstream of society. (Driedger, 1989: 2)

The recent history of disability has witnessed a shift in the response of society and social policy to disability. This is primarily attributed to the growing demand for change articulated by disabled people themselves. The increased organisation by disabled people resulted in the emergence of the independent living/disability rights movement, initially in the United States in the 1970s and expanding into Europe in subsequent years. Referred to as the 'last of the civil rights movements' (Driedger, 1989: 1), it manifested itself primarily through the emergence throughout the world of large numbers of organisations comprising disabled people. The disability rights movement, with disabled people acting as catalysts of change, is now, like all social movements, finding expression in social and public policy. Oliver (1990: 90) views the disability rights movement as a 'contemporary struggle to tilt the balance of history in favour of a fairer and more equitable future for disabled people'.

From an Irish historical context, Colgan (1997) points out that a range of elements have contributed to the significant improvement in the quality of life of disabled people over the past 50 years. These include legislation, economic development, medical and technological advances, advances in thinking about service delivery methods, political and cultural influences. She also notes the influence of the British welfare state on Irish social policy and how European and American thinking has shaped the responses to disability issues in Ireland. The newly established National Disability Authority in Ireland (2001a) refers to the manifestations of historical neglect in relation to the denial of disabled people's rights in the plethora of policy responses. It also identifies the historical emphasis on the charitable model, which has significantly influenced attitudes and curtailed the potential of disabled people to actively engage and contribute to society and achieve independent living. The predominant view historically in Ireland has been the 'special needs' approach in terms of access, in which the 'normal' environment should be modified, as far as is reasonable, to be made usable by people with impairments. Viewing access as an 'add-on' rather than as an integral part of the planning and design process further compounded this approach.

Despite overall improvements in the quality of life for disabled people in the last number of decades, many commentators conclude that disabled people's needs in relation to the built environment are poorly articulated in social and public policy (Barnes, 1991; Imrie, 1996). The consequence of history, as well as other factors, has meant that the design of the built environment is 'disablist' (Imrie and Kumar, 1998) in that it continues to restrict and discriminate against disabled people's mobility and access requirements.

European Union and the international context

The commonality of the issues pertaining to disability has meant that they have traversed regional and national borders. According to Driedger (1989: 1) the formation of Disabled Peoples' International (DPI) represents the first successful effort of people with various disabilities to create a 'united voice at the international level'. DPI represents ten per cent of the world's population who are disabled, one way or another. As discussed by Quin and Redmond (1999), the process of politicisation of disabled people has been particularly strong in the United States. The growth of the grassroots consumer movement in the United States has had a great impact internationally, especially in promoting the concept of independent living. The Commission on the Status of People with Disabilities (1996) acknowledges the growth and development of the Irish disability rights movement, specifically identifying the resurgence towards the end of the UN Decade of Disabled Persons (1981–90). The influence of disability activism in Europe is acknowledged as a key impetus for the emergence of the Irish disability rights movement.

Barrier-free design as a key to independent living is of interest to disabled people everywhere. Examples of good practice in designing an enabling environment have universal application and the exchange of experience and ideas at international and European level is an important tool of empowerment, which is apparent in the work of organisations such as Disabled Peoples' International, the European Network on Independent Living and the European Disability Forum (Driedger, 1989; Oliver and Barnes, 1993; Davis, 1993).

One significant piece of legislation that has influenced disability issues on the world stage is the American with Disabilities Act (ADA) of 1990. The ADA has been used extensively by disability activists as a model to promote anti-discrimination legislation at a national level in many countries. It also serves as a model of excellence in the Irish context, as recommended by the Commission on the Status of People with Disabilities (1996).

Tubridy (1996: 245) points out that at an international level, one of the most important recent developments, in terms of consciousness raising on disability issues, was the adoption of the United Nations Standard Rules on the Equalisation of Opportunities for Persons with Disabilities in 1994 by all member states. The UN Standard Rules set out standards and targets for member states in a wide variety of areas relating to disability including, among others, access, education, employment, income, information and recreation. They are not legally binding, but as Colgan (1997) argues, the Rules provide a legal standard for programmes, policies and laws concerning participation and equality. Colgan (1997: 123) concludes that the Standard Rules offer 'ready-made performance indicators for any government seriously committed to the task of securing inclusion and participation'. Rule 5 of the Standard Rules (UN, 1994: 22) sets out guidelines for accessibility:

> States should recognise the overall importance of accessibility in the process of the equalisation of opportunity in all spheres of society. For persons with disabilities of any kind, states should (a) introduce programmes of actions to make the physical environment accessible; and (b) undertake measures to provide access to information and communication.

From the European perspective, many countries have developed a range of policy and programme responses which attempt to address barrier-free design and create increased accessibility for disabled people. Imrie (1996: 97) argues that within Europe most if not all responses in relation to creating an accessible environment have been 'piecemeal, *ad hoc* and poorly resourced' and tend to be an add-on to social policies rather than being an integral part of them. At the supranational EU level, he argues that the response has been singular, with the emphasis being on 'socio-technical' solutions towards access in which 'design' alone would overturn disabling barriers. Despite the limitations, the European and international contexts remain critical for influencing disability policy in general and as fora for exchange of best practice, the development of standards and lobbying for change at the national level.

Current policy on access and independent living in Ireland

Irish disability policy has undoubtedly experienced a significant philosophical shift in emphasis away from institutionalisation and segregation towards inclusion and mainstreaming. However, the reality is that the shift in policy has not necessarily been translated into practice. Much of the philosophical shift is accompanied only by the rhetoric of creating the necessary conditions for disabled people to achieve independent living. As the analysis in this chapter shows, disabled people are still operating on the margins, excluded from the mainstream. The lack of appropriate social policy responses to disabled people's access needs has denied their access and right to participate in the socio-institutional fabric of society.

A policy document, the Report of the Commission on the Status of People with Disabilities (1996), has had major influence in the field of disability in Ireland. The Commission Report (1996: 1) acknowledges access as being 'the gateway to full participation'. It further acknowledges that access is not just about access to buildings but about the right to access a broad range of activities in mainstream society. The Commission Report highlights the frustration and anger caused to disabled people through inaccessible environments and confirms their isolation and marginalisation from society. The Report contains a set of recommendations to promote access and recommends the introduction of standards for the design and maintenance of the external built environment as well as recommending a set of actions that would promote access and opportunities for Irish disabled people.

Part M of the building regulations

The Department of the Environment and Local Government is one of the key statutory agencies with responsibility for ensuring access to the built environment and housing for disabled people, with each local authority having an important role in building control and the maintenance of the external environment. A vital instrument governing environmental access for people with disabilities is Part M of the Building Regulations (established under the Building Control Act, 1990). Part M provides for 'Access and Facilities for Disabled People' requiring that all new buildings for public use be accessible to disabled people. Part M and the associated Technical Guidance document emerged in 1991, was revised in 1997 and again in 2000.

In 2000, Part M of the building regulations was amended to make houses 'visitable' by people with disabilities. This requires that houses that are subject to application for planning permission must now comply with Part M. Any new house commencing on or after January 2001 should therefore be designed so that disabled people can safely and conveniently approach and gain access to the main habitable rooms as well as having a WC provided at entry level. The National Economic and Social Council (1999: 525) argues that this amendment represents a significant shift towards the concept of 'lifetime adaptable housing' and the enhancement of the housing rights of citizens with disabilities.

The revision of Part M reflects a major improvement and progression in the policy response to the access needs of disabled people. In particular, the inclusion of private dwellings for the first time in the Regulations is laudable, as is the more stringent legal requirement for public buildings. Access provisions will have to be 'adequate' not just 'reasonable' as in the 1997 Regulations. A positive element of the process of the review of the 1997 Regulations was the consultation with the key stakeholders, including organisations of and for disabled people. This represents the first serious attempt by policy makers to engage disabled people in discussions about the type of environment they wish to live in.

However, the lack of enforcement with very few sanctions for non-compliance means that Part M is very weak and effectively ignored in relation to creating a more accessible built environment for disabled people. The UK experience mirrors the situation in Ireland; Imrie and Kumar (1998: 359) conclude that while planning and building control departments have some statutory responsibility for regulating access, evidence shows that few local planning authorities have adopted access policies, while fewer seem to insist that developers incorporate access into proposed building schemes. Moreover, they argue that local authorities tend to regard disability as a medical rather than an environmental issue, which potentially 'absolves planning and/or other officers, of their responsibilities to overturn inaccessible spaces in the built environment'.

Policy on access and public services

A commitment to improving accessibility of public services is made in the national social partnership agreement, the Programme for Prosperity and Fairness (Government of Ireland, 2000). According to this agreement, each government department will ensure that reasonable steps are taken to make its services and those of agencies under its remit accessible to people with disabilities within five years. To facilitate effective action and acceptable standards, the National Disability Authority (NDA) will issue guidelines in accordance with national norms and will award an accessibility symbol to compliant public offices. Adequate resources will be provided to the NDA and the Department of Justice, Equality and Law Reform to monitor, guide and audit progress towards the achievement of this commitment. The NDA (2001a) has incorporated this commitment as one of its strategic priorities in its strategic plan 2001–3. This commitment is important in that it represents recognition on behalf of the government that disabled people need access to public buildings and services. It is a national recognition of the issue, with commitment to producing national guidelines and allocation of resources as well as monitoring of implementation. Some progress has already being made on this commitment, and 'the need to render as many public buildings as possible to persons with disabilities is accepted' (Department of Justice, Equality and Law Reform, 1999a: 25). A number of constraints are highlighted which impact on the speed with which government departments can make their premises accessible to disabled people. Such constraints include the costs associated with the adaptations, the fact that public bodies are often lessees of buildings in private ownership, the physical and space constraints and the need to account for the 'heritage value' of some buildings (Department of Justice, Equality and Law Reform, 1999a).

Access and the broader environment

In relation to broader environmental access – streetscapes, signage, parking, roads, outdoor amenities, street furniture – the situation is even more acute as there are no legal standards or agreed national guidelines. The Commission on the Status of People with Disabilities Report (1996: 26) called for structures to be put in place to develop policy and practice as well as monitor progress in relation to the universal right of access to the built and external environments. However, there are no plans by the Department to establish a national committee for the purposes outlined in relation to broader environmental access as this is viewed as a responsibility of each local authority (Department of Justice, Equality and Law Reform, 1999a).

The absence of a national policy and standards for the external environment represents a major and detrimental gap, resulting in the first instance in very poor levels of awareness and understanding of the access needs of disabled people. With the non-existence of policies and legislation in this area, disabled people have very little ability to influence the development of the environment they live in. Tubridy (1996) remarks that one of the key ways in which awareness in relation to environmental access has been raised is through the emergence of local access groups in towns and cities throughout Ireland. While having the capacity to raise the awareness, local access groups still rely on the goodwill of local authority officials and other key stakeholders to instigate change. They operate in a vacuum, lack any contextual framework at a national level and remain powerless at the local level.

A new national 'good practice' initiative that has recently emerged is the Barcelona Declaration Project, delivered by the Institute of Design and Disability (2002) on behalf of the National Disability Authority. The aim of the project is to encourage local government to make provision for the inclusion of people with disabilities in the community which it represents, specifically in the area of environmental access. The Barcelona Declaration is the manifesto outcome of a European Congress, 'The City and the Disabled', held in 1995, which has since been adopted by many European countries. The project will involve a number of elements including promoting awareness of the needs of disabled people among local authorities; developing and delivering disability proofing programmes in terms of local authority decision making and activities; providing good practice guidelines and facilitating local authorities to meet the needs of disabled people. A number of local authorities in Ireland have already adopted the Declaration. While the project represents a move towards the promotion of 'good practice' in local authorities, it is not binding and therefore there is no obligation on the local authority to adopt or implement the Declaration.

Access and the law

Recent legislative developments impacting directly on the question of access for disabled people have resulted from equality legislation, the Employment Equality Act, 1998 and the Equal Status Act, 2000. The latter outlaws discrimination against disabled people in the provision of goods and services, the former in terms of the workplace. The Equal Status Act, 2000 contains a separate section (Section 4) dealing with disability discrimination, which states that a person selling goods or providing services, a person selling or letting accommodation or providing accommodation, educational institutions and clubs, must do all that is reasonable to accommodate the needs of a person with a disability by providing special treatment or facilities in circumstances where, without these, it would be impossible or unduly difficult to make use of goods, services and accommodation. However, they are not obliged to provide special facilities or treatment when the cost would be more that what is called nominal cost. What amounts to nominal cost depends on the circumstances of each individual case (Equality Authority, 2000).

O'Connell (2000: 1) sees the Equal Status Act 2000 as finally giving full legal effect to the principle of 'reasonable accommodation', a feature of other countries' disability rights legislation. However, he points out that we did it 'Irish style' and the form of reasonable accommodation which we have enshrined in law is qualified by the now 'infamous nominal cost criterion'. In practice, this means that if in making 'reasonable accommodation' for a disabled person, the service provider entails more than a nominal cost, then the 'reasonable accommodation' does not have to be made as a matter of law. Effectively, the nominal cost qualification counteracts any meaningful right of access in terms of the provision of goods and services. As a result of the nominal cost clause, the potential for this legislation to impact on the built and external environment both in the public and private sectors is extremely curtailed. Of the 675 cases dealt with by the Equality Authority under the Equal Status Act, 2000, only 46 were brought under the disability grounds, and of these, 22 relate to 'access to pub/club/restaurant' and 'wheelchair access' (Equality Authority, 2002: 29). It is acknowledged that legislation forms only the basis through which disabled people have the right to access services and goods and that significantly more is required to ensure full and active participation by disabled people in the mainstream. However, the absence of rights-based legislation remains a fundamental weakness in addressing the inclusion of disabled people in Irish society.

Critique of current policy

Current Irish social policies in relation to access clearly point to deficient and ineffectual statutory controls governing access needs. Overall, a number of elements within Part M of the building regulations, as well as the lack of regulation in the broader external environment, militate against the creation of a barrier-free environment for disabled people. Despite advocating the need for a rights-based approach, current policy provisions are not aimed at establishing an enabling environment but at making special provision for special cases, endorsing the view that disability is an individualised, medical problem and not as a social responsibility (Commission on the Status of People with Disabilities, 1996). The policy approach as set out in the current regulations is to 'separate out the requirements of people with disabilities from those of the general public of which they are actually a part'. By presenting their contents in the form of 'special provision' the regulations and guidance do not offer advice on the full and positive potential which accrues from making buildings and the environment accessible (National Rehabilitation Board, 1998: i).

As is the case in the UK's Disability Discrimination Act 1996, the *right* to access is not reflected in either Irish policy or legislative provision. The equality legislation has, to date, not managed to fully embrace the rights-based approach. Conroy (2002: 12) comments that the Irish legislative framework in relation to disabled people's rights is problematic because of its piecemeal nature, and concludes that the result of this piecemeal approach is that existing legislation is not comprehensive enough, not enforced or not delivered.

In addition, Part M of the Building Regulations remains vague and ambiguous with no standards or legislative provision at all governing the external environment. While progress at a national level in relation to the national social partnership commitments and good practice initiatives are positive steps, there remains little strategy or coherence in the overall policy approach to access for disabled people. Disabled people's capacity to achieve independent living therefore continues to be seriously curtailed. A hostile built and external environment is a significant barrier to the achievement of independent living. By denying disabled people the right of access, they have very little opportunity to exercise self-determination, choice and control over their own lives.

Universal right of access and *access for all* are now the associated articulation with access policies for disabled people, both nationally and internationally. The reality of the Irish policy response in this area is that it has been *ad hoc* and fragmented, mirroring the policy approach in the field of disability in general.

Independent living

In order to understand the central and critical role access plays in relation to the achievement of independent living, it is necessary to examine what is meant by independent living and in particular how it is defined by the independent living/disability rights movement, a radical consumer movement led by disabled people themselves.

The philosophy of the independent living movement is based on four assumptions: that all human life is of value; that anyone whatever their impairment is capable of exerting choices; that people who are disabled by society's reaction to physical, intellectual or sensory impairment have the right to assert control over their lives; and that disabled people have the right to fully participate in society (Morris, 1993a). Essentially, the independent living philosophy espouses living like everyone else; being able to have control of one's own life; having opportunities to make decisions that affect one's life and being able to pursue activities of one's own choosing, regardless of disability. Disabled Peoples' International, as a worldwide consumer-led organisation, sees independent living as a process over which disabled people must have individual and collective control. This philosophy:

> emphasises our right to self determination. Self-determination implies that we take responsibility for our own lives and see ourselves not as objects of care or humanitarian concern but as citizens with all the rights and duties that full citizenship entails. (1991: 3)

The philosophy also includes the possibility of failure and risk. DeJong (1979: 442) points out that the 'dignity of risk' is what the independent living movement is all about. Without the possibility of failure the disabled person is said to lack true independence and the mark of one's humanity is 'the right to choose between good and evil'.

Independent living is a relative term and what is important is the freedom to choose the degree of independence or dependence most suitable to an individual's lifestyle and social pattern. Furthermore, independent living expands the notion of independence away from physical achievements towards political and socio-economic decision making. It is concerned with the personal and economic choices that disabled people make. As Crewe and Zola (1987: 347) argue, to retain the 'old physical criteria' of independence only 'contributes to the very isolation we seek to avoid'.

The independent living movement has now developed into something much more than a grassroots effort on the part of disabled people to acquire new rights. It is beginning to reshape the focus of disability policy, promote new forms of service delivery and revise the thinking of professionals, policy makers and researchers. In other words, the movement has led to the emergence of a new analytical paradigm (DeJong, 1979), which is at variance with the dominant and traditional medical model.

The focus of the problem of disability within the independent living paradigm lies in both the environment and the social control mechanisms in society at large, rather than with the individual, as the medical model suggests. To cope with the environmental barriers, the disabled person must shed the 'patient' role for the consumer role. Advocacy, peer support, self-help, consumer control and barrier removal are the trademarks of the independent living paradigm. DeJong (1979: 444) summarises the key characteristics of this alternative model. The independent living model:

> offers us an opportunity to steer away from the myopic pre-occupation with unalterable individual characteristics that direct our attention from the larger institutional and environmental context in which disabled people live. The institutional and environmental context has for too long been accepted as given.

Independent living in Ireland

From an Irish perspective, the Independent Living Movement had its genesis in the early 1990s. A number of key factors influenced the emergence of the Irish disability rights movement, among them, the significant role played by individual disability activists, the influence of developments in the European and international Independent Living Movement and the lack of appropriate national responses from existing disability policy and services for people with significant physical disabilities. The practical manifestation of the Independent Living Movement in Ireland is witnessed in the development of Centres for Independent Living (CILs) throughout the country, as well as the emergence of a small number of organisations *of* disabled people, including the Forum of People with Disabilities and People with Disabilities in Ireland.

The first Centre for Independent Living (CIL) was established in Dublin in 1991; there are now almost 30 CILs nationwide. CILs have brought together a critical mass of disabled people who are working at the grassroots level, demanding their rights as equal citizens. The first Dublin-based CIL was instrumental in pioneering the first-ever pilot personal assistance service (PAS) programme in Ireland in 1992 which gradually expanded to other parts of the country over the last decade. Personal assistance services, viewed as the cornerstone service of the Independent Living Movement, involve the provision of a consumer-managed service, providing support to a person with a disability to carry out everyday activities with assistance. The PAS plays a critical role in enabling people with significant physical disabilities to achieve independent living at an individual level. In Ireland, as has been the experience elsewhere, the development of personal assistance has been successful in supporting disabled people to come together as a collective to address and work on common issues, lobby for policy and service changes and campaign in areas affecting the achievement of independent living – including housing, transport, environmental access, education, employment, PAS, rights-based legislation and promoting the social model approach in policy and service provision. While such issues have always been on the disability agenda, the unique element offered by the Independent Living Movement is that it is disabled people themselves acting as agents of change. The Irish Independent Living Movement, with its slogan 'Nothing about us, without us', continues to remain a significant force on the disability landscape, challenging existing boundaries and creating new opportunities for disabled people who traditionally have remained on the margins.

Two major criticisms of the Independent Living Movement nationally and internationally are, first that, it has almost exclusively remained in the domain of those with significant physical disabilities. Its lack of a cross disability focus has meant that people with learning disabilities and mental health problems have not successfully engaged in the process to date. Secondly, the inability of the movement to engage non-disabled people in the struggle as supporters and allies has been criticised. Indeed, both criticisms present significant challenges to the movement for the future.

Independent living and the environment

The independent living paradigm proposes that the presence of environmental barriers critically affect the level of independence of disabled people (Dunn, 1990). Fundamentally, it suggests that the cause of 'disability' resides not within the individual but within the various environments. Swain *et al.* (1993) assert that an individual's experience of 'disability' is created in the various interactions with a social and physical world designed for non-disabled living, thus reaching barriers of exclusion from participation and full citizenship. The creation of disabling barriers resulting in the lack of access has contributed significantly to the marginalisation and segregation that disabled people experience in their lives on a day-to-day basis.

It is clear that the environments need to be altered to enable the disabled person to achieve independent living. This means that the myriad of barriers that exist including physical, architectural, socio-economic, communication, attitudinal and institutional, have to be broken down. Imrie (1996: 7) purports that inaccessible environments are an expression of social inequality rein-forcing disabled people's 'subordinate and marginal status in society' and one of the crucial contexts underpinning disabled people's experiences of oppression and domination. Varela (1983), in discussing the struggle in the United States for a barrier-free environment, indicates that the fight for accessibility added a singular perspective to the debate on disability rights – people are disabled by a poorly designed environment (social, political, intellectual and physical) that fails to meet their needs.

By defining disability in terms of disabling barriers that prevent disabled people accessing social and economic life, the independent living paradigm has been successful in engaging a whole range of policy and professional areas – architects, town planners, lawyers, sociologists, economists and social policy makers. This also reflects, however, the significant level of complexity of disability issues and the need for a cross-disciplinary and integrated response. Furthermore, the interdependency of the issues also adds to the complexity. For example, the need for physical access is a prerequisite for giving a physically disabled person access to education. The disabled person's participation may well be dependent on the availability of accessible public transport, the pro-vision of personal assistance in the educational setting and the existence of a non-prejudicial attitude among staff and students of the educational establish-ment. This interdependency of issues is highlighted in a study carried out on employment and disabled people in County Donegal (Kitchin *et al.*, 1998). Participants (disabled people) in the study felt that whether they could manage to persuade employers to employ them remained largely redundant until the problems of accessibility of work environments and transport were tackled.

Developments and future challenges

The existence of an enabling environment is essential to the achievement of independent living. Environmental access is inextricably linked to broader socio-economic relations in society and societal prejudices. Without basic access disabled people are systematically excluded and segregated from the mainstream. In order to achieve independent living in Ireland, a radical shift is required at many different levels. Specifically, the creation of an enabling environment to allow for independent living requires a holistic, integrated and multi-disciplinary response. In addition, a completely new way of thinking and operating by social and public policy makers, designers, architects, planners and the public in general is essential.

Anti-discrimination legislation, as the European and international contexts illustrate, is the essential future first step if a society is committed to ensuring and upholding the rights of people with disabilities. Therefore, one of the most fundamental elements that needs to be addressed by policy makers in Ireland is the introduction of rights-based legislation which would include making access provisions for disabled people in the built and external environments enforceable.

In addition to comprehensive rights-based legislation, national standards for the built and external environments, best-practice guidelines, strict enforcement and substantial sanctions for non-compliance with the standards should be put in place. In addition, a process of re-education and awareness-raising of all the key stakeholders is an important element. The creation of an accessible environment should be part of the mainstream policy-making and planning processes. The process of 'disability proofing' all social and public policies, practices and activities is one of a number of tools that can be utilised to ensure that disabled people's requirements are considered and addressed in mainstream policy making. Disability proofing is necessary not only at the national, but also at the regional and local levels. Irish social and public policy needs to move beyond the medicalised and static concepts of disability towards reconstructing disability as residing in 'disabling' environments that are socially and environmentally created. Furthermore, the solution to disability is in the creation of enabling environments providing 'a society that is fit for all' (Swain *et al.*, 1993: 6).

In the process of creating an accessible environment, people with disabilities, although one of the key stakeholders, have to date been excluded. The environments have been created and developed without reference to their needs. One major challenge for Irish policy making is how best to achieve full and democratic participation by disabled people in the decision-making processes and in shaping society in general. A challenge for the disability rights movement is to build its capacity to engage effectively in international, European, national and local policy-making fora. The future role of the disability rights movement is crucial in addressing the rights-based agenda and promoting the policy and practice of independent living. Central to this agenda is the promotion of an enabling environment as one of the essential elements to achieve access and participation along with the movement acting as an agent for social change in general.

The disability rights movement is moving inexorably to the centre of the stage and its significance lies not in the legacy it will leave behind but in the new forms of social relations it will be instrumental in creating. (Oliver, 1990: 93)

Recommended Reading

Commission on the Status of People with Disabilities (1996) *A Strategy for Equality.* Dublin: Stationery Office.

Crewe, N.M. and Zola, I. K. (eds) (1983) *Independent Living for Physically Disabled People.* San Francisco: Josey-Bass.

DeJong, G. (1979) 'Independent living: From social movement to analytic paradigm', *Archives of Physical Medicine and Rehabilitation,* 60: 436–46.

Imrie, R. (1996) *Disability and the City: International Perspectives.* London: Paul Chapman.

Swain, J., Finkelstein, V., French, S. and Oliver, M. (eds) (1993) *Disabling Barriers: Enabling Environments.* London: Sage.

Chapter 6

Health services and disability

Suzanne Quin

Health policy and disability are inextricably linked. At some or all stages of their lives, people with disabilities will come to the attention of health providers and require their services. Health care has been traditionally linked to disability since the inception of medical interventions. Throughout history, to quote Winzer (1997: 84), 'the medical aspects of disabilities have been paramount; other concerns relating to disability have been secondary, where they have been considered at all'. The link between health care and disability is particularly strong in Ireland given that personal social services are subsumed under the umbrella of health. This includes a substantial input from voluntary organisations in this field which have played and continue to play a significant role as support, conveyors of information, and service providers in different types of disability.

This chapter will begin with a brief historical overview on the relationship between health services and disability. It will discuss current policy and provision of health services for people with disability in Ireland. Attention will be directed to the role of voluntary bodies in service development and delivery. The particular health issues facing women with disabilities, those who are dependent on others for aspects of personal care and people from different ethnic minorities will be considered. Finally, the chapter will address the challenges of new and future developments in the interrelationship between disability and health care.

Historical overview of disability and health services

According to Winzer (1997), documented evidence of interest in the causes and effects of different types of disability dates back to the papyrus manuscripts of ancient Egypt. Amongst the disabilities referred to in the hieroglyphics are epilepsy, deafness and visual impairment. Medical understanding and philosophical assumptions were inextricably linked for the Greek and Roman civilisations where the primary focus of concern was the aetiology of disabilities, particularly insanity, deafness and blindness. This linking of moral explanations with physical effects was also evident in medieval society and resulted in some disabilities attracting more negative attributes in comparison to others. Hence, blindness attracted more sympathy and support than deafness, which, because of the difficulties in communication, was assumed to be associated with mental incompetence.

The provision of services for those with disabilities was subject to the living conditions, beliefs and personal relationships in medieval society. At a time when, for the population as a whole, survival was uncertain, life expectancy short and living conditions poor, those with any form of disability had little chance of survival. The creation of hospices and almshouses provided some succour for a fortunate few. It was the development of understanding of the physical cause of certain types of disabilities, in tandem with improvements in the material conditions of the population as a whole, that specialist services to meet the needs of those with different types of disabilities began. However, the medicalisation of disability had inherent drawbacks from the viewpoint of those affected. Borsay (1998: 655) argues that 'while Social Darwinism and the Eugenics Movement are of the nineteenth-century origin, medical practice before 1800 was also instrumental in disempowering disabled people'.

Medical model *v* social model of disability

It was 'the medicalisation of the body' which led to what Barnes (1993) describes as the systematic exclusion of people with impairments from the mainstream of community life. Thus, while the medicalisation of disability was instrumental in the creation of service provision, focus on the medical aspects of disability distracted from other aspects of disability such as those of education, employment, transport and social relationships. The medical model of disability has been criticised for viewing disability in terms of physical deficiencies resulting from impairment in relation to 'ideal type' norms of the able-bodied person (Oliver, 1996). As such, the disability was the prime focus with the service provider acting as an expert whose task was to redress the defined deficiencies as far as possible. Service recipients were expected to participate in this task, reluctance being perceived as lack of motivation or inability to accept reality. Hence, the target for change was the person with the disability whose prime task was that of physical adaptation and psychological acceptance.

Critics of the medical model point to its failure to take into account the social context in which the disability occurs. Living and working conditions, it is argued, are not organised to take account of differences. In this way, many people, in addition to those who are defined as disabled, are impeded or even excluded from one or more aspects of everyday life. A public transport system that is not wheelchair accessible, for example, is also likely to create difficult if not impossible conditions for frail older people or parents with babies and/or toddlers. A social model of disability, it is argued, requires change in the social world rather than in the people who inhabit it. It further requires a radical change on the part of professional service providers to adopting a rights perspective in relation to disability and to planning and creating services in partnership with existing and potential service users.

Proponents of the social model have criticised health professionals for perpetuating the medical model by focusing on physical impairments and viewing disability as a form of personal tragedy for the individual and his/her family (Oliver and Sapey, 1999). This may represent the attitudes and feelings on the part of professional staff, rather than the reality of the experience from the subjective viewpoint of those affected. Bogdan *et al.* (1992), for example, found staff of a neonatal unit where some of the babies were likely to survive but had disabilities to 'take the five-stage model of adjustment popularised by Kubler-Ross for terminally ill patients and apply it unchanged to the parents they encountered'. Likewise, staff in a rehabilitation context, working with patients with impairments arising from accidents or illness, can see it as their task to redress, insofar as it is possible, deficits in physical functioning, without reference to patients' priorities. Rehabilitation, according to Oliver (1996), has been based on the principle that disabled individuals must be restored to as near to 'normal functioning' where cure was unavailable.

French (1994), in a review of research studies on health professionals' attitudes towards people with disabilities, found conflicting evidence as to whether or not they differed from the population in general. Of particular concern was some evidence that health professionals' attitudes could become more negative in the course of their careers. As a result of the studies examined, French (1994: 162) emphasised the importance of health professionals receiving 'high quality disability equality training, that they understood the meaning of disability as disabled people define it, and that they are informed about the important role disabled people have played in the development of services'.

The controlling influence of health care on many aspects of the lives of people with disabilities has been commented on by writers such as Barnes (1993), French (1994), and Oliver (1996). French (1994: 109) states that 'because disability has been medicalised, disabled people often find they are compelled to go through a medical professional, or a bureaucratic agency, to get a service they require or a piece of equipment they need'. Hence, she argues that while medical care may form only a small part of their everyday lives, people with disabilities can find that the health professionals have considerable control over their lives as gatekeepers to limited resources. Professional dominance can thus render services for disabled people 'limited, inconvenient, inefficient and frustrating'.

On the same theme, Finkelstein (1993: 41) suggests in the British context that the 'Department of the Environment rather than Health and Welfare should be the main "home" for organising disability-related services in the community'. This is on the grounds that those services focused on reducing physical and social barriers are the ones most relevant for people with disabilities. This view that health care is limited in what it can offer the majority of people with disability is reflective of the social model which emphasises the importance of rights, not needs, as a basis for service provision.

Wendell (1996) views the social and physical barriers as significant problems for people with disabilities. However, she expresses concern that exclusive focus on their elimination could distract from the 'hard physical realities faced by many people with disabilities'. She is also critical of the social model insofar as it tends to put all those with disabilities into one social group, thereby ignoring differences in gender, ethnicity, socio-economic circumstances age and different disabling conditions. While people with disabilities had social experiences in common, she argues, differences cannot be ignored.

Differences in diagnostic conditions and in the experiences of different people sharing a similar condition are important in understanding the wide-ranging nature of disability in relation to health care. The extent to which 'disability' is an umbrella term covering a range of conditions, many of which can vary in their effects from minor to profound, makes it difficult even to identify the extent of disability in a population. In Ireland, the lack of statistical information on the numbers and needs of people with physical and sensory disabilities has made service planning difficult (Department of Health and Children, Strategy Document, 2001b: 142). The recent establishment of a database in relation to physical disabilities, in tandem with the longer standing database on learning disability provides a much needed basis for effective service planning.

Health services and disability in Ireland

The Department of Health and Children has overall responsibility for the ensuring that the health care needs of the population are met. The function of the health boards is to provide health services to meet the needs in accordance with policy and available resources. In some respects, the title of 'Department of Health and Children' and of 'Health Board' is a misnomer, since the brief also encompasses policy and provision of personal social services. The proposal was put forward in the document *Health: The Wider Dimensions* (Department of Health, 1986) to rename the health boards to reflect more accurately the extent of their involvement in the provision of welfare supports. This is echoed in a recommendation of *Report of the Commission on the Status of People with Disabilities* (1996) that Health Boards should be described as Health and Social Service Authorities to better reflect their brief. The Health Strategy (Department of Health and Children, 2001b: 141), *Towards Quality and Fairness: A Health System For You*, states that the principle underpinning policy in this area is 'to enable each individual with a disability to achieve his or her full potential and maximum independence, including living within the community as independently as possible'.

The amalgam of personal social services with health has important implications for those with disability. On the one hand, it can be argued that a holistic definition of health properly incorporates care needs of different sections of the population. On the other hand, the inextricable linkage of health with continuing personal-care needs can serve to perpetuate the linking of inability to carry out tasks of daily living without help with pathology.

The *Report of the Commission on the Status of People with Disabilities* (1996) argued for a rights approach to the provision of services. It cited three principles informing recent international legislation and practice: the recognition of disability as a social rather than a medical issue; the adoption of a civil rights perspective; and recognition of equality as a key feature of the human rights approach (1996: 8). In relation to health services and disability, the Commission (1996) listed a total of 36 recommendations relating to different aspects of the service. The areas addressed ranged from physical inaccessibility, deficiencies and disparities in availability of community-based services, and lack of consumer control, to greater disability awareness on the part of health professionals.

An earlier report specifically focusing on health and personal social services for people with physical and sensory disabilities, *Towards an Independent Future* (Report of the Review Group on Health and Personal Social Services for People with Physical and Sensory Disabilities, 1996), had identified a number of deficits and had made proposals both in relation to structures and service provision to address them. A key recommendation in this report was to address the lack of reliable information outlined above by creating a comprehensive database on the health care needs of those with physical and sensory disabilities. This task had already been undertaken in the area of learning disability following the Report of the Review Group on Mental Handicap Services in 1991 (Review Group on Mental Handicap Services, 1991).

The Report published in 1999, *Towards Equal Citizenship* (Department of Equity and Law Reform, 1999), reviewed in detail the progress made in the interim on the numerous recommendations made by the Commission in 1996. In relation to health services, the Department of Health and Children pointed out that there were a significant number of recommendations that would take a number of years to address fully. In terms of establishing a comprehensive database as a basis for service planning, a Database Committee, established in

1998, formulated guidelines for the collection of data nationally, which is now in process. Health Board Co-ordination Committees, already in place since the early 1990s in relation to services for those with learning disability, were established in connection with physical and sensory disabilities in 1998. These committees comprise representatives of the local health board, and of voluntary organisations that are service providers and service users (where appropriate, parents of service users). The purpose of the committees is to promote a partnership model of service delivery, to address any gaps and overlaps in existing services and to identify priorities for the development of services such as home helps, day centres and personal assistants based on local knowledge and local needs.

Eligibility for health care

People with disabilities share the same general conditions for eligibility to public health care as the population in general. Essentially, there are two categories of eligibility.

Category One
Those in Category One are entitled to what is known as a medical card from their local health board. This is subject to a means test, the amount of which is reviewed annually to keep pace with the overall cost of living. Those holding a medical card can avail themselves of free general practitioner services, free public hospital care including accident and emergency (with a GP referral) and out-patient clinics. Prescribed medicines are available free of charge and the holder is entitled to free dental, ophthalmic and aural services and appliances, although the actual provision of these can be limited in reality. While a basic means test is the condition for eligibility, discretion is allowed to go beyond this for anyone with greater than average needs of health services that result in their inability to provide for themselves without undue hardship. At present, approximately 30 per cent of the general population hold medical cards (Department of Health and Children, 2001b). The proportion of people with disabilities holding medical cards would be considerably above average given the link between poverty and disability as discussed in the chapter by Harbison in chapter 11.

Category Two
The remainder of the population falls into this category. As in Category One, they have cover for public hospital care, in-patient and out-patient and consultant services in public beds. They are liable for limited charges for in-patient and out patient care and are not entitled to free GP services or free

prescribed medicines. There is also a list of prescribed conditions such as multiple sclerosis, epilepsy, Parkinsonism. Those with any of the listed conditions are entitled to medicines for its treatment free of charge. In addition to this list, there is a further Drugs Payment Scheme whereby an individual or family will only have to pay up to a stated limit per month on prescribed drugs, medicines and appliances.

Parallel to the public hospital system is private hospital care, access being based on ability to pay. Most costs of hospital care in the private sector are met through health insurance rather than direct payment. A significant percentage of the population take out private health insurance. Even amongst those with medical cards, the percentage also holding private insurance is substantial, with approximately 45 per cent of the total population covered (Deloitte and Touche, 2001). Demand for health insurance has proved to be relatively impervious to increases in its costs, an indicator of the high value placed on health care coupled with concerns about the public system indicated above.

Until the mid-1990s, the Voluntary Health Insurance Board had a monopoly position in the provision of health insurance in Ireland. Following the Third Directive on Non-Life Insurance for the European Union in 1994, any insurance company can now offer health insurance in Ireland. However, any health insurance on offer must be on the basis of community rating, that is the same premium charged regardless of age and health status. To date, only BUPA (Ireland), a company with a well-established base in the UK, has entered the Irish health insurance market. As a new company in the Irish market, it has been in a position to offer competitive rates aiming to attract young, low health risk subscribers.

The community rating system should, in theory, work for the benefit of those requiring higher than average usage of health insurance cover such as those with a range of disabilities. In practice, this is not necessarily the case. First of all, health insurance is not a right; therefore, a company can refuse cover for an existing condition at the time of application. Secondly, where an existing subscriber develops a condition, while they may be entitled to cover for it at the same rate, their changed health status may result in decreased income and hence an inability to pay their subscription. Moreover, private insurance may set limits in the amounts to be paid in any one year. Thus, those whose conditions require lengthy, continuing hospital stays may find their cover insufficient at a given time.

The role of the voluntary sector

There are a large number of voluntary bodies in relation to disability in
Ireland. Most are created to address the particular issues of a single type of
disability or illness such as Cystic Fibrosis or Muscular Dystrophy. Fewer,
larger organisations such as the Irish Wheelchair Association encompass a
wider range of different disabilities in their brief. The aims and resources
available to each organisation are very varied. Some rely solely on the work of
volunteers to provide supports such as information fact sheets and a newsletter. In the middle are those that rely mostly on volunteer activity but
employ a small staff to coordinate the organisation's activities. At the other
end of the scale are the small number of large organisations such as the MS
Society, the Irish Wheelchair Association and Enable Ireland, employing a
range of professional staff providing services in lieu of, or ancillary to, the
health boards' functions.

Traditionally, voluntary organisations have played both a pioneering and
a reactionary role in the development of services for people with disabilities in
Ireland. In the absence of state provision, voluntary bodies have had a major
role in creating and providing a wide range of health and personal social
services such as physiotherapy, occupational therapy, speech therapy, social
work, domiciliary care and institutionally based care. Some of these services
have been taken over or are now funded by health boards. In recent years,
there has been a shift from a degree of laissez-faire in such arrangements to a
contracted agreement between the health board and the voluntary body in
which the respective obligations of accountability and transparency are defined.
Voluntary organisations in the field of disability have also played a key role as
pressure groups in trying to place and keep the disability agenda to the forefront of government policy.

At the same time, many traditional voluntary organisations have been
rightly viewed as a reactionary force in the development of policy in relation
to disability. This is for a number of reasons. In the first instance, a voluntary
organisation can be created as a vehicle for change. Over time, however, its
own existence becomes its *raison d'être* and it can outlive its relevance and
usefulness. Also, voluntary organisations rely to a greater or lesser extent on
private funding. This leaves them open to the danger that presenting images
of helplessness and tragedy may maximise donations while those presenting a
message of independence and autonomy may receive less financial support.
There is also the danger that organisations representing lesser-known or less
sympathy-provoking conditions will attract less funding. In addition, voluntary
organisations dedicated to a single condition can be seen to reinforce the
medical model in that they 'specify their purposes in relation to one or a
family of medically defined conditions' (Drake, 1996a: 151). In so doing, they

can distract from shared concerns of across a range of differently named conditions and focus on the search for a cure that may be out of reach of current knowledge and technology.

Voluntary organisations have also been accused of speaking and acting on behalf of people with disabilities rather than genuinely representing them. A study by Drake (1996b) of voluntary groups in Britain working in different areas of disability found differences between respondents in the same organisations depending on whether or not they themselves had a disability. In relation to agency purpose, for example, he (1996b: 10) found that 'disabled people focused their efforts upon lobbying, campaigning and empowerment'. Non-disabled respondents, in contrast, viewed their organisation's role as being to provide services for other agencies, support families and carers and to respond to 'need'. In terms of the services provided, Morris (1991: 108), highlights the issue of enforced dependency, commenting that 'although charities collect money from the general population, they very rarely give disabled people money; this would be to give us too much power. Instead the help is in the form of equipment, holidays and so on.'

Drake (1996b) also found considerable variation in the extent to which people with disabilities were employed and/or involved in any significant ways in planning. He (1996b: 13) observed that 'where disabled people are absent from both the governing body and the staff, they are severely limited in their influence over the decision-making processes. They may be consulted, but have no direct voice.' Commenting on the situation in Britain overall, Drake (1996a: 153) pointed out that 'most of the largest, richest, and best known charities are governed by non-disabled people who control what should be included, and what excluded, from the purposes, objectives and work of their enterprises.' This point is also valid in relation to the proportion of people with disabilities on the boards of voluntary organisations created to serve their needs. The development of organisations by people with disabilities to represent themselves in the policy arena has brought a new dimension to the role of people with disabilities' own involvement in planning and provision.

In regard to state funding of formal voluntary involvement, Faughnan and Kelleher (1993) found in their study that the majority of voluntary and community organisations were very dependent on state financing. Funding has largely come to voluntary organisations involved in services for people with disabilities via Section 65 of the 1953 Health Act. These arrangements tended to be *ad hoc* and the amount of state support varied between agencies (Faughnan and Kelleher, 1993). More recently, as O'Farrall points out (2000: 268), 'governance and management has become a key policy concern in the relationships between the State and voluntary organisations in Ireland'. The focus now on the concept of partnership and the development of contractual agreements has created a clearer brief for the voluntary sector. This enables voluntary agencies engaged in service provision to undertake medium rather than short term planning where state funding for their services is guaranteed for a given length of time. This is in line with the recommendations in the *Report of the Working Group on the Implementation of the Health Strategy in Relation to Persons with a Mental Handicap* (Department of Health, 1997) which emphasised the need for new partnerships between the health boards and voluntary agencies based on service agreements. The Health Strategy, *Towards Quality and Fairness: A Health System for You* (Department of Health and Children, 2001b: 89) states that service agreements between health boards and the voluntary sector will be extended to all service providers in association with performance indicators to measure outcomes against funding. These developments are designed to bring 'greater clarity and accountability to the delivery of services'.

Community-based health services for people with disabilities

While overall responsibility for policy in relation to healthcare for those with disability rests with the Department of Health and Children, it is the health boards that are the statutory service providers and service developers within the overall policy framework. There are ten health boards in total since the Eastern Health Board was divided into three health board areas within the umbrella of the now Eastern Regional Health Authority. As pointed out in the Strategy Document, *Towards Quality and Fairness: A Health System for You* (Department of Health and Children, 2001b: 141), health services have an impact on people with disabilities both through the use of primary, secondary and tertiary services used by all and the specialist services 'developed specifically to meet the needs of people with different types of disability'.

Community-based services for people with disability are provided on a local basis. This can enable them to be more responsive to local need. However, it has also resulted in wide variation in provision for those in similar circumstances depending on where they happen to live (*Report of the Review Group on Health and Personal Social Services for People with Physical and Sensory Disabilities*, 1996). Core community-based services provided by health boards include public health nursing, occupational therapy and physiotherapy, home help as well as meals on wheels. The fact that many of these services are primarily geared towards service provision for vulnerable older people (in the case of public health nurses for young children and their mothers also) means that the resources available to people with disabilities can be very limited in reality.

Specifically designed for the needs of people with significant physical disabilities are the personal assistant services. There are two levels of assistance available. Home Care Attendants provide help in the person's own home, the type and extent of the help varying from person to person depending on need and availability. Personal Assistants undertake tasks of daily living such as washing, feeding, dressing and associated personal or household tasks to facilitate the person with a disability to live independently. They may also accompany the disabled person and provide personal assistance to enable them to participate in education, work and leisure activities. This is a particularly important service, as it offers real opportunities for the person with personal care needs to determine how and when such needs are met and the opportunity to participate more fully in social, educational and employment spheres. However, the limited availability of the service overall, along with the limited hours per person, means that the potential of this specialist provision is not maximised at present.

Other community-based services are day centres offering a range of recreational, sport and aspects of health care facilities to older people and those with significant levels of disability. Geographical disparities occur in the actual availability of day centres, the range of services on offer, the numbers and types of needs catered for and whether they are provided directly by a health board or by a voluntary agency in conjunction with the local health board. Respite care is another service with varying availability throughout the country. It is specifically provided for by a few voluntary organisations or the person may be admitted to a health board nursing home for a limited period. The primary purpose is to give the carer a break from the demands of providing ongoing physical care of a family member. The extent to which it meets the needs of the person with the disability may be less clear, especially in the case of those who are admitted to facilities primarily for the care of older people.

Women with disabilities and health care

As Begum (1996: 170) points out, 'more work remains to be done on how disability interacts with other dimensions of social inequality to influence people's experiences of health care'. The aspect of social inequality she was concerned about was that of women with disability. She sought responses from women about GP services through advertisements in the disability press. Out of over 100 responses, forty per cent declared problems in their face-to-face contact with their current GP. The most common difficulties cited were access and negative attitudes. Those with conditions that can be more difficult to diagnose in the early stages, such as multiple sclerosis, were particularly vulnerable to their symptoms being ascribed to 'nerves' or 'psychological problems'. Interestingly, there was little difference between male and female

GPs in levels of reported dissatisfaction. What was appreciated by the respondents was a GP with good communication skills who recognised their expertise in relation to their own disability.

Health care needs specific to women can be experienced as problematic for women with disabilities. Kallianes and Rubenfeld (1997: 208) state that 'medical professionals often respond with surprise when disabled women request contraception or pregnancy information and may be ill prepared to provide appropriate care'. At the root of the problem, they argue, citing numerous authors in support of their contention, 'is the widespread belief that disabled women are asexual and could not possibly have concerns regarding sexuality' (1997: 205). Even the practical difficulties of accessing routine screening can be problematic. A case study (Sandra) in Tighe's (2001) small qualitative study, demonstrates in graphic terms the difficulties encountered in trying to get a routine gynaecological examination. Such examples demonstrate that for a woman with a disability, as Tighe (2001: 517) points out, 'barriers such as inaccessible health care facilities, require considerable energy reserve, as well as sometimes placing her at distinct health risks.'

Vulnerability to abuse and disability

An area of particular concern for health care is that of domestic violence and women with disabilities. As McPherson comments (1991: 55), 'the disabled community has the same social problems as the community at large – and violence against women is one of them'. Violence against women is now recognised as a major health hazard for women in general (Department of Health, 1997a). However, there are particular difficulties for a woman with a disability in a situation of domestic violence. She may be even less able to remove herself from the threat of violence or protect herself from physical injury. Furthermore, the paucity of accessible housing can reduce her opportunities to leave and there is the concomitant risk that she could lose parental custody to a non-disabled partner (Calderbank, 2000).

It is not only in situations of domestic violence that women with disabilities are at risk of physical, sexual and/or emotional abuse, nor is this issue confined to women only. As Calderbank (2000: 521) points out, all those 'who need assistance with personal care and are reliant to some degree on others, are in a vulnerable position which could become abusive'. According to Shakespeare (1996b), people with disabilities are twice as likely to experience physical or sexual abuse in comparison to non-disabled people. Enforced dependency for physical assistance may make avoidance of repetitive abuse difficult or impossible. Moreover, there may be obstacles to accessing help from others, particularly for those who are physically isolated or with communication difficulties.

Clearly, health care professionals must be cognisant of the potential for abuse of people with disabilities. Physical abuse as a concept is wide ranging to encompass physical contact not initiated or desired by the recipient which causes them pain and/or distress. In its extreme form it can result in serious injury or death. However, any form of physical abuse will lead to lessening of the person's sense of control and dignity. It is in this context that Shakespeare (1996b: 206–7) draws attention to experiences of disabled people in their encounters with health care professionals. He argues that 'the process of medical examination is deeply invasive, and disabled people are not considered to be bothered about this. . . . Evidence reveals the medical encounter to be a powerful relationship with oppressive repercussions. It can undermine a disabled person's feeling of ownership of the body.'

Ethnicity, disability and health care

A growing challenge for all aspects of Irish health services is the shift from what has been a largely mono-cultural to a more ethnically and culturally diverse population. As stated in the Health Strategy (Department of Health and Children, 2001a: 54), 'Ireland is now moving towards a more multiethnic/ multicultural society. In health, as in other areas of public policy, this brings a need to plan for diversity with a wider range of needs to be addressed – affecting both the health workforce and the patient/client group.' The diversity of disability adds a further dimension to the challenges of providing ethnically sensitive health care. The complexity of this area is demonstrated in studies from other countries such as the UK with longer histories in service provision in this respect. In relation to families having children with disabilities, for example, Fazil *et al.* (2002: 238) cite growing research evidence that such families 'face widespread disadvantage and discrimination, particularly if they are members of minority ethnic groups'. In their own study of families of Pakistani and Bangladeshi origin with a severely disabled child, Fazil *et al.* (2002) found language difficulties and misconceptions of service providers about extended family support and attitudes to respite care to be significant barriers to appropriate service provision. The research findings led the authors (2002: 239–10) to conclude that, 'while all ethnic minority parents of disabled children face significant additional disadvantage compared to the white majority . . . there are deep differences between different ethnic minority groups.'

Language and attitude barriers were also features of a study by Bhakta *et al.* (2000) of Asian carers' usage of primary care teams. This study found considerable variation in individual experiences of different professionals amongst the survey population. The fact that a health professional was from the same ethnic origin did not automatically lead to greater satisfaction on the part of the service recipient. What was of greater import was the extent of the service provider's capacity to listen and respond appropriately to articulated needs and concerns. Also of importance were the carers' own preconceptions of professionals' ethnic sensitivities. Some of the Muslim carers in the study, for example, did not make use of community nursing services because of concerns that 'cultural and religious rules of hygiene would not be followed' (2000: 135).

Katbamna *et al.* (2000: 12) comment on the dearth of knowledge about two crucial aspects of disability and ethnic differences. The first is whether the focus on western definitions of dependence and independence (on the part of people with disabilities and family carers) has equal validity for South Asian populations. They cite Kalyanpur's (1996) suggestion that cultures which place emphasis on family and community rather than the individual may be less likely to regard providing or needing personal care as being a burden. The second area raised by Katbamna *et al.* (2000: 12) is the lack of research 'on how disabled people within minority ethnic communities perceive their disabilities'. The latter they contrast to the vast literature on white majority experiences of people with disabilities and family carers.

New developments in health care
and their implications for disability

Ongoing developments in knowledge, technical expertise and technology in health care have opened up new possibilities and new dilemmas in the area of disability. Achieving some (or even complete) alleviation of a condition hitherto incurable may be possible now or at some time in the foreseeable future. A well-publicised example of this is spinal injury and the determined, high profile accounts of the actor Christopher Reeves.

The possibilities for changes in the field of genetics have the most far-reaching consequences for many disabilities. Shakespeare (1998: 666–7) comments that 'the boundaries between health and disease are altered and social experience is increasingly "geneticised"'. However, at present, genetic developments have been primarily in the area of identification rather than curative interventions. As a result, Shakespeare (1998: 666) argues, 'genetic screening creates additional moral and political dilemmas for prospective parents'.

In Ireland, abortion is legally forbidden in the Constitution. Hence, the detection of genetic abnormalities in the foetus must be addressed by counselling and information. In countries where abortion is legal, prenatal screening raises significant and complex issues. Those concerned with the status and rights of people with disabilities are critical of legislation such as that of the UK which enshrines foetal abnormality as an acceptable ground for termination. Such an approach, it is argued, accepts the premise that life with disability is of lesser value. By inference, those with disabilities are of lesser worth in society. This is an area in which the feminist movement and the disability rights movement can appear to be diametrically opposed. Feminist emphasis on the right of a woman to choose whether or not to proceed with a pregnancy has incorporated foetal abnormality as additional grounds for opting for termination. Disabled feminists, such as Morris (1991), have highlighted the importance of not negating disability rights through the promotion of feminist rights.

Rock (1996: 126) is critical of medical intervention in reproductive technology in that its intent is to eradicate disability. This, she argues, is an impossible goal since 'disability is part of life' which can also occur as a result of accident, illness and old age. The danger of undue focus on its eradication is that resources may be devoted to its elimination rather than addressing the social barriers to participation in society. If disabled people are not equally valued to all others in society then, argues Rock (1996: 126–7), 'disabled people, especially disabled women, are becoming an endangered species' who may never achieve life in the first place. She views the medical profession as having to bear some responsibility for this in the unquestioning acceptance of social values and attitudes in relation to disability. This theme is reflected in Shakespeare's (1998: 677) comment that 'there is much anecdotal evidence that negative accounts of living with impairment are presented by professionals at the ante-natal stage'.

Developments in knowledge and understanding of conditions are major challenges facing health care in the coming decades (Koop, 1999). The prospect for health care in relation to disability is an exciting one. The principles of rights and partnership are now the internationally accepted keystones for the provision of services to meet existing and emerging needs (World Health Organisation, 2000a). In Ireland, the development of a comprehensive database provides for the identification of need and delivery of services based on its analysis. Of critical importance is the provision of adequate resources to provide people with disabilities a comprehensive range of services offered by health professionals with the knowledge and commitment to the principles of rights and partnership into practice.

The *Report of the Commission on the Status of People with Disabilities* identified a number of aspects of health care where there was scope for improvement. Three years after the Commission's Report, *Towards Equal Citizenship* (Department of Justice, Equality and Law Reform, 1999) undertook a review of progress to date and plans to implement change and targets yet to be achieved. What has been evident is an ongoing commitment to monitor progress towards agreed goals and a change of approach with greater emphasis on partnership between service providers and service users. Of critical importance is the level of resources allocated towards the development of comprehensive, accessible and appropriate services and the inclusion of people with disabilities at all levels of service planning. In addition, educating professionals to ensure high quality practice must be continuing to ensure a disability-friendly, partnership and person-centred approach to the provision of health care.

Chapter 7

Gender and disability

Patricia Noonan Walsh

Introduction

Consider the prospects for Rosa, a pretty young woman with intellectual disabilities growing up in a village in Mexico at the start of the twenty-first century. Without any natural family of her own since infancy, she depends on a small rural community for shelter, nurturance and friendship. She has learned to meet her personal needs, to keep a home, to read and write, to travel on the local bus. When Rosa reached the age of 15 years, she celebrated this landmark with the festive party typical in her culture for young women entering adulthood. Rosa is vulnerable to exploitation and has no family members to protect her interests. Her prospects for marriage are slender. Soon, she must earn her livelihood. But the regional economy is sluggish and offers few work opportunities, only a handful of which apply to women with Rosa's skills. Any job will offer a precarious future and a modest income at best. Her country's government aspires to provide reliable social and health service systems for millions now living in poverty, but these goals have yet to be achieved. Does the fact that Rosa is a young woman help to determine her personal prospects for a long life of good quality? How might public policies make a difference?

This chapter examines the complex bonds between a private domain – personal identity interwoven with the presence of a disability – and the public domain where social policies are forged. First, it reviews some defining moments in the recent past, leading to present understanding of the relevance of gender issues in shaping policies related to people with disabilities. Next, it outlines recent EU and global policy initiatives affirming the need to link disability and gender. The impact of gender is considered across three areas of human experience – the individual's development in the context of his or her family, health, and ageing. Current policies are examined to determine how effective they may be in ensuring that men and women with disabilities are agents in directing the course of their lives in the family, society and the wider cultural and physical environment. Finally, strategies for policy makers and for people with disabilities themselves are suggested.

A brief history

To revisit the past 150 years in Ireland and much of Europe and North America unearths a groundswell of institutional living as the first option for men and women with disabilities that peaked sometime in the sixth and seventh decades of the twentieth century (Braddock *et al.*, 2001). Today, the landscape is marked by inroads leading to individual support devised so that people may lead self-determined lives as equal citizens in their own homes and communities.

Separate and unequal

Only faint light reveals the distant lives of thousands of people with disabilities who lived their lives in institutions. It may be assumed that the lens of gender identity focused on them rarely. Separate care for people with disabilities dominated the policy landscape in the recent past. It was meted out to people living in groups by age, or the category by which they were labelled – perhaps having epilepsy, or being blind. A high percentage of individuals with physical, sensorial or intellectual and other developmental disabilities as well as those with mental health difficulties were encouraged to live in institutions in Ireland (Robins, 1986), in the UK (Race, 1995), and in other countries with developed market economies and formal social or health service systems (Braddock *et al.*: 2001). Not so long ago, a single large psychiatric hospital might house all, opening its doors to those with *no fixed abode* – the homeless, the very poor and those deemed vulnerable to abuse. Children, too, entered the doors of institutions. Many grew apart from their families and stayed for a lifetime. Often, the shadow of a brother or sister who had gone away dimmed in the memories of younger siblings.

Gender was useful in organising groups of people with disabilities to live and work in convenient arrays. Adults lived in single-sex dormitories or wards. Men worked in gardens, women in kitchens and laundries. In Ireland, religious bodies established residential centres to care for people with disabilities that reflected the gender of their respective founding fathers, mothers, sisters and brothers. Hence, nuns might accept only girls or women into lifelong care.

More recently, purpose-built residences obviously larger than family homes – hostels, chalets, bungalows, or *de-designated units* (Department of Health, Ireland, 1993) – replaced hospital wards dating from the Victorian era. Whatever the shape or decor it has assumed, this congregate model of social care flourished throughout much of Europe during the twentieth century and persists even now (Emerson *et al.*, 1996).

Cradle to grave

Benign initiatives dedicated to care for people with disabilities and other groups sprang up in many countries in the middle of the last century. Some offered lifelong care at the price of isolation from society. Darker forces promoted the systematic euthanasia of people with disabilities in Germany in the 1930s and 1940s, when thousands of children and adults with disabilities were killed outright (Friedlander, 1995). Legal sterilisation of people with disabilities, usually without their consent, persisted in many countries during the twentieth century. Evidence suggests that this drastic intervention was aimed in part at controlling the sexual and reproductive lives of women and men with disabilities (Parish, 2002).

Elsewhere, people with disabilities were treated as anonymous members of administrative groups – childlike, dependent and genderless at any age (Walmsley, 1996; McCarthy, 2002). Not so long ago in Ireland, the bodies of many women – some, it is safe to assume, with disabilities – who had lived in a walled residence all their adult lives, doing laundry work for a token wage, were disinterred from a common plot which did not record their names or ages and reburied respectfully (Raftery and O'Sullivan, 1999).

Labels and categories

Group treatments ironed over individual differences, quenching personal aspirations, family life, and adult identity as a man or woman in society. The misuse of formal procedures to determine who had a disability and was thus unworthy of life in the last century turned the process of assessment to an evil purpose (Friedlander, 1995). These memories rightly provoke caution in assigning people with disabilities to categories. Today, some decry any efforts to label or enumerate personal characteristics – such as the person's gender – or even to establish the number of people with disabilities in a given population. By contrast, Fujiura and Rutkowski-Kmitta (2001: 69) remind us that we are compelled nonetheless to take account of the human condition, and thus galvanise the ground between disability and society:

> From the Hippocratic division of the Four Humors through contemporary efforts to catalogue variations in genome sequences, people have sought to systematize the measurement and subdivision of their own.

Current debates probe questions long taken for granted: what disability means, who may be said to have a disability, and how many people in a certain population are so identified. There is considerable variation in the answers proposed, and even in the language used. For example, it is difficult to compare the prevalence of impairments, disabilities or handicaps across countries, as the figures depend on the age structure of the groups surveyed and the indicators used in a particular country or region (Barbotte *et al.*, 2001).

In Ireland, the number of individuals with disabilities is estimated at about 350,000, or ten per cent of the Irish population (Commission on the Status of People with Disabilities, 1996). A National Intellectual Disability Database was established and is renewed annually, drawing on fresh information submitted by statutory and voluntary agencies throughout the country (National Intellectual Disability Database Committee, 1997; Mulvany, 2000; 2001). Data on about 27,000 individuals are currently entered. A second database relating to people with physical or sensory disabilities was launched in March 2002 (Department of Health and Children, 2002b).

Current approaches

Consensus remains elusive on a single definition of disability, or an all-purpose model of disability, although current thinking considers the universal phenomenon of disablement as part of the fabric of the human condition (Bickenbach *et al.*, 1999). Two conceptual shifts dominate much of today's thinking about people with disabilities. First, there is a sharpened focus on the lived experience and authority of the individual as a boy, man, girl or woman with a personal and gender identity in a given culture. Each person negotiates developmental tasks of growth, maturation and ageing in a given social and environmental context. Assuming an appropriate adult gender role in society – rural Mexico, urban Nigeria, suburban Ireland – is paramount in this array of developmental tasks that each person must complete (Santrock, 1995; Eagly and Wood, 1999). Understanding the individual's life course development and experiences within the context of family, society and the wider physical environment is of equal importance. For example, the forthcoming revised International Classification of Functioning, Disability and Health (the ICF), developed by the World Health Organisation (2001a), integrates the impact of the environment on impairments, disabilities and handicaps (Barbotte *et al.*, 2001).

A second conceptual revolution has sparked an emerging field of study. Disability studies draws on many scholarly disciplines and professions to explore all aspects of disability – the lived experience of individuals, the history of discourse and interventions driven by social policy (Albrecht *et al.*, 2001). Students of disability studies approach gender as a topic of great importance from each aspect of their field. First, gender is often neglected, and yet it is at the heart of personal experiences and self-identity of people with disabilities. Second, gender is a recurrent theme, telling both benign and oppressive stories, in the past treatment of people with disabilities in society. And third, gender is recognised as a crucial determinant of health and of economic outcomes, and is thus an essential factor in efforts to shape appropriate social policies today.

Recent forces favour more gender-sensitive approaches to the lives of people with disabilities. Deinstitutionalisation and the shift to community living endorsed by the Irish government mirror similar directives in the Nordic countries (Tøssebro, 1996), the UK (Department of Health, United Kingdom, 2001) and elsewhere. Providing supports so that people with disabilities may choose where and with whom to live and work is a current policy objective in many countries. The growth of person-centred, individualised models of devising supports so as to achieve desired outcomes is even a matter of government policy in the UK (Department of Health, United Kingdom, 2001). Such new approaches place the person with disabilities firmly in the centre of all efforts to plan supports so that he or she may lead a life of quality.

Until recently men and women with disabilities were more often talked about than consulted directly when policies on their behalf were decided. Latterly, their voices have emerged to inform policy and practice (Tubridy, 1996) and to set the tone for a discourse of advocacy swelling across geographical boundaries. In the next section, key developments in European and international policies related to disability and gender are examined.

Global context

Irish policy about people with disabilities has kept pace with many international directives related to people with disabilities, although it has lagged somewhat in enacting legislation to mandate or fund required changes. Many global policies are rooted in a human rights approach to disability, recognising that each individual must have equal opportunities for personal dignity, family life and participation in society. Gender is at the heart of the expression of these rights in daily lives.

EU policy

The European Union, of which Ireland has been a member state since 1973, made a radical shift in social policy by moving from a welfare-based to a rights-based model of disability that specifies equality of opportunity as the benchmark. This landmark supplants an earlier model in which the person with disability was the locus of the problem rather than a social and physical environment (Quinn, 1999). The rights-based model of disability serves as the engine of the EU's social policy for this population of about 30.5 million people (Commission of the European Communities, 1998).

While disclaiming direct responsibility for housing or educating citizens of the Member States, the EU reserves competence in directing and also funding initiatives aimed at social and vocational integration. Employment is thus a core target. In Ireland, as in each of the 15 Member States, *National*

Action Plans for employment should be shaped to promote equal opportunities for men and women and also for people with disabilities, as endorsed in the Treaty of Amsterdam (Commission of the European Communities, 1997). Have these opportunities been realised? Without reliable data, identifying gender differences in living circumstances, employment history or dependency on benefits and other income transfers among people with disabilities – or comparing these indicators with those reported for the general population – is beyond our grasp. Specifically, it is not yet possible to determine the impact of EU employment or other integration policies on the lives of men and women with disabilities in Ireland by gender. Are women with disabilities experiencing the feminisation of the workforce reported for European women in the general population? Are older men with disabilities as disadvantaged as their peers by the dearth of traditional manufacturing jobs and the growth of the information technology and financial services sectors? Such questions lead beyond current data.

International policy
In the international arena, the United Nations (UN), the International Labour Organisation (ILO) and the World Health Organisation (WHO) highlight gender issues in recent policy statements related to people with disabilities. Although lacking the force of law, the *Standard Rules on Equalization of Opportunities for People with Disabilities* (United Nations, 1994) explicitly endorses measures to meet the distinctive needs of men and women with disabilities. The United Nations appointed a special rapporteur, Bengt Lindqvist, a Swedish expert who monitored progress in observing the rules in each country, according to its capacities.

The ILO, an international body affiliated with the UN and based in Geneva, has consistently included people with disabilities in vocational training and employment initiatives. It specifically links gender equality with employment opportunities for people with disabilities (Epstein, 1997). The World Health Organisation recognises that gender is a critical determinant of both physical and mental health (World Health Organisation, 1997).

Gender also exerts a bias in the treatment of mental illnesses: doctors may diagnose more quickly for women compared with men. Women around the world are more at risk due to socio-economic disadvantage, income inequality, low social status and unrelenting care for others. Men are more likely to report problems with alcohol use (World Health Organisation, 2001b).

People with intellectual disabilities are also at risk for incurring additional physical or mental health difficulties, yet these are often overlooked. In partnership with the World Health Organisation, the International Association for the Scientific Study of Intellectual Disabilities (IASSID) prepared a set of reports on healthy ageing with a focus on gender issues (World Health

> **The United Nations Standard Rules**
>
> Grace, a single parent with four children, is blind. Aged 37, she lives in a small city in a West African country with an as yet flimsy base of social and health services. Grace's lifelong prowess in sewing makes her the family breadwinner. In addition to her work and her duties in the home, she has made a name for herself as advocate for other women with disabilities in her region and travels to international meetings. As she says, even if her own country has not yet developed laws to guarantee appropriate income and health supports for people with disabilities, the UN Standard Rules must and should apply to every country, whether prosperous or still developing. Grace points often to Rule 18, which declares that . . . 'States should recognize the right of Organisations of people with disabilities to represent persons at national, regional and local levels.'

Organisation, 2000b). A key policy recommendation was for sound national policies targeting special populations and providing both moral and fiscal substance to shore up lifelong supports (Janicki, 2001).

In summary, these authoritative international bodies specifically target people with disabilities in their over-arching policy statements. Each organisation endorses gender sensitivity and equality in implementing policies about social, economic and health status of all people. Are these objectives merely aspirational? In the next section, we examine three thematic areas – families, health and ageing – to explore the impact of gender in the lives of people with disabilities.

The impact of gender

What is the impact of gender on three key themes in the lives of people everywhere, not least those with disabilities? Why are these important in shaping social policy?

Families

In most parts of the world, families give essential care, protection from risk and economic support to members who have disabilities. Family care dominates, and most carers are women. People with intellectual disabilities living in countries with formal service systems, tend to live outside the family home as they age (Braddock *et al.*, 2001). Yet more than 25 per cent of Irish adults with intellectual disabilities aged over 50 years live in the family home (Health Research Board, 2001). More and more, siblings step into the breach when parents die or simply become too old to care – sisters lead the way (Egan and Walsh, 2001).

In a study of informal care – care that is unpaid and administered by family members – among elderly men and women in the United States, Katz, Kabeto and Langa (2000) found that older women with disabilities, whether married or single, received fewer hours of care than their male counterparts. Female children were the most likely caregivers of women with disabilities, whereas wives cared for men. The authors suggest that disparities are due to a cultural tradition in which women care and nurture, rather than the physical limitations of men surveyed.

Often, informal care from kin and formal care from professionals blend in the daily lives of people with disabilities. In their longitudinal study, Miltiades and Pruchno (2001) assessed predictors of formal service use, waiting list use and care-giving burden among 305 mothers with an adult child and found that formal service use remained stable over time. These authors suggest that wait list use and placement outside the mother's home are aspects of an evolving process, rather than discrete events, and they urge researchers to explore further the relationship between specific formal service use and continued co-residence (Miltiades and Pruchno, 2001).

Gender, poverty and disability interweave in lives of children with disabilities, with grave consequences for family well being and for social policy. Data from the United States indicate that poverty is a root cause for the increasing likelihood that children will be born with or acquire disabilities (Birenbaum, 2002: 217): 'when both the mother and the child have disabilities, or when there are two children with disabilities in the family, then reliance on welfare is over-determined'. Also, trends towards the proportion of children living in poverty and greatest concentration of poverty among single parent households – mainly headed by the mother – are exacerbated in households with a child who has a disability (Birenbaum, 2002).

Among women in the general population in the United States, Porell and Miltiades (2002) found regional differences in functional status – a core indicator of level of disability – among ageing people, notably among women, living in areas of relative poverty. Families protect women and children likely to be affected most harshly by events in the wider environment, for example by violence, civil wars and displacement of income due to economic catastrophe (United Nations Development Programme, 2000). Women with disabilities are also at heightened risk of physical and sexual abuse (Walsh and Murphy, 2002) and these threats may be exacerbated in times of political upheaval.

Health
Health is a core indicator of quality of life for all people. However, countries differ greatly both in their expenditure on health, and in the years of life that their new citizens may expect at birth (Table 1). More prosperous countries have more to spend on health, but the results are not always predictable.

Looking close to home, it may be seen that Ireland and the UK spent the same proportion of GDP on health in 1998, with slightly poorer outcomes for life expectancy for Irish men and women (Table 1). Apparently, while financial expenditure is necessary, other factors play their part in advancing good health outcomes.

Table 1 **Selected indicators: Health expenditure and life expectancy in 1998 for five countries**

	Ireland	Mexico	Romania	UK	USA
Life expectancy at birth:					
Female	79.4	75.7	74.1	80	80.2
Male	73.8	69.7	66.5	74.7	73.5
Total expenditure on health as % of GDP	6.8	5.3	3.8	6.8	12.9

Sources: Health expenditure data from *WHO Report 2001* (World Health Organisation, 2001c): Annex Table 5; life expectancy data from *Human Development Report 2000* (United Nations Development Programme, 2000: 161–2).

Health is paramount among indicators of Quality of Life outcomes achieved for individuals with disabilities (Felce, 1997; Schalock and Verdugo, 2002). Gender-specific health risk factors have been identified for the general population. For example, there are greater risks of depression for women, and of alcohol dependence among men (World Health Organisation, 2001b). Risk factors have to date been less systematically identified for people with disabilities. Strategies to promote the mental health of people with intellectual disabilities are the focus of recent international reports (World Health Organisation, 2000c). Mental health problems may be masked by the presence of developmental or other disabilities and hence elude treatment (Thorpe *et al.*, 2001). Antecedent conditions may include life stressors, limited social networks and fewer opportunities for social learning. In addition, adverse reactions may be exacerbated among adults with intellectual disabilities due to cognitive impairments, poor self-esteem and relatively poor social support.

Ageing
Greater life expectancy is a worldwide trend, with rates of increase even greater in developing countries. This 'agequake' will have a profound impact on every aspect of life in every region of the globe during this century (Alvarez, 1999). Life expectancy at 65 years is increasing rapidly, and more people live to be one hundred years old, or even older (Robine, 1999). There is evidence that a woman in Ireland reached the age of 110 as early as 1930

(Robine, 1999). Some of the millennium babies born as January 2000 dawned may well live into the twenty-second century. Certainly, the proportion of people in Ireland aged over 65 and even over 85 years – the *very old* – will increase steadily. It is estimated that 14 per cent of Irish people will be 65 years or older by the year 2011 (National Council on Ageing and Older People, 2001). Some particular risks for various age-related health conditions will extend coverage as more men and women grow older. While there is no evidence for gender differences in the incidence of Alzheimer's Disease in the general population, more women live longer and are thus at greater risk of incurring this form of dementia.

Major mental disorders are more frequent among elderly people with intellectual disabilities (Thorpe *et al.*, 2001). For example, the prevalence of Alzheimer's disease among people with Down Syndrome is higher than for other older people in this population. In Ireland, greater life expectancy is already apparent for people with intellectual disabilities (Mulvany, 2001). This upward trend marks the success of various social and health policies to date – better housing in domestic rather than institutional settings, medical and technological advances. However, it signals an increase in the numbers of middle-aged and older people with disabilities who will need new forms of support in the future.

Summary

Gender is interwoven with the personal and social experiences of people with disabilities throughout the lifespan. Effective social policies recognise the impact of gender on family life, health promotion and outcomes and ageing. In the next section, some current policies in Ireland relevant to the experiences of men and women with disabilities are reviewed in the light of research evidence.

Current policies

Many current Irish social and health policies are inclusive, referring to citizens with disabilities or their families. Not all explicitly link gender with the presence of disability.

Children and families

The *National Children's Strategy* (Department of Health and Children, 2000) targets all Irish children, resting on three fundamental principles: children will have a voice; children's lives will be better understood; and children will receive quality supports to promote all aspects of their development. Elsewhere, the Strategy (2000: 47) states that: 'children with a disability will be entitled to the services they need to achieve their full potential'. The Strategy proposes interventions that are as yet untried. How will desired outcomes be achieved for infants and for young boys and girls with disabilities? Will all families have access to the array of supports, including early intervention programmes, shown to have optimal impact on both family functioning and the well being of vulnerable children (Guralnick, 1998; Blacher, 2001)? Will all Irish children have equal opportunities for education? Will the voices of Irish children with disabilities be heard in their homes and schools?

Employment
The process of transition from school to work is a critical path to good outcomes in terms of income, employment and social status for young adults with disabilities (Wehman and Walsh, 1999). Will this process be eased by the recent policy of *mainstreaming* vocational and employment initiatives? Or will some aspiring Irish employees find themselves awash on minor tributaries? It remains to be seen whether employment strategies for Irish adults with disabilities will be embedded with national plans to extend gender equality in the labour force.

While legislation to advance gender equality has been introduced in Ireland, its impact on men and women with disabilities at different stages of their working lives, for example, planning for retirement, is not fully understood. Evidence from the United States suggests that gender differences do affect labour force participation among older men and women with disabilities (Loprest, Rupp and Sandell, 1995). These authors found that while a similar percentage of men and women reported having disabilities that limit work, there were gender differences in functional limitations and specific conditions.

Health
Recent health policies in Ireland take account of gender differences in health risks, in distinctive needs for health care and also in optimal strategies for health promotion. *A Plan for Women's Health* (Department of Health, 1997) links gender with the presence of disability as a crucial element in health policy and practice, and highlights specific health requirements of women with disabilities in Ireland. It recommends direct consultation with women who have disabilities themselves in order to develop appropriate health services. Barriers of many kinds – at environmental, service system and physical levels – impede access to health care for women with disabilities (Schrojenstein Lantman-de Valk *et al.*, 2001; Lunsky and Havercamp, 2002).

Irish men, too, are at risk as they age, for cardiovascular illness and certain types of cancer, as well as mental health difficulties (Western Health Board, 2000). It remains to be seen whether gender-specific health initiatives will consult with men who have disabilities in shaping policies to meet their distinctive needs.

Healthy ageing

Michael lives in a suburb of an Irish city: he has had mobility difficulties throughout his adult life. A few years ago the pharmaceutical factory where he worked part-time was closed, putting Michael and many of his friends and neighbours out of work. This year he celebrates his 65th birthday, and has learned that the Disability Allowance he had received for many years will be replaced by the Old Age Pension. Lately, Michael's wife has become concerned about him – he is moody and withdrawn and has lost his appetite. Getting out more would help, she thinks, perhaps to keep in touch with his former workmates or to visit a nearby gym. But Michael finds that local taxis are slow to respond to his telephone calls, especially once it is known that he uses a wheelchair. Using public transport poses so many obstacles that a day out demands Olympic vigour and at the moment, he simply does not have the resolve to make such an effort.

Disability policies

Finally, Irish policies and legislation measures in the past decade have specifically addressed social issues related to disability, while others have been mooted. These measures reflect substantial changes in the structure of services. A new relationship obtains between the Department of Health and Children and the health boards, with the latter assuming greater responsibility for planning, funding and evaluating services regionally while the Department reserves a strategic role (Department of Health and Children, 1998). It has initiated a new practice of agreeing time-limited service contracts with the voluntary bodies that provide services for many thousands of Irish people with disabilities (Working Group on the Implementation of the Health Strategy in Relation to Persons with a Mental Handicap, 1997). More recently, in June 2000, the devolution of the NRB to the NDA signalled in *A Strategy for Equality* (Commission on the Status of People with Disabilities, 1996) was accomplished (Establishment Group for the National Disability Authority and Disability Support Service, 1998).

Other legislation, which targeted people with disabilities:

- *Employment Equality Act* (1998), initiated by the Equality Authority, spelling out nine grounds with potential for discrimination in the workplace: gender, religion, marital status, age, family status, disability, sexual orientation, race, or membership of the travelling community. While the Irish census (April 2002) attempted for the first time to capture data on the living circumstances and employment histories of household members with various disabilities in Ireland, there is as yet no national body of data analysed by gender and age of adults with all disabilities.

- *Education Act* (1998) aimed to introduce children with special educational needs to mainstream education.
- *National Disability Authority Act* (1999): the new authority adopted a national role in the areas of policy, research, standards and monitoring.
- *Comhairle Act* (2000) has an information and advocacy role.
- *Equal Status Act* (2000) prohibits discrimination in public in securing goods or services.
- *Mental Health Act* (2001) covered areas of involuntary admissions to psychiatric hospitals, where, it may be noted, more than 800 persons with intellectual disabilities live even now (Mulvany, 2001).

As of 2002, other legislation is pending: a Disabilities Bill; a Disabilities (Education and Training) Bill (Department of Education and Science); and Incorporation of the ECHR into Irish Law (Mulvany, 2001).

Summary
Current policies in Ireland address life domains such as education and employment, health and equality, and childhood and old age. These documents often refer to gender differences and always extend to all citizens including those with disabilities. But it is apparent that the important links between gender and disability evident in recent research findings are not explicitly forged. Nor is it evident that the various government departments and agencies work in harmony to implement policies targeting men and women with disabilities throughout their lives. In the final section, some strategies to effect seamless policies are proposed.

Challenges

How can Ireland achieve seamless policies targeting the person in the context of the family, society and the wider environment? Two strategies – wider coverage and stronger coherence – are proposed here.

Coverage
First, policies in every domain should be sensitive to the link between gender and personal identity for people with disabilities at different stages of their lives. Supporting families of young children is no mere expression of sentiment. Rather, it is the best guarantee of long-term support and of positive gains for both persons with disabilities and family members – a sound investment in social capital and predictor of quality of life (Seltzer, Krauss, *et al.*, 2001). Rather than an intricate puzzle of rules and entitlements varying across Irish health board areas, an optimal approach might be to consult with each family

to find out what it needs most to nurture all the children in the family, including children who may be especially vulnerable. Special supports should be directed towards single-parent households, often headed by mothers, to ensure that poverty does not gain a silent victory.

Employment remains the critical path to social and vocational integration in Europe. It is true that the mainstream is the fastest, most direct and most accessible route. However, considerable numbers of Irish men and women with disabilities work in separate pools, far from the mainstream. Future employment policies should incorporate measures to follow the progress of all navigators to see whether the mainstream peters out, or the source of funding dries up, or some voyagers – women, or people with particular disabilities, or those living in rural settings – founder and are lost from sight.

Coherence
Second, policies should embed crosscutting principles – consultation, reference to trends in wider society, and a lifespan perspective – relevant to all citizens. Doing so will help to move towards an array of coherent policies aiming at the lifelong pursuit of a good quality of life for all. Gender equality is neither a discrete bundle, nor an annex to policies in a single domain. It is as important in transition planning for young people with disabilities, as it is for men and women in their fifties or sixties planning for retirement. Why is it that people with disabilities age out of a lifelong condition and become simply *old* when they reach 65? A more coherent policy would take into account the increased life and health expectancy of older people around the globe. It would recognise that older people with disabilities share the same gender-related health risks as their peers as well as distinctive risks associated with the condition giving rise to their disability. Older people with disabilities will weather the same changes in their functioning, family composition, housing needs and leisure preferences experienced by any other Irish person of their age, albeit with different levels of support.

Summary
The knowledge base about what works for early intervention in the family, for education, for transition to adult life, for employment, for personal growth and satisfaction and for healthy ageing is substantial. Such evidence seldom informs coherent and extensive policy formation targeting men and women with disabilities. Research should drive Irish policy initiatives and monitor subsequent changes in practice. As advocacy gains strength in Ireland, people with disabilities will increasingly take a place at the centre of any consultation or debate when policies are being shaped. It follows that people with disabilities should inform any evaluation process carried out to determine how well policies are attaining targets.

Chapter 8

Ethnicity and disability

Maria Pierce

Introduction

This chapter examines the issue of ethnicity as it intersects with disability, a subject that has been noticeably absent from Irish social policy literature and debates. It discusses the growing importance attached to diversity in debates about disability. The situation of ethnic minority people with disabilities in Ireland is briefly introduced, and the development of rights and standards for ethnic minority people with disabilities at a European and international level is examined. Although studies of people with disabilities from ethnic minority backgrounds tend to focus on generic issues, some consideration has been given to ethnicity and the different areas of disability and these studies are referred to in this chapter. Current Irish policy relating to ethnic minority people with disabilities is outlined, followed by an analysis of some of the likely developments and future challenges facing Irish social policy.

Disability and diversity

The social model of disability has been instrumental in enabling disabled people to express their experience of disability as an oppression. The social model of disability has gained widespread support, especially within the disability movement itself. This model lies in direct contrast to the medical model of disability, which places an emphasis on individual impairment and classification systems. The social model focuses on 'disablism' and on the issue of how society physically and attitudinally disables people who have impairments. Parallels have been drawn between 'disablism' and the discrimination and oppression faced by other minorities such as ethnic minority groups who encounter racism, women who encounter sexism, and gay men and lesbian women who encounter discrimination on the basis of their sexual orientation (Oliver, 1990; Vernon, 1998).

  In recent years there have been calls for the social model of disability to be further developed. Feminists argue that there is a need to take account of the complex and often variable interaction between different forms of social oppression as well as drawing parallels between different forms of discrimination such as disablism, racism and sexism (Fawcett, 2000). The feminist movement has been instrumental in broadening the social model of disability by examining how gender impacts on disability. Others, such as Oliver (1996) and Shakespeare (1996a), have drawn attention to the need to portray people with disabilities as a heterogeneous grouping and to explore issues of difference and diversity. Increasingly, the significance of recognising diversity among people with disabilities is emphasised. The European Year of People with Disabilities, 2003 illustrates this. One of its objectives is 'to make people aware of the heterogeneity of people with disabilities and of people with disabilities facing multiple discrimination'.

The experience of disability and disability identity are structured by a range of crucial dimensions (Barnes *et al.*, 1999). Ethnicity is one of these, which can be defined as:

> involving at least some of the following attributes: a notion of 'personhood'; a distinctive language; the identification of a community with a particular religion . . . and a distinctive culture, which may be expressed in a variety of ways, including social etiquette, dress and diet (Drake, 1999: 148).

The need for a greater exploration of issues related to ethnicity in discussions of disability has been emphasised (see, for example, Begum, 1992; Morris, 1991; and Abu-Habib, 1997).

There have been attempts to conceptualise the experience of ethnic minority people with disabilities. For example, the term 'double discrimination' has been employed to refer to the two levels at which ethnic minority people with disabilities can encounter discrimination. At one level, ethnic minority people with disabilities experience racial discrimination by virtue of their ethnic minority status within the wider population. At a second level, they experience discrimination and barriers within their own community and the wider society on the grounds of disability. There are, however, differing views on the significance of racism in structuring the experience of disability. Stuart (1993) argues that the experience of oppression excluding ethnic minority people with disabilities from mainstream life is specific to them and an experience that differs substantially from that of disabled 'white' people. Stuart (1993) rejects the term 'double discrimination' and instead adopts the notion of 'simultaneous oppression', which he uses to refer to how the structures of racism and disablism operating separately but at the same time shape the experience of disabled ethnic minority people. In contrast, Vernon (1998) argues that simultaneous oppression is not just experienced by disabled black people. She believes that Stuart places too much emphasis on racism in the experience of disabled people, and argues that despite differences such as 'race', gender, sexuality, age and class, there are important similarities in the experience of all disabled people.

Disability and ethnicity are two characteristics shaping the experiences of a person with a disability. Other factors can be just as important. Begum (1992) describes the 'triple oppression' of being a black disabled woman, who experiences racism, sexism and handicapism. McDonagh (2002: 133), a feminist activist and academic, writing about the complex experience of Travellers with a disability in Ireland, argues that 'it is important and relevant to put experiences of racism and discrimination [on the grounds of disability] into different categories'. She gives examples of the categories of gender, age, and whether a particular condition is genetic or the result of an accident or disease. Although there are many overlapping characteristics structuring a person's experience, it is beyond the scope of this chapter to address the influence of a range of complex factors other than ethnicity and disability, both of which are, in their own right, complex concepts.

People with disabilities in a multi-ethnic Ireland

Until recently there has been little focus on the experiences and needs of ethnic minority people with disabilities in Ireland. Yet Ireland is, and historically has been, a multi-ethnic society. The Traveller community, which constitutes the largest ethnic minority group in Ireland estimated at approximately 27,000 (National Consultative Committee on Racism and Interculturalism, 2001) has a history dating back to the twelfth century in this country. As well as a shared history with the Travelling community, there is a longstanding presence in Ireland of a small Jewish community and the arrival of Hungarian, Chilean, Vietnamese and Iranian Bahá'i programme refugees in 1956, 1973–4, 1979 and 1985 respectively. However, Ireland has only recently become conscious of its internal multi-ethnicity. This new multi-ethnic consciousness coincides with the arrival and settlement from the early 1990s onwards of new communities of migrants, asylum seekers and refugees from the European and non-European world. While there is no precise information on the ethnicity of newly emerging communities in Ireland, it can be said that there is considerable variety amongst them. Legally resident nationals from non-EEA countries[1] come from a wide range of ethnic backgrounds including Latvian, Lithuanian and Polish (Woods and Humphries, 2001). The range of over 100 countries from which asylum seekers applying for refugee status originate (Woods and Humphries, 2001) gives some indication of the ethnic diversity of this group of people. Ireland also has expanding Chinese and Muslim communities.

People with disabilities come from multi-ethnic backgrounds. There are people with disabilities within the Traveller Community and each of the newly emerging ethnic minority groups. While the availability of information on ethnicity is poor, there is even less information on people with disabilities amongst ethnic minority communities. There are an unknown number of Travellers with a disability. Similarly, there are an unknown number of asylum seekers and refugees with a disability. Asylum seekers and refugees with a disability include those with a pre-existing disability who may have had their situation exacerbated by the conditions from which they were fleeing. Others may have acquired a disability arising out of war, conflict or torture. Ireland has admitted refugees with disabilities under the 'Medevac' programme. For example, a number of Bosnian refugees were admitted into Ireland specifically to receive medical attention for injuries sustained during the war in former Yugoslavia. SPIRASI, the Spiritan Asylum Services Initiative, estimates that at least ten per cent of the asylum seeking population in Ireland have survived torture (SPIRASI, 2001). The psychological trauma inflicted by conditions before and during flight may lead to debilitating mental illness for some asylum seekers and refugees. They will all require special attention and care on arrival in Ireland.

There are also people with disabilities amongst migrant workers from non-EEA countries. Migrant workers in Ireland now outnumber asylum seekers and refugees (Woods and Humphries, 2001). The UN points out that migrant workers often suffer from discrimination, poverty and social exclusion on arrival in the host country and the situation for disabled migrant workers is one of double disadvantage. While it is likely that people with disabilities are less inclined to migrate to Ireland for the purposes of taking up a job than able-bodied people, there may be a family member with a disability accompanying them. Again, there are no data in Ireland in this regard. It is important to mention that a proportion of children from a minority ethnic background who have come to Ireland through inter-country adoptions will have a disability. It should also be noted that the profile of ethnic minority people with disabilities is changing and will continue to change at the same time as the ethnic profile of Irish society evolves.

Rights, standards and commitments: the EU and the international context

Some developments are taking place at international and European level concerning the rights of ethnic minority people with disabilities. The United Nations from its early days has been concerned to advance the rights of disabled people and improve their lives. A considerable body of international norms and standards can be used to promote the advancement of rights of persons with disabilities within a broad human rights framework. Under the UN Charter, the Universal Declaration of Human Rights, International Covenants on Human Rights and other human rights instruments, people with disabilities are entitled to exercise their civil, political, economic, social and cultural rights on an equal basis with non-disabled people. Attention is also paid to the rights of ethnic minorities in UN conventions and human rights instruments. Noting that ethnic minority people with disabilities belong to both sorts of minorities and are likely to be subject to both kinds of discrimination, the UN has emphasised that ethnic minority people with disabilities are a special group that has to be strongly protected. Under the Standard Rules on the Equalisation of Opportunities for Persons with Disabilities, the UN calls for special attention to be directed towards ethnic minorities, migrant workers and the large number of refugees with disabilities. The Rules, which were adopted by the UN General Assembly in 1994, affirm the need for prevention, rehabilitation, access and equality of opportunity. They commit member states to take action, and provide guidelines by which action can be taken, for promoting equal opportunities for persons with disabilities. They also offer people with disabilities and their organisations an instrument for influencing policy making and action.

The UN Rules were formally endorsed in 1996 by the Council of the European Community as a blueprint for the European Union's disability policy.[2] Rights-based approaches to disability and 'race' have subsequently been underpinned in the Amsterdam Treaty. Article 13 of the new Treaty gave the EU the power to combat discrimination on grounds of disability and 'race' as well as on the grounds of sex, religion or belief, age and sexual orientation. Using Article 13 as a point of departure, the Council adopted two Directives addressing discrimination that may be encountered by people with disabilities from ethnic minority backgrounds. The first was a framework Directive to implement the principle of equal treatment and prohibit discrimination on the grounds of racial or ethnic origin.[3] The second was a Directive establishing a general framework for equal treatment on four discriminatory grounds including disability in employment and occupation.[4] A further initiative was the Community action programme to combat discrimination (2001–6),[5] which recognises the particular difficulties for people facing multiple discrimination. The programme is aimed not only at combating discrimination on single grounds, including on the grounds of racial or ethnic origin and disability, but also on multiple grounds. As such, the programme supports measures to combat multiple discrimination facing ethnic minority people with disabilities.

Concern is expressed in some countries that people from minority ethnic backgrounds do not receive appropriate information and advice about their rights as people with disabilities. In Britain, for example, the Disability Rights Commission has drawn attention to the low utilisation of its services by ethnic minority people, which it considers to be 'failing people from an ethnic minority background' (Woods, 2002: 2). Communication to ethnic minority communities requires more than simply the translation of information into languages other than English. This, it recognises, is not a 'magic solution'. Under the Commission's theme of 'An Effective Legal and Statutory System', the Disability Rights Commission is piloting a project aimed at encouraging and supporting the involvement of civil society organisations as partners at regional level in providing quality, sustainable and new services in the areas of disability rights information, advice, casework and representation at local level. A central objective of the project is to advance the dissemination of information to ethnic minority people with disabilities by addressing the issues preventing ethnic minority people from accessing information in relation to disability rights from organisations such as the Disability Rights Commission. To achieve this goal, the Disability Rights Commission is seeking to build relationships and form partnerships with key ethnic minority networks and organisations, including organisations of disabled ethnic minority people, with a view to developing structures through which information can be channelled to ethnic minority people with disabilities (Woods, 2002). The Regional Development Agency[6] is piloting the project in Yorkshire, a region with a large population of ethnic minorities. If successful, it is intended that the project will be extended to other regions in England as well as to Scotland and Wales (Disability Rights Commission, 2002).

Special attention has been focused on migrant workers at international and European level. The labour standards of the International Labour Organisation (ILO) offer an example of how international organisations contribute to advancing the situation of disabled migrant workers. Certain ILO Conventions relating to migrant workers, for example the Migration for Employment Convention (Revised),[7] make some provisions for disabled people's protection. Additionally, the provisions of some ILO conventions and recommendations regarding disabled people, such as the Vocational Rehabilitation and Employment (Disabled Persons) Convention 1983,[8] apply to migrant workers, as they do to all disabled workers.

Attention has also been drawn to the situation of refugees with disabilities at international level. The UNHCR, which is committed to the principles of the UN Standard Rules, has played a central role in highlighting the plight of refugees with disabilities. It has also been a key actor in promoting community-based rehabilitation for refugees with disabilities in both countries of asylum and return. It has stressed the importance of drawing on the experience of organisations of persons with a disability to develop unique approaches to assisting refugees with disabilities within a number of host countries (UNHCR, 1999). Consideration has been afforded to refugees with disabilities in some countries. For example, each year New Zealand, which became the first country in the world to accept refugees with disabilities in 1959, provides for the resettlement of 75 refugees with medical, physical or social disabilities along with their spouse and dependent children under its Refugee Quota Programme (UNHCR, 2002). The Netherlands too accepted a sub-quota of 100 disabled refugees falling under one of the following UNHCR categories of Medical at Risk, Disabled or Victim of Torture for the years 1999, 2000 and 2001 (UNHCR, 2002). The Canadian Task Force on Mental Health Issues affecting Immigrants and Refugees began in 1988 to highlight the ways in which the experiences of prosecution and torture might create significant problems for refugees and immigrants and the need for appropriate services in Canada (Stienstra, 2002). In Australia, the adequacy and appropriateness of Australia's treatment of child asylum seekers with disabilities held in immigration detention are being considered under the National Inquiry into Children in Immigration Detention announced by the Human Rights Commissioner in 2001.

Ethnicity and the heterogeneous nature of disability

People with disabilities come from all sections of society and from different ethnic backgrounds. As with the 'white' Irish majority, ethnic minority people may be disabled by physical, sensory or intellectual impairment or by mental illness. There are generic issues for people with disabilities, irrespective of ethnicity. For example, the lack of access to buildings for people with physical disability, which is seen as one of the greatest forms of disablism, faces people with disabilities from both ethnic majority and minority communities. Nonetheless, a sense of diversity must inform debates about the different areas of disability.

Much of the literature exploring the intersection of ethnicity and disability does not emphasis the heterogeneous nature of disability. Rather, the focus is on disability in a generic sense and the common problems of inaccessibility and inappropriate services that ethnic minorities encounter, irrespective of whether they are people with physical or sensory disability, intellectual disability or mental illness. There is a strong emphasis upon the under-utilisation of disability-related services by those from ethnic minority backgrounds. Language, cultural differences in communication styles and modes of non-verbal communication are identified as major barriers in cross-cultural communication (Bau, 1999). Racism, either individual or institutional, is often identified as a major factor preventing ethnic minority people from accessing services (see Vernon, 1998; Shah and Priestley, 2001). Ethnic minority people with disabilities, far from being exempt from racial discrimination may be even more vulnerable to racial discrimination. The focus on disability as a generic issue is likely to be a reflection, at least in part, of the importance attached to the social interpretation of disability in discussions on disability as it relates to ethnic minority communities. Following this argument, 'the lives of individuals with disability are usually far more limited by prevailing social, cultural, and economic constraints than by specific physical, sensory, psychological or intellectual impairments' (Groce, 1999, cited in Stienstra, 2002).

There are examples of studies on ethnic minorities that focus on distinct areas of disability. For instance, a number of British studies focus on disabling diseases such as sickle cell disorder (SCD), which some ethnic minority groups are most at risk of inheriting[9] (see for example, Atkin and Ahmad, 2000; Atkin, Ahmad and Anionwu, 2000). Ethnic diversity amongst deaf people has also been addressed in the British literature. Ahmad, Darr and Jones (2000) focus on the issues concerning identity and ethnicity in the lives of minority ethnic deaf people. In a separate study, Jones *et al.* (2001) address the welfare service needs of South Asian deaf young people and their parents in Britain. In this study, parents of deaf children from South Asian communities expressed concern that deaf culture was contributing to the estrangement of deaf people from their families and hearing ethnic group peers. Furthermore, the study found that deaf people from ethnic minority communities and their families might perceive deaf culture to be an extension of the dominant white culture and a threat to their ethnic and religious heritage.

Some studies have paid attention to the service needs of people with learning difficulties from ethnic minority communities as well as the support needs of their carers. For example, Baxter (1995) focuses on racial discrimination in services for people with learning difficulties in the UK. She examines a number of areas within such services. For instance, in relation to education, she refers to the dissatisfaction that parents of ethnic minority children with intellectual disability have expressed with the ethnocentric nature of the curriculum in special schools. This has implications for services in an increasingly multi-ethnic Ireland, where 'there has been a growing realisation of the importance of education for those with intellectual disability' (Quin and Redmond, 1999: 157).

Acute difficulties face ethnic minority people with mental health problems. A body of research concerned with estimating the prevalence of mental illness within and between ethnic groups (for example, see Berthoud and Nazroo, 1997), seeks to explain differences and question the appropriateness of diagnostic tests and responses. However, the experience, and information and service needs of ethnic minority people with mental health problems have generally been given scant regard.

Current policy including recent research findings

In Ireland, policy makers tend to consider ethnicity and disability in isolation from each other. The problems facing people from ethnic minority backgrounds are rarely addressed in policy documents and reports concerning people with disabilities. In recent years, people with disabilities from the Traveller community have become more visible in policy documents. For example, the Task Force on the Travelling Community (Government of Ireland, 1995: 280) recommended that the Commission on the Status of People with Disabilities 'should make specific reference in its work to the distinct needs of Travellers with a disability'. The Report of the Commission on the Status of People with Disabilities (Government of Ireland, 1996a), which is the most recent major report on the overall situation and service provision for people with disabilities in Ireland, identified Travellers with disabilities as a group of vulnerable people. Together with a number of other specific groups, Travellers with disabilities were considered to have particular concerns and needs over and above those of the general population with disabilities. The inclusion of Travellers with disabilities in the Commission's Report suggests that policy makers are beginning to recognise ethnic diversity among people with disabilities. However, McDonagh (2002) argues that including Travellers with disabilities in policy documents is inadequate if policy makers do not acknowledge Travellers' separate ethnic nomadic culture. Furthermore, Travellers are invisible in other major reports concerning people with disabilities. For example, in the Report of the Review Group on Health and Personal Social Services for People with Physical and Sensory Disabilities (Government of Ireland, 1996b), the Traveller community is mentioned only in the context of the Group's concern about the low uptake of immunisation services among some groups.

The marginalisation of the Traveller community within disability discourses can be seen to be a consequence of a focus on disability as a unitary category. In this analysis, unity rather than diversity is emphasised (Fawcett, 2000), so that disabled people are presented and treated as an undifferentiated, homogeneous group of people. This is a form of institutional racism. Institutional racism can be said to exist 'where things are done in a way which assumes that all clients are from the same racial, cultural and linguistic background as the rest of the white population' (Baxter, 1995: 205). This means that Travellers with disabilities face institutional racism. Faced with institutional racism and institutional disablism, Travellers with disabilities tend to be marginalised by policy makers. McDonagh (2002: 133) makes the following point:

> While carrying out research for both the Task Force [on the Travelling Community] and the Commission on the Status of People with Disabilities, it would appear that Travellers with a disability were ignored or lost in the area of service provision.

In addition, Travellers with a disability form a discrete minority within the Traveller community. The Traveller community itself, being numerically and culturally overshadowed by the dominant settled community, faces many significant obstacles. It is not surprising then that Travellers with a disability suffer from invisibility, as the recent Traveller Health Strategy points out (Department of Health and Children, 2002a).

In a similar way, asylum seekers and refugees with a disability face significant obstacles of racism and disablism. Unlike the Traveller community, policy makers have not considered ethnic minority groups with disabilities. Asylum seekers and refugees face the additional challenge of coping with the demands of post-migratory integration. Maintenance of mental health is among the factors identified as promoting integration (Begley *et al.*, 1999). Policies aimed at promoting mental health and at developing psychiatric services therefore need to take account of the special needs of asylum seekers and refugees. An Irish-based study found that 'informal networks of friends and self-help groups can offer an invaluable source of psychosocial support' to asylum seekers and refugees (Begley *et al.*, 1999: 76). Furthermore, the study revealed that professional counselling and psychological services were deemed to be culturally unacceptable and, if they were to be delivered, would be best mediated through training helpers from amongst the refugee community. Moreover, a preference for interventions addressing core post-migratory stressors was documented. These include long delays in the determination process and the uncertainty of their situation, hostility from Irish people, loneliness and boredom, serious fears of being sent home, difficulties visiting home in an emergency, worry about the safety of family members, lack of information, language and communication difficulties and unemployment. The Interdepartmental Working Group on the Integration of Refugees in Ireland acknowledged that there might be psychologically and emotionally vulnerable refugees[10] who would require psychological services. However, the Working Group appeared satisfied that the 'need for the provision of additional resources for these groups, and for other emerging client groups, should be monitored' (Interdepartmental Working Group, 1999: 31). Undoubtedly, asylum seekers and refugees with a physical, sensory or intellectual disability have additional difficulties as they share many of the barriers to integration experienced by asylum seekers and refugees including risk to mental health as well as the many barriers to participation experienced by Irish people with disabilities.

Government policy in relation to asylum seekers has serious implications for the mental health of this group of people, for example policy determining asylum seekers' right to work. Currently, some groups of asylum seekers are entitled to take up employment while others are not. Asylum seekers who made their application for asylum in Ireland after the 27 July 1999 are not permitted to work. Instead they are forced to endure unemployment (Fanning *et al.*, 2000). Much research has shown that the onset and maintenance of common mental disorders are strongly associated with financial strain and that unemployment has a variety of mental health effects including alcohol abuse, depression, suicide and parasuicide (Begley *et al.*, 1999). Begley *et al.* (1999) point out that asylum seekers facing into a period of uncertainty are already susceptible to mental health problems and are placed at an even greater risk due to enforced unemployment. They argue that this kind of enforced unemployment, where asylum seekers spend long periods of occupational inactivity in a host country, far from their homeland, is extremely destructive and a major risk factor to the mental health (as well as physical health) of asylum seekers. Moreover, they argue, it is avoidable. Begley *et al.* (1999) recommend that the necessary steps are taken to ensure that all asylum seekers be afforded the right to work after six months, a recommendation that is endorsed by Fanning *et al.* (2000). Attention has also been drawn to the negative impact on the mental health of children and adults living under the conditions of direct provision, a system introduced by the Irish Government in 2000 (Fanning *et al.*, 2001).

In Ireland, equality legislation addresses discrimination on nine grounds including the grounds of 'disability', 'race' and 'membership of the Traveller Community'.[11] The Employment Equality Act, 1998, addresses discrimination in relation to employment, while the Equal Status Act, 2000, deals with discrimination outside employment, including in the areas of education, provision of goods, services, facilities, accommodation and disposal of property on the same grounds. The Equality Authority has statutory responsibility to work towards the elimination of discrimination and the promotion of equal opportunities in Ireland. The Equality Authority tackles discrimination and promotes equality on single ground issues (that is, activities focusing on a single ground such as disability) and on multiple ground issues (that is, activities that focus on all nine equality grounds simultaneously) (National Economic and Social Forum, 2002). With a view to developing an integrated approach to equality, the Equality Authority is simultaneously involved in activities that focus on cross-ground issues (that is, activities that reflect the multiple identities that people hold) (National Economic and Social Forum, 2002). For example, the Equality Authority has recently published research in relation to gays, lesbians and bisexuals with disabilities. Other Irish bodies such as the National Disability Authority and the National Consultative Committee on Racism and Interculturalism support this cross-ground approach to inequality.

Multiple identities were explored in a recent report jointly commissioned by the Equality Authority and the Equality Commission in Northern Ireland (Zappone, 2002). The Joint Equality and Human Rights Forum,[12] in seeking to build on the suggestions contained in this report, embarked on a joint research project (Zappone, forthcoming). As part of this project, the Equality Authority commissioned a small-scale, exploratory piece of qualitative research on the identity, situation and experiences of ethnic minority people with disabilities in Ireland in 2002. The research examines the usefulness of the concept of multiple identities for equality strategies. It highlights some of the difficulties that rise with regard to profiling ethnic minority people with disabilities in Ireland using existing national statistical data. It looks at multiple identities and the experience of participating in employment and accessing health services from the view of people with disabilities from ethnic minority communities (Pierce, forthcoming).

Likely developments and future challenges

Many challenges face policy makers with respect to ethnic minority people with disabilities. Owing to unequal power relations in society, marginalised groups, which would include groups such as ethnic minority people with disabilities, have limited access to resources and welfare (Williams, 2000). Williams (2000) suggests that a framework of principles of recognition and respect could contribute to a rethinking of social policy and a reordering of the social relations of welfare. One of the principles outlined in the framework is that of 'recognition and respect for identity'. This principle involves, amongst other things, recognising the differences amongst groups such as ethnic minorities and people with disabilities. This would mean that those with multiple identities, in this case ethnic minority people with a disability, are given due recognition and respect. This principle is useful for thinking about challenges facing policy makers in Ireland with regard to ethnic minority people with disabilities. Travellers with disabilities have endured particular invisibility within the Traveller community and the wider Irish society (Crowley, 1999; McDonagh, 2002). In recent years, Travellers with disabilities are becoming visible in policy documents (for example, see Department of Health and Children, 2002). However, there is a need for the ethnic distinctiveness of Travellers with disabilities to be recognised. Other ethnic minorities with disabilities remain largely invisible and also need to be recognised. Travellers and other ethnic minorities with disabilities can be marginalised as a result of institutional discrimination. This issue needs to be acknowledged and addressed.

The principle of 'recognition and respect for identity' is particularly relevant given the significant absence of data relating to ethnic minority people with disabilities in Ireland. Scant information is available relating to either the prevalence of Travellers or to other ethnic minority people with disabilities, which renders these groups invisible (Pierce, forthcoming). For the first time, new questions on disability and membership of the Traveller community have been included in the Census of Population 2002. It is expected that this could provide information on the prevalence of disability among the Traveller community. However, policy makers and statisticians are confronting a challenge to develop an appropriate question on ethnicity, which can identify similar needs within other ethnic minority communities.

The Department of Health and Children (2002a) is examining the development of ethnic identifiers for Travellers and other ethnic groups for use in health information systems. This is consistent with the provision under the Programme for Prosperity and Fairness to adapt data systems to enable disaggregation of health access and outcomes by ethnicity (Government of Ireland, 2000). Pilot projects to develop a Traveller identifier in two health information systems are currently underway. It is envisaged that the experience gained from these projects would be extended to other ethnic groups and be used to extend Traveller identification to other health information systems (Department of Health and Children, 2002a). It is considered that the development of an ethnic identifier is vital to the systematic and regular gathering of data relating to ethnicity within health services, and would make it easier to plan and monitor services for ethnic groups. The extension of an ethnic identifier to the National Intellectual Disability Database and National Physical and Sensory Disability Database would generate a picture of ethnic minority people with a physical or sensory or intellectual disability currently receiving and/or requiring specialised health and personal services and help to improve the planning of services for this group.

The principle of 'recognition and respect for identity' is relevant for the voluntary and community sector. The importance of including marginalised groups within civil society is an important dimension of any strategy for equality and social inclusion. Ethnic minority people with disabilities often find themselves doubly excluded from mainstream voluntary organisations. Recent research has shown that voluntary and community organisations are, for the most part, at a relatively early stage of working with new ethnic minority communities (Faughnan and O'Donovan, 2002). Some voluntary organisations – both those providing services to people with disabilities and their families, and organisations of people with disabilities – have signalled their awareness of the importance of recognising ethnic diversity among people with disabilities. For example, in its submission to the Working Group on the National Anti-Poverty Strategy and Health, St Michael's House raised this issue. It pointed out that it is important to identify people with learning disabilities among disadvantaged groups such as Travellers and refugees and that they are provided with the extra supports needed for their health and educational needs (St Michael's House, 2002). There is a challenge for organisations of and for people with disabilities to become aware of ethnic diversity within their own organisations. They also face the challenge of working towards full inclusion of people with overlapping identities in the organisation at every decision-making level. Equally, organisations of and for ethnic minority people need to recognise and involve ethnic minority people with disabilities in their organisations.

Certain groups require special mention in a discussion of future challenges relating to ethnic minority people with a disability. People with disabilities amongst refugees and asylum seekers have not been visible, a situation that has parallels with Britain, where the presence of refugees and asylum seekers with disabilities has largely been ignored (Roberts, 2000). Organisations such as the Irish Refugee Council (IRC) have highlighted the trauma experienced by asylum seekers and refugees and point out that any failure to deal with this trauma may result in their mental health deteriorating (IRC, 2002). Since 2000, asylum seekers arriving into Ireland have routinely been dispersed outside Dublin into hostels and reception centres. A particular concern in relation to dispersal is that the few very important specialised services that currently exist, including the Psychology service, are available only in Dublin. The IRC (2002: 10) states that 'access to appropriately qualified and culturally sensitive counsellors, psychologists, doctors and care workers is essential in order to assess their particular health needs, irrespective of where they are accommodated'. The particular needs of women, children and unaccompanied minors must be considered.

There is no formal acknowledgement of the needs of asylum seekers and refugees who have survived torture. SPIRASI, the Spiritan Refugee and Asylum Services Initiative, has been to the forefront in highlighting issues that should be considered when providing health services for this group of people. SPIRASI (2001) identifies a number of factors that negatively affect the health of survivors of torture. These include the lack of a specialist service with training in torture related health provision and follow up psychosocial support services and the inability of the existing health structures to meet the needs of torture survivors. SPIRASI (2001) suggests a number of improvements to help people who have survived torture. These include funding for a centre dedicated to the care and rehabilitation of survivors of torture, information dissemination on torture related health issues to all relevant statutory and NGO services, education and training of all government personnel involved in asylum cases on the issues of torture and its after-effects and fulfilling the criteria stated in the UNCAT regarding Ireland's responsibility towards torture survivors.

An issue that is likely to emerge in the future relates to the needs of disabled people among migrant workers from non-EEA countries. Migrant workers are reported to suffer from higher rates of occupational accidents and disability than native workers (Bollini and Siem, 1995). Although the reasons behind the higher incidence have been insufficiently investigated, Bollini and Siem (1995) point to a number of contributing factors. These include a greater tendency for migrant workers to be employed in hazardous occupations, higher mobility, insufficient training, language difficulties and the additional stress of adapting to a different environment. Furthermore, access to rehabilitation services and disability benefits tends to be more difficult for members of ethnic groups than for natives. As Ireland is receiving increasing numbers of migrant workers from non-EEA countries, the higher incidence of disability among migrant workers is likely to have implications for Ireland's social security and health systems, as well as for migrant families. Ireland needs to acknowledge in its immigration policy the higher incidence of disability among migrant workers. There is also a requirement to take account of the needs of disabled migrant workers and their families by adopting policies aimed at promoting the health and safety of migrant workers and removing any barriers preventing them from accessing benefits and services.

Increasingly, ethnic minority children come to Ireland from a wide range of countries via inter-country adoptions. The importance of parents being able to assist adopted children from ethnic minority backgrounds in understanding and appreciating the cultural, religious and linguistic values of their heritage and prepare them to cope with certain forms of discrimination has been highlighted (O'Brien and Richardson, 1999). However, disability among adopted children from ethnic minority backgrounds has received little or no attention in Ireland to date. In addition, practically nothing is known in Ireland about ethnic minority children with disabilities or about the family care of ethnic minority adults and children with disabilities or about the ethnic dimension to ageing with a disability. These areas warrant further attention.

Conclusion

An awareness of the particular difficulties facing ethnic minority people with disabilities is increasing. At a European and international level, a number of measures and initiatives have emerged aimed at advancing the situation of people with disabilities facing multiple discrimination. Ireland is a multi-ethnic society, yet people with disabilities from ethnic minority backgrounds have been largely invisible both within their own communities and the wider society. In Ireland the problems Travellers with disabilities face are beginning to come to the fore in policy debates and discussions. However, people with disabilities in the newly emerging ethnic minority groups have been conspicuously absent and have not as yet been formally recognised by policy makers. Due recognition and respect should be given to ethnic minority people with disabilities, and other people with multiple identities. This is as pertinent for civil society organisations and service providers as for policy makers. The additional problems facing asylum seekers and refugees with disabilities are noted. The voluntary and community sector has been to the forefront in highlighting the needs of asylum seekers and refugees who have survived torture and outlining the responses that are required. A growing number of migrant workers and their families live in Ireland. The particular needs of people with disabilities among this group are likely to emerge in the future.

Acknowledgement: The author would like to thank Bryan Fanning for comments on an earlier draft of this chapter.

Chapter 9

Ageing and disability

Bairbre Redmond and Jennifer D'Arcy

The inevitability of ageing is one of the few human absolutes and, as Matt Janicki (1999: 289) wryly reminds us, the alternative to ageing is a much less attractive proposition. In terms of the developed world, Ireland still has a relatively young population with 45 per cent of the population aged 25 years or younger (O'Donevan, 2002), and therefore has yet to face the policy implications of large ageing populations such as those in the UK and the US. The Population Division of the United Department of Economic and Social Affairs (United Nations, 2002b) projects that the population of people in Ireland aged 60 years or older will increase from 15 per cent of the overall population in 2002 to 28 per cent in 2050. While these percentages are low in terms of the developed world, this 13 per cent increase is significant in terms of policy challenges for Ireland in the years ahead.

Many previously able-bodied adults experience both physical disability and diminishing mental health for the first time in older life and there is a close association between advancing years and increasing rates of disability (McGlone, 1992). Studies of those termed 'frail elderly' and those with age-related disabling conditions such as dementia (Jette, 1995; O'Shea, 2000), show a high probability, particularly for those over 80 years of age, that irrevocable disability will occur.

The interrelationship between ageing and disability is complex. The objective of this chapter is not primarily to focus on those who may become disabled as a result of natural ageing. Rather, it concentrates on the impact of advancing years on those who have always had a disability – in other words, how people with a lifelong disability cope with growing older. The chapter will explore the double stigma of 'ageism' and 'handicapism' and how the social oppression of those with disability can be joined in later life by a matching prejudice towards older people. It analyses the impact of age-related change on disabled people, with particular emphasis on the recognition of the needs of those whose disabilities become more complex as they grow older. Family care and alternative accommodation for older disabled people is also discussed along with the concepts of belonging and loss in later years. The importance is demonstrated of including those with lifelong disability in the planning of high-quality policies for effective ageing and of recognising that the needs of older people with lifelong disability have far more similarities to, than differences from, the ageing population as a whole.

Demographic background

The proportion of those aged over 65 years is considered to have particular implications for social policy in Ireland. Fahey and Fitzgerald (1997) projected a large increase in the Irish population aged over 65 years, from 402,000 in 1991 to over 690,000 in 2026. There is therefore a projected increase of approximately 72 per cent in this period. A report commissioned by the Joint Committee on the Family (Fahey, 1997) compared the ratio of older people to young people in Ireland. In 1981, there were almost three times as many children as old people. The Central Statistics Office forecasts that by 2026 the numbers of children and old people in Ireland will converge at around 700,000 each. While the above figures suggest a substantial increase in Ireland's older population (over 65 years) relative to others, it is not as high as most other European countries (Quin, 1999; Fahey, 1997). NESC (1999: 24–5) argues that 'while the increased figure will be low by EU standards, the experience on countries with currently high old-age dependency points to the need for long-term planning for the increase in pension costs and the associated caring needs of an increasing dependent aged population'.

While much work has been conducted on the policy implications of an ageing population at both national and European level, what do we know of the population of disabled people in Ireland? The Health Research Board has been compiling a national database of people with intellectual disability in Ireland since 1996 and has produced three reports on their findings (National Intellectual Disability Database Committee, 1997; Mulvany, 2000; Mulvany, 2001). The database information can also be compared to data collected in the 1974 and 1981 Censuses of Mental Handicap (Mulcahy, 1976; Mulcahy and Ennis, 1976; Mulcahy and Reynolds, 1984), thus allowing for the observation of trends in this group over 26 years. The latest report (Mulvany, 2001) represents a national census of people with intellectual disability in the Republic of Ireland as of April 2000. This report shows an increase in longevity in those with intellectual disability with those aged 55 years and over who now represent 11.3 per cent of all those with intellectual disability in Ireland. However, a most significant change in the 2000 database is the large increase in those with disability currently in the 34–54 year group. This cohort has now grown from 19 per cent of the overall population of those with intellectual disability in 1974 (Mulcahy, 1976) to 32 per cent of the overall population in 2000, see Figure 1.

Figure 1 **Prevalence of moderate, severe, and profound intellectual disability (combined) by age group: 1974, 1981, 1996, 2000. National Intellectual Disability Database, Ireland 2000.**

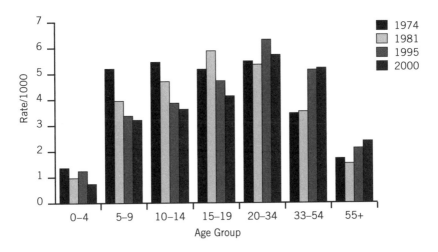

Source: Mulvany, 2001: 8. Reproduced by kind permission of the Health Research Board.

As a companion resource to the Intellectual Disability Database, the Health Research Board is also currently in the process of compiling the Physical and Sensory Disability Database (Gallagher, 2001, 2002). The Database comprises information on the specialist services currently being used or needed within the next five years by people with a disabling condition. Importantly for this discussion, the Database is confined to those people with a physical or sensory disability below the age of 66 years of age. An analysis of the data in phase 1 areas[1] for the National Physical and Sensory Disability Database shows a significant proportion of respondents in an older age group. In a total 1683 disabled people in the Phase 1 Data Set, 26.20 per cent were between 35 and 54 years, and 17.83 per cent were between 55 and 65 years (Gallagher, 2001: 56). Therefore just over 44 per cent (741 people) of the total numbers included in the database were above the age of 35, suggesting a correlation between physical and sensory disabilities and ageing.

The changing age profile noted in both the most recent Intellectual Disability Database Report (Mulvany, 2001) and the early data from the National Physical and Sensory Disability Database (Gallagher, 2001, 2002) have considerable implications for future service planning and delivery. The growing number of people with disability now in their middle age who will start to enter old age over the coming twenty years is likely to put extra demands on residential services and on those services that support independent living. The database figures also point to a pressing need to plan and design services specifically focused on the needs of older people with both intellectual and physical disability and to see how the needs of these groups can also be recognised in policy decisions for older people in general.

Double stigma: ageism and handicapism

The desire to achieve and maintain a healthy and dignified old age is common to all, but may be difficult to achieve in a Western society that places considerable value on youth, perfection and the ability to make money. Many people with disability have already learned to live in a society that places little worth on imperfection, but as they grow older they may well encounter a companion prejudice against older people – the concept of ageism (Janicki, 1999). Stigma is a term used interchangeably in both the field of gerontology and disability denoting the concept of labelling an individual on the basis of superficial characteristics or as a term 'used to refer to an attribute that is deeply discrediting' (Goffman, 1990: 13). Robert Butler (1969) coined the term 'ageism'. He likened it to other forms of bigotry such as racism and sexism, defining it as a process of systematic stereotyping and discrimination against people because they are old. Scrutton (1990) argues that such commonly held ideas restrict the social role and status of older people, structure their expectations of themselves, prevent them achieving their potential and deny them equal opportunities.

Gerontological research has pointed to a number of societal influences and factors contributing to ageist attitudes in Western society including the connection between old age and death (Butler, 1969), emphasis on youth culture, and economic productivity (Traxler, 1980). Many of these factors are useful in comparing prejudicial attitudes to older people and to similar attitudes towards those who are disabled. Eisenberg (1982: 5) has argued that:

> because some disabled persons exact a cost from society, either because of their inability to be self-sufficient or because they are prevented from becoming so as the result of compensation legislation, they are viewed as bad or inferior in some way and hence, deserving of their fate.

Hockey and James (1993) offer an analysis of the social construction of old age, drawing a parallel between older people and people with disabilities who meet with disempowering practices in society. Hockey and James contend that while many older people are able-bodied, fit and active, a conceptual linkage of dependency with old age exists. They go on to suggest that 'it may be the social milieu in which elderly people find themselves which proves more disabling than the biological fact of growing old' (Hockey and James, 1993: 32).

Oliver (1990) and Abberley (1987) contend that any theory of disability must reconceptualise disability as a system of social oppression. Barnes and Mercer (1996: 25) examine disability from the social oppression viewpoint and argue that 'disability is not the resulting limitations caused by chronic illness, impairment or trauma, but the way such matters are responded to and categorised by the wider society'. Barnes and Mercer (1996) locate theories around stigma and social oppression within the sociological viewpoint of labelling theory. They suggest that the inherent nature of disability is irrelevant and that it is the labelling process 'which categorises people by virtue of their position in relation to the dominant structures and values of the society' (Barnes and Mercer, 1996: 25). In addressing the social aspects of ageing and visual impairments, Hendricks (1992) argues that being old and blind constitutes a jeopardy as people have stereotypical beliefs about blindness and that similarly this is also true for age. Therefore, people may often experience cumulative disadvantage or social oppression on the basis of both age and disability.

How old is old?

The World Health Organisation (WHO) report on ageing and intellectual disabilities (World Health Organisation, 2000b) recognises that there is no generally accepted age that defines exactly when a person has become old. The report took the age of 50 years as a chronological point for determining age-related change. However, certain disabilities cause new problems or 'secondary conditions' in later adulthood. This results in an accelerated ageing for some individuals who may face ageing-related difficulties chronologically earlier than those in the general population. Probably the best-known secondary condition associated with a disability and ageing is the link between Down Syndrome and dementia (Dalton and Janicki, 1999). However, Janicki (1999) notes that the most problematic of these age-associated difficulties can be those faced by older adults with physical disability, where musculoskeletal problems normally associated with advanced age can emerge much earlier. In their study of the experience of ageing for those with physical disability, Zarb and Oliver (1993) revealed that many of their respondents found the effects of the ageing process itself, combined with their existing disability, to be very limiting in terms of their overall independence. Certainly, for those with a lifelong disability who have achieved an independent or semi-independent life-style, ageing can sometimes deliver a devastating blow in the form of a new, different disability that can threaten their hard-won self-sufficiency.

Successful ageing depends largely on disease prevention and the maintenance of good health into old age. These goals need to be supported by long-term proper nutrition, exercise and sound preventive health services.

Writing in relation to ageing and physical disability, Dolsen (1992) claims that successful ageing or 'ageing well' is essentially making the best use of one's remaining resources to maintain one's independence and quality of life. Walsh *et al.* (2000) reported that many older men and women with intellectual disability in the United States were overweight, took little exercise and had levels of obesity and cholesterol higher than those of the population in general. Gill and Brown (2002) report that many older women with intellectual disability have inadequate information about and access to good age-related health services. The scarcity of adequate training for health professionals in working with disabled people can result a lack of respect and sensitivity in the provision of intimate health procedures for women, particularly in the area of breast and uterine cancer screening. This is compounded by a lack of health education for those with intellectual disability that would allow them to take more control over their own health. This issue of self-determination in health care is similar for many of those with physical disability. Zarb and Oliver (1993) found that many older people with physical disability wanted health services that were more responsive to their specific needs. Respondents in their study reported an overall lack of understanding and interest by medical personnel in the long-term effects of physical disability and a dismissive attitude by doctors towards the opinions of the person with disability.

However, a lifelong experience of disability may also provide unexpected strengths for those now entering old age. In his report for the Eurolink Age Seminar on Age and Disability, Daunt (1990) makes an important and relatively optimistic observation in his profile of those who have a life-long disability. He notes that those with disability who have established an autonomous and active way of life in their early years will have an advantage in their later years over those who will become disabled for the first time as a result of ageing. Those with a disability who have achieved independence have also, by default, learned to overcome, or a least work around, much of the stigma associated with their disability and to access such suitable technological aids and adaptations, facilities and transport as may be available. Furthermore, those with a lifelong disability will have developed life strategies and social habits and may well have made plans for their old age that accommodate their disability. This point has considerable relevance in terms of the long-term value of supporting those with disabilities to live as independent and autonomous a life as possible.

A sense of belonging in old age

Fry *et al.* (1997) looked at the factors necessary for achieving and maintaining a good old age and noted that, prominent amongst these, were family and kinship ties and a sense of belonging within a community. Hawkins (1999) also noted that the need to develop dignity and choice in the social, residential and daily environments for older people with disability was a major challenge for policy makers if they were to combat existing, pervasive negative stereotypes. For those with disability, finding an appropriate place to live in adulthood has never been easy. Until the 1980s most adults with disability faced a stark choice in terms of long-term accommodation – either entering often quite restrictive residential care settings or staying with their families. However, because of the chronic shortage of any alternative accommodation, the reality for many people was that long-term family care was frequently their only option. The 2000 Report of the Intellectual Database in Ireland (Mulvany, 2001) shows that one third of all people with intellectual disability in Ireland aged 35 years and older still live with their families, with 22 per cent of those aged 55 years and older still in family care. These figures are on a par with data in the United Kingdom (Grant, 2000) and in the United States (Heller, 1999) and are characterised by family caregivers also struggling with issues associated with their own advancing age. Heller (1999) and Walker *et al.* (1999) suggest that many cases of older people with disability still living in their family home are marked by a lack of long-term planning by the family. Walker *et al.* (1999) also suggest that many older people with disability living in long-term family care may lack appropriate control and autonomy over their own lives owing to long-standing, habitual restrictions placed upon them when they were still very young. However, Irish research (Redmond, 1996) indicates that such a lack of long-term planning may be more associated with a lack of alternative service provision being available for these families, rather than an unwillingness to surrender their caring role. Also, few parents now in their seventies and eighties could ever have anticipated the dramatic increase in the life expectancy of those with disability in the latter half of the twentieth century and many may well have simply assumed that they would be able to provide care for their son or daughter for their whole life.

A longer lifespan also brings with it the inevitability of loss as the years progress. For those with disability still living at home, the loss of their parents may also mean a move into new accommodation, often as an emergency measure. Such 'emergency' placements can come at a time of deep bereavement for the individual and Heller (1999) refers to the 'transfer trauma' associated with such unplanned moves. Also the inevitable experience of grief and despair that is normal after the loss of a parent may not be full appreciated in the case of an older person with disability. Either their grief becomes subsumed into the practicalities of moving to a new care setting or, in the case of those with intellectual disability, it may be misdiagnosed as 'challenging behaviour' or non-compliance (Harper and Wadsworth, 1993; Kloeppel and Hollins, 1989). Many of these factors could be addressed by involving those with disability and their families in what Ludlow (1999) terms permanency planning, i.e.

reviewing alternative and appropriate accommodation options and starting a move into such accommodation while parents are still around to act as support to their family member.

The WHO report on health ageing for those with disability (2000b) acknowledges the rights of the person with disability to live in a dwelling appropriate to his or her culture in the mainstream of that society. Therefore, if high-quality permanency planning is to become a reality, it will depend on the existence of sufficient appropriate and enriching settings to accommodate older people with a disability. However, the Irish Intellectual Disability Database for 2000 (Mulvany, 2001) showed that 1,171 people living at home were in immediate need of alternative accommodation. A further 471 people with an intellectual disability now resident in psychiatric hospitals would also require alternative accommodation within five years. The reality is that if there are not enough places for those in immediate need, then the idea of planning for the future becomes a meaningless aspiration.

Empowerment and inclusion in planning

The development of adequate and appropriate services to support the 'greying' of those with a lifelong disability must address the issue of human rights and social justice that Barton (1996) saw as necessary in combating stigma and exclusion. 'Disabled People are increasingly involved in challenging . . . stereotypes and developing an alternative dignified perspective, one that recognises disability as a human rights issues. This involves the struggle for choice, social justice and participation' (Barton, 1996: 13). Such a struggle for participation and social justice must involve the voices of those older people with disability in the planning of their own futures. In a submission to the Commission on the Status of People with Disabilities, the National Rehabilitation Board (NRB) criticised the lack of inclusion of older people in considering the requirements of disabled people. This 'limited vision' is seen as insidious to the 'notion that quality of life automatically and inevitably diminishes in later years' and the perception of older people as being 'incapable of advocating for themselves' (NRB, 1994: 10). Daunt (1990) also addressed this serious under-representation of older people in the planning, delivery and co-ordination of services in European member states. He criticised the lack of 'lobbies or pressure groups able to identify and articulate the special needs of this population'. He noted that potential future opportunities to effect change may only occur when the first generation of those people who have acquired motor or sensory disabilities and who have championed the cause of equal opportunity themselves encounter the realities of ageing (Daunt, 1990: 16). The World Health Organisation (2000b) report on healthy ageing for adults with intellectual disability also highlighted the necessity that service development must include a commitment towards respect for the individual and his or her family, the inclusion of the person's needs and wishes in any support plan, and the development of support plans that are minimally restrictive, culturally sensitive and which foster the growth and autonomy of the person.

Conclusions

As new and numerically larger generations of Irish people with disabilities begin to enter their third age, they present a clear challenge to policy makers. Firstly, there is a need to understand the quite blurred margins that exist in the identification of those that are labelled 'old' and those labelled 'disabled'. In particular, policy makers have to appreciate the subtle, yet essential, difference between older disabled people and those who have become disabled as part of the ageing process. In order to begin to properly address important issues for older disabled people it may be necessary, in policy terms, to redefine or reinterpret the definition of old age, particularly for those who may have accelerated ageing – in other words, to appreciate the third age as a personal, adaptable concept. In practice, this may be best achieved by the introduction of flexible lifestyle changes and retirement plans driven by individual need rather than by strict chronology. Specific pre-retirement and retirement programmes for those with intellectual disability, where they have been attempted, have proved effective (Sutton *et al.*, 1993; Laughlin and Cotten, 1994). Interestingly, in the evaluation of such a programme established in west Dublin in the mid-1990s, the participants requested the reintroduction of a small enterprise activity in their primarily leisure-type retirement programme (Koornneef, 2000), demonstrating the importance of not underestimating the capacity of the semi-retired. There is also evidence that some older adults with disability may also benefit from inclusion in general programmes for older retired people in the community (Heller, 1999).

Janicki (1999: 300–1) emphasises the need for 'ageing in place' – recognising the changing needs of people as they age, while finding and providing the supports to help people to remain where they are. The ideal of ageing in place also demands the provision of more individualised supports to meet the unique needs of individuals as they age. Such supports may be community based for those already living in the community, and Zarb and Oliver (1993) highlight the importance of providing adequate information on such supports to those with disability to allow them to maintain a self-determined and self-defined future. Greater flexibility in residential settings is also needed that will allow those with diminishing physical or cognitive capabilities to stay where they are living with extra help where appropriate, rather than being moved to specialist, separate 'elder' services for those with disability. Interestingly, in terms of planning and delivery of services in Ireland, the National Physical and Sensory Disability Database Development Committee (Gallagher, 2001) suggests that it is more appropriate for services for older disabled peopled to be funded from the budgets for services for older people in general. This raises policy issues with regard to defining the age that one is deemed 'old' and for the co-ordination and integration of services for ageing disabled people. The Committee acknowledges the need for further review and consideration on this matter and identifies the importance of 'liaison concerning service delivery' (Gallagher, 2001). Adaptability in terms of service provision should also accompanied by adaptability in terms of paying for such services. If such a flexible policy approach is to be adopted to support older people with disability, then new, more flexible service funding will also have to be considered. Current Irish research (Nolan, 2002) into the feasibility of direct payment options for those with disability may be best suited to support innovative and pragmatic service provision for those who are ageing with a disability.

The amount of interest paid by policy makers to the ageing of those with disability is dependent on a nation's population demographics and on the quality of existing services for those with disability. From an international perspective, many developed countries are starting to come to terms with the forthcoming increases in their older populations. Janicki (1999) notes that one of the most fundamental policy issues to be tackled is how to make society more sensitive to the needs of older people in general, and to the unique needs of disabled people who are entering old age. If Ireland is to begin to respond in an innovative way to the ageing of its disabled population, Irish people will have to be educated about the specific needs and the not inconsiderable strengths of this growing cohort. What is particularly important is that professionals who work in the area need to be challenged both in their training and in ongoing work supervision to recognise and avoid the adoption of easy, stereotypical perspectives and to work in a way that advances positive and inclusive options. Although originally designed as guidelines for designing policies for all older people, the UN Principles for Older Persons (United Nations General Assembly, 1992) have considerable resonance for those ageing with a disability – they include independence, participation, care, self-fulfilment and dignity. Those who plan, design, fund or deliver services to older, disabled people would benefit greatly from focusing and keeping true to those five simple guidelines if the ideal of a 'good old age' for those with long-term disability is to become a reality.

Chapter 10

The mixed economy of welfare: state, NGOs and the private sector

Anne Good

'A Welfare State exists where government organisations provide material benefits for those who are unable to support themselves adequately through paid employment.'   **Giddens (1993: 313)**

Introduction

State welfare provision is crucial to the well-being and social citizenship of the estimated 370,000 to 400,000 people with disabilities in Ireland.[1] Giddens's (1993) definition shows clearly that this is the case, given that only an estimated 20 per cent of Irish people with disabilities are in paid employment (Kearns and Lynch, 2002; Goodbody Economic Consultants, forthcoming), while the remaining 80 per cent depend to various extents on the welfare provisions of the Irish state, as delivered through a mixed economy of public, NGO and private provision. The nature of this mixed economy must be understood and analysed if change in disability policy is to be more than aspirational and if the lives of people with disabilities are to be improved in practical ways.

Drake's (1999) theoretical framework categorises state disability policies along a spectrum, from those that actively damage people with disabilities and deny their human rights (such as Nazi Germany), through to those which guarantee full social citizenship for all (such as contemporary USA). It can be argued that, according to Drake's typology of disability policy, Irish disability policy can be termed as currently piecemeal, but as moving slowly towards a hybrid system (such as that in Australia). Thus it is argued here that, despite recent changes, the Irish state is still a long way from guaranteeing and resourcing full social citizenship for people with disabilities (exemplified by the USA). The chapter examines the historical development of what is termed Ireland's mixed economy of welfare, especially with regard to disability. It uses the case study of transport to illustrate the continued gap during the period 1996 and 2002, between the vision of equality and inclusion presented in the 1996 Report of the Commission on the Status of People with Disabilities, and the reality of people's lives as documented in some recent research. The chapter concludes with a discussion of the way forward in the form of NDA work on national standards for all services, both mainstream and specific, which impinge on the lives of people with disabilities.

Understanding welfare and the state

In modern advanced capitalist countries such as Ireland, welfare provision is considered to be an important aspect of the role of the state, and welfare benefits to be part of the entitlements due to people as a key dimension of their social citizenship. How the state prioritises and delivers on welfare is often a measure of the state's perceived legitimacy and a major factor in the outcome of elections in democratic states. This welfare role has been a matter of contestation across Europe since the rise of new right politics in the 1980s, with some arguing for state withdrawal from direct provision, except in the most extreme cases of deprivation and as a last resort. Instead the state should concentrate on a neo-liberal agenda of competition and trade as a basis for economic growth and thus, it is further argued, aims to improve the standards of living for most citizens. This neo-liberal agenda gained dominance in both the United States and the EU during the 1980s and early 1990s, although in the case of the EU it was modified by the influence of a strong social democratic tradition which tried to ensure that moves towards a single free market in Europe from 1986 onwards were accompanied by effective social policies to mitigate any adverse effects of such change (Bailey, 1992; Lambert, 1994).

Clearly, in Ireland, as elsewhere, this dominant discourse of competition and individualism has presented particular problems for those unable to compete without some State intervention to 'level the playing field' by tackling entrenched exclusion and discrimination. Among these are many people with disabilities. So the emphasis on paid work as the core strategy for meeting citizens' needs is particularly problematic for those structurally excluded from the labour market by intrinsic and embedded inequalities, discriminatory attitudes and stigmatisation (Cantillon *et al.* 2001). The countervailing force of equality laws and policies in Ireland has so far been weak in relation to people with disabilities. Recent research has documented the structural exclusion of Irish people with disabilities from paid work (Bergeskog, 2001) as compared with those in Germany for example (Kearns and Lynch, 2002). The barriers documented in this research have ensured that only 40 per cent of those with a disability/health problem between the ages of 15 and 64 were in employment in 2002, compared to an overall rate of 65 per cent for the total population in that age category (Central Statistics Office, 2002b: 1). This means that the safety net of state welfare remains the main personal resource available to the majority of people with disabilities in Ireland and so it is a particularly important aspect of their social citizenship.

Theorising disability welfare policies

Drake (1999) proposed a model for understanding disability policies in which policy models exist along a spectrum from negative to positive with regard to the core principle of the social citizenship of people with disabilities.

Typology of disability policy models

The negative policy model
The state actively seeks to deny the human and civil rights of people with disabilities.

Laissez-faire model
The state plays a minimal role in the lives of disabled people, who are left to fend for themselves.

Piecemeal policy making
The state makes some response to disablement but only in a reluctant and haphazard way, being provoked to action as a result of pressure and circumstance rather than through any desire to construct and implement a cogent and carefully planned strategy.

Maximal policy model
The State's purpose is to identify and respond to the several disadvantages caused by disability but the focus remains on the individual and his/her impairments with services aimed at integrating people with disabilities de facto operating in a segregationist way.

Social or rights-based model
The State accepts that it has a responsibility to serve all citizens and recognises that disablement is a product of society and environment designed by non-disabled people for non-disabled people. The emphasis is on the guarantee of citizenship and the exploration of that concept for its implications with regard to policy and services.
(Drake, 1999, pp. 36–7)

Further: Hybrid model
The state promotes service provision and civil rights legislation in a twin track approach, with neither perspective dominating.

(Drake, 1999: 104–5)

This chapter will apply Drake's model to the Irish context, using the example of transport policy, and will argue that while the Irish state has the aspiration to be a hybrid such as Australia, in reality it is making only slow progress from being piecemeal in its impact on the lives of people with disabilities. Furthermore, the aspiration of the Irish disability movement is to achieve the rights-based model. These dichotomies between rhetoric and practice, and between aspiration and reality, are key factors in the growing anger and militancy of the disability movement in Ireland.[2] They can be explained in part by the failure of the State to impact effectively on the mixed economy which forms the system of welfare for people with disabilities. The macro-level change of the late 1990s needs to be translated into micro-level change across all services, both mainstream and special, before it will have meaning in the lives of most people with disabilities.

Welfare and the Irish state

The Irish state developed a piecemeal approach to welfare in general, including that for people with disabilities, as a result of historical developments. These included the particular role of the Catholic Church in service provision in Ireland, the influence of Catholic social theory on the new State in the 1930s and 1940s, the role of women in Irish society and the weak economy until the late 1990s. Each will be considered briefly.

The Catholic Church was given a very strong role in the provision of welfare services in Ireland from the late nineteenth century onwards, that role being particularly concentrated on the health and educational sectors.

> The historical development of welfare institutions, and thus many of the service delivery aspects of the Irish welfare state, is intrinsically tied up with the expanding role of the Churches in Irish social life . . . the Catholic Church became increasingly involved in a wide range of institutions, from hospitals . . . to homes for 'unmarried mothers' . . . elite boarding schools and borstals and residential homes for young people. (Tovey and Share, 2000: 322)

Services for people with disabilities could also be added to that list.

Furthermore, Catholic social theory, with its emphasis on corporatism and what has become known as subsidiarity, was extremely influential in the formation of the state, the writing of the constitution, and, perhaps most importantly, the resistance to the development of the kind of welfare state created in the UK (including Northern Ireland), after the Second World War. The Catholic Church actively opposed a broader role for the state, resistance which was displayed most dramatically during the 'Mother and Child' confrontation of the early 1950s.

In this context, it is no surprise to find that very many services for people with disabilities are delivered through Church controlled agencies, even if they are primarily state funded. So those working and campaigning to improve welfare provision for people with disabilities in Ireland have been faced with the challenge of changing not only the state but also the myriad of large and small non-state organisations which deliver services on behalf of the state. As well as Church organisations these include other long-standing charities and new service providers which emerged from the disability movement and its independent living section.

The changing role of women in Ireland since the early 1970s has also been a crucial factor in recent developments in state welfare policy. In particular, the unprecedented movement of Irish women into paid work since the early 1980s (Good, 2000) has had a double effect. Firstly, it has changed the nature of Irish families (Kennedy 2001; O'Connor, 1998) by dramatically reducing their capacity to continue caring for children, elderly people and people with disabilities, through the private economy of love labour (Lynch and McLaughlin 1995). Secondly, it has provided most of the human resources for an emerging paid economy of care, funded by the state. Thirdly, the more radical agenda of some forms of contemporary feminism have added to the voices of those calling for a more just society for all and for a broad equality agenda to inform state policy and welfare provision (Good, 2000; O'Connor, 1998)

The fourth contextual factor in the production of Ireland's current welfare system was the relative economic underdevelopment of the State until the 1990s. This peripherality in relation to the majority of EU members meant that Ireland was slow to develop the kind of universal welfare provisions which emerged elsewhere in the EU and which then came under threat during the new right dominance of the 1980s. Instead, Irish welfare developed in an *ad hoc* way, as state resources permitted and political pressure demanded, and with a particular character determined by social factors such as the power and influence of the Catholic Church and the unusual but rapidly changing role of Irish women. Into this welfare system, as it related to people with disabilities in particular, came a new force for change when the international movement for the rights of people with disabilities began to make its presence felt in Ireland.

The disability movement in Ireland

This international movement for equality and human rights for people with disabilities began to have a major impact on Ireland during the 1990s (Lundstrum *et al.*, 2000), under the influence of the international disability movement especially from the UK and USA, and also of some international initiatives, most importantly the development of the UN Standard Rules on the Equalisation of Opportunities for People with Disabilities (1993). Pressure for change culminated in the groundbreaking report of the Commission on the Status of People with Disabilities in 1996 which was framed around the Standard Rules. That report, based as it was on the deliberations of a body whose majority comprised people with disabilities, and on consideration of some 600 submissions from individuals, groups and organisations, set out in its findings a radical programme for change. That programme included recommendations on detailed aspects of service provision across all policy areas. Furthermore, a new state body, the National Disability Authority, was to be established with a mandate to develop standards for service provision across the disability sector.

A further, and related, development came with the broad equality legislation of the late 1990s, the Employment Equality Act of 1998 and the Equal Status Act of 2000, followed by the creation of two equality bodies: the Equality Authority with responsibilities in the areas of policy, research, advice and public attitudes and the Office of the Director of Equality Investigations whose role is to take equality cases under the two laws. Finally, in 2000, the National Disability Authority was also established with the remit of setting national standards for disability services which were mainstreamed across a range of government bodies.

These two factors, a strong new disability rights movement and new legislation and policy agencies in Ireland, along with further international developments, created a climate of change in the late 1990s and early years of the twenty-first century. However, a recent evaluation of those changes concluded that they occurred mainly at the macro level of law and policy without as yet having a significant impact on the lives of people with disabilities (Lundstrom *et al.*, 2000). This conclusion was confirmed by the message received by the NDA during a series of regional consultations with people with disabilities and their families and carers, which were held during June 2002. At every meeting the message was that services were still at a most unsatisfactory level and could be described in the same language as that used by the Commission on the Status of People with Disabilities in 1996:

> Existing supports and services for people with disabilities are poorly coordinated. People with disabilities and their families have great difficulty and experience serious frustration getting information about their entitlements and accessing them from the multiplicity of agencies which are involved in undertaking assessments and providing services. Professionals working in the field waste much time and energy on duplication. (1996: 97)

The challenge facing the state now remains that of moving more swiftly from macro-level change to micro-level improvement in the services delivered to people with disabilities across the country. This means addressing the mixed economy of welfare and ensuring that decentralisation of service delivery and welfare provision no longer means unsatisfactory experiences for the people intended to be helped by the state and its agencies. How this might be achieved will be considered next through the case study of transport services for people with disabilities.

Transport

The policy area selected as the case study for this chapter is that of transport. Transport is a critical area as it plays a gatekeeping role with respect to the full participation of people with disabilities in education, training, employment and all aspects of social life. Without comprehensive, integrated, accessible and affordable transport, people with disabilities are *de facto* excluded from mainstream economic and social life, and so other initiatives in these areas are reduced in effect. This is especially so for those who live in rural areas and less developed regions such as the West of Ireland. As the Commission on the Status of People with Disabilities pointed out:

> In practical terms, one of the single largest areas of concern raised in the sub-missions and at the listening meetings was the question of access and transport. Clearly the built environment and most forms of transport are very inaccessible for people with disabilities . . . These problems are not just mechanical ones but ones that have several important consequences. They mean that people are denied full access to education, to employment and training, to cultural and leisure events. They mean that the overall cost of living for people with disabilities is higher than for other people. (1996: 6)

We shall see that by 2002, the situation, while beginning to improve as some of the relevant aspects of the National Developmental Plan were implemented, had still not dramatically changed from that of 1996, and that the principle of universal access was still a considerable way from realisation.

State involvement in transport for people with disabilities in Ireland is characterised by the mixed economy of welfare, with direct involvement by the state, mainly through the CIE group of companies, as well as indirect involvement through state support for large service providers, small private initiatives, the private sector and privatised provision within families. Furthermore, the state provides direct financial support to some people with disabilities through mobility allowances, tax concessions for disabled drivers and passengers and the Free Travel Scheme.

This case study will:

1 examine the transport sector critique in the Strategy for Equality (1996)
2 summarise progress between 1996 and 2002
3 summarise research evidence regarding the micro-level experiences of people with disabilities, 1996–2002
4 map out the way forward post 2002.

Strategy for equality: recommendations on transport

The Commission report made a series of detailed recommendations regarding transport, as in other policy areas (1996: 46–50, 197–206). These 29 recommendations covered all areas including public transport systems (bus, train, ferries and airlines); private transport by taxi or hackney; specialised transport services in the disability sector; state supports, facilities and services for private car usage by people with disabilities and their carers/family members. Emphasis was placed on the varied transport requirements of all people with disabilities, whether they have mobility impairments, sensory impairments, intellectual disabilities or experience mental distress.

Progress between 1996 and 2002

Progress in implementing the transport recommendations made in 1996 was assessed in 1999 and was found to be slower than in other policy areas (Department of Justice, Equality and Law Reform, 1999a). The report evaluated the developments to date and listed ten aspects of the way forward (1999: 186), including the provisions in the PPF (Programme for Prosperity and Fairness, 1998–2002) and the NDP and the actions under way in the CIE group of companies.

The Programme for Prosperity and Fairness and the National Development Plan (2000–6) both include provisions relating, either directly or indirectly, to transport and people with disabilities. In particular, the PPF made a commitment to achieving accessibility of public services, and thus to ensuring that all government departments take reasonable steps towards making their services and those of the agencies within their remit, accessible to people with disabilities. The NDA views the creation of a fully accessible transport system as a key dimension of this commitment (NDA, March 2001). Several commitments were undertaken as part of the NDP (2000–6), including new purchases to comprise only accessible stock; rendering new and improved rail and bus stations accessible and the establishment of a Public Transport Accessibility Committee in 2000. By the end of 2002 there was evidence of significant progress in some areas, while others lagged behind.

However, we will see that research findings indicate that these measures have, as yet, had very limited practical impact on the lives of people with disabilities. The gaps between aspiration, promises and reality remain large.

Research evidence regarding the transport experiences of people with disabilities 1996–2002

Transport is one of the least researched areas of disability policy, according to the Report on Disability Related Research published by the National Disability Authority in 2002. Only eight studies were identified since 1996, in comparison with 144 in the area of health or 79 in the area of education (NDA, 2002d: 37–8, 77). No national study on transport for people with disabilities had been carried out[3] and this gap, accompanied by the lack of national baseline data in all areas including transport, means that an overall picture is not yet available. This gap in the knowledge base will be filled in 2003. Meantime, the findings of local studies from 2000–1 add together to provide a consistent 'broad stroke' picture which is likely to be true for the country as a whole up to 2002, even if some details vary.

A number of local studies were identified, in areas such as Clare, Dublin, Mayo, Meath and Limerick. A locally based study in Kerry also included transport as one of the services considered. Findings from these local studies will be examined in some detail in order to identify the mixed transport economy of welfare in the regions specified and to examine the barriers experienced by people with disabilities in these areas when trying to access transport. These studies were concerned with land transport only, no equivalent research having as yet been done on air or sea transport.

The research showed that the economy of transport, as experienced by people with disabilities was indeed mixed, but that the private car still dominated. The sectors and modes of transport identified were:

- public transport (rail, public bus)
- NGO sector provision (private buses and vans)
- private sector (taxis and hackneys)
- privatised and personal (lifts in private cars from family members and neighbours)

All of these areas have a welfare component, in that the state either provides services, funds services and service providers, or provides various types of indirect support such as tax relief or funding for service users.

The range of transport options provided through this mixed economy might thus appear to be wide. However, when research on usage was examined it was found that the private car dominated, especially in rural areas. So, in one county: 'the picture is one of very low usage of communal forms of transport, and a high dependency on private cars' (Kerry Network of People with Disabilities, 2001: 10).

All studies identified a complex range of barriers, from the physical to the attitudinal, to the use of all other modes of transport by people with disabilities.

So, when needs and aspirations were quantified and analysed the patterns were:

- significant barriers to transport use, especially public transport
- high levels of unmet transport needs
- low aspirations regarding transport due to bad experiences in the past
- exclusion of people with disabilities from all aspects of life consequent upon lack of transport leading to isolation and poverty

As one person expressed it: 'I feel like a prisoner in my own home. I feel I am being punished for a crime [i.e. his disability] that's not my fault.' (Kerry Network of People with Disabilities, 2001: 20)

In short, it is clear that, as in the UK (Drake, 1999: 88), transport in Ireland has until recently, been designed and run by non disabled people for non disabled people, and that transport continued to play a key role in the social exclusion and marginalisation of people with disabilities up to, and including 2002.

Experiences in each of the main sectors within the mixed economy will be outlined.

Public transport, 1996–2002

While no overall statistics were available, some indication of the situation could be gleaned from the fact that, in December 2002, only 35 per cent of the buses operated by Dublin Bus were fully accessible. However, it was also clear that progress in implementing the NDP provisions began to accelerate during 2002, since the equivalent figure in February was 24 per cent, showing an 11 per cent increase in ten months. Furthermore, by the end of 2002 all buses in the other large cities (Cork, Limerick, Galway and Waterford) were accessible. In contrast, changeover to accessible coaches was slower on intercity routes with a pilot project of 20 accessible coaches being planned at the end of 2002. Bus services in rural areas remained inaccessible.

Accessibility to trains was also very limited with most stations having access to one platform only. Again, some progress was made in 2002, when two main Dublin stations (Heuston and Connolly) were refurbished and made accessible. But in many cases, people in wheelchairs still have little choice about where to sit on trains (there is a designated space on most mainline trains) and sometimes had to travel in the baggage car. Furthermore, people in wheelchairs and others with special transport needs had to contact Iarnród Éireann twenty-four hours prior to their travel date to ensure their needs were met. In contrast, DART services in Dublin and Arrow services on the Dublin commuter belt and in Cork and Cobh were almost completely accessible.[4]

Thus, by the end of 2002, it was clear that progress had been made through the PPF and NDP provisions outlined above, but the experiences reported by people with disabilities in the recent research indicated that much remained to be done. Research on the impact of the 2002 developments was unavailable until 2003. The Kerry study (2001) revealed that public transport was less used than private buses or taxis. Respondents (who included people with all types of disabilities) reported that public buses to meet their needs were simply not available (49 per cent) or not accessible (a further 35 per cent). In the Limerick study (Disability Federation of Ireland, 2001), which focused mainly on people with physical/sensory disabilities, the most frequently identified difficulty in using public buses was problems of wheelchair use (56.6 per cent), the second was that waiting for the bus was tiring (30.1 per cent) and the third was getting on (26.5 per cent) or getting off (24.1%) the bus (2001: 11).

Participants in the Meath (2000) and Dublin (2001) studies pointed out the need for consideration of the whole journey to be undertaken by the person with a disability, given that, if any aspect of that whole journey is inaccessible or otherwise unsuitable, it renders the journey impossible. For many people with disabilities, it was argued, the only realistic option is a door-to-door appropriate service, something which is clearly not provided by public buses or trains.

From the Limerick study, some detailed comments were:

A year ago I was told that I couldn't use a public bus because there was only one access door and I would block the other passengers

There is no public transport in my area

I would like more ramps on footpaths to make buses more accessible

Some bus drivers can be very helpful but others are very uncooperative

There is a bad attitude towards disabled people on buses.
                                        (Disability Federation of Ireland, 2001: 17–18)

Clearly, a range of factors, from the structural, to the organisational and the attitudinal, still impede the use of public buses by people with disabilities. Trains were shown to be even more problematic.

NGO transport
Usage of bus/van services provided by organisations for people with disabilities was relatively high, second only to private car usage in the Kerry study. These services, while more successful in meeting the needs of people with disabilities than public buses, were seen as underfunded, as leaving some needs unmet and as adding to feelings of exclusion and stigmatisation. The Mayo study

(South-West Mayo Development Company, 1999) examined the range of bus and van services provided in the county, usually to transport people with disabilities to services. A number of areas were identified as problematic, most especially the reliance on the Community Employment scheme for provision of drivers, and reported bullying and some dangerous practices which occurred in some services. The Dublin report, which focused on the Vantastic model that had emerged from the Independent Living movement, also highlighted the need to move beyond the CE scheme for supplying drivers, as well as drawing attention to underfunding and consequent unmet needs. A more strategic response to the transport needs of people with disabilities was clearly required.

Comments in the Limerick study included:

The only transport available to me in the past 20 years has been the I.W.A. bus

I'm frustrated by the lack of support from the Health Board to organisations providing transport to disabled people, for example CIL. The Health Board were unwilling to fund it, there's a lack of help and assistance from them

Even though I am a member of IWA I was denied a lift to work. I was told that they didn't have enough space and wouldn't be going out that way

I would like if there were no logos on the sides of buses so I wouldn't be embarrassed.

(Disability Federation of Ireland, 2001: 18–20)

Private sector
People with disabilities rely heavily on taxis and hackneys, but they express dissatisfaction with the service provided and with the attitudes of some drivers. Taxis came second to private NGO buses in usage rates of non-private car modes of transport in the Kerry study. High dependency on taxis was also reported in other studies but significant barriers remain.

Comments in the Limerick study included:

I was in Dublin and a wheelchair accessible taxi wouldn't come and pick me up. I was supposed to have an appointment for 15 minutes but it only lasted two minutes because of the delay and I was still charged £60 for the appointment.

I was in Dublin in a taxi and my wheelchair was taken apart and I was charged for each piece as separate luggage.

I find taxi drivers very rude as they have come to pick me up and then refused to take me.

(Disability Federation of Ireland, 2001: 18 –19)

The private sector option of taxis/hackneys is often used, despite these problems, for lack of an alternative rather than because of satisfaction with the service provided. Research has also been carried out on the supply side and recommendations made. National Radio Cabs, for example, made a submission to the Department of the Environment and Local Government in May 2002. The submission argued for greater government involvement in laying down standards and regulations for the provision of a better taxi service for people with disabilities, and for assignment of responsibility to a dedicated authority for monitoring those standards. It also called for a more coherent government approach to the funding of taxi services rather than the current situation of some *ad hoc* funding of initiatives along with health board voucher systems. These do not ensure that needs are met: 'only a minority of those in need of public service provision are currently served' (2002: 19). The long-term solutions proposed included the establishment of a dedicated wheelchair accessible fleet of taxis, providing door-to-door service, with a free phone direct contact line, drivers trained to serve the needs of customers with disabilities and government funding to ensure viability (2002: 20–1).

Individualised private solutions
In the absence of any fully satisfactory alternative within public transport or private/NGO provision, most people with disabilities, especially those living outside the main urban areas, are heavily reliant on the private car, whether their own, or those of family members or neighbours and friends. This can push people into driving more than they feel able to do; it can be an expensive alternative; it increases levels of dependency and feelings of obligation; it can mean that people refrain from travelling out of concern for family members:

> I feel my sister and brother need a break. I would like more transport so I'd be able to make more friends.

> I could live my life to its full potential and be more independent if there was reliable transport. I wouldn't have to depend on my family so much.

> If I didn't have family members/friends to bring me into town I would have no social life and I like socialising just as much as an able-bodied person.

> I can only drive myself locally.
>
> (Disability Federation of Ireland, 2001: 20)

Further problems are presented by lack of disabled parking spaces, misuse of such spaces by other people, and lack of dished kerbs on paths. Finally, the Meath study found that there was a need to change the certification system used as the eligibility criterion for state support to disabled drivers through VAT and Vehicle Road Tax.

Way forward

The way forward towards improved transport services for people with disabilities was comprehensively mapped out by the Strategy for Equality in 1996. However, implementation in this area has been slower and less complete than that in other areas, as revealed in the progress report of 1999. Developments between 1999 and 2001 were patchy and less than satisfactory. Change then accelerated during 2002 but, at the end of that year, much still remained to be done before the concerns expressed by people with disabilities were comprehensively met.

It is clear from this evidence that the current mixed economy of welfare in transport requires further state intervention to ensure better standards, implementation of commitments already made, and funding of required initiatives in all sectors. Most of all, what is required is the establishment of a coherent overview of the transport needs of people with disabilities and a comprehensive plan to ensure that all elements of the mixed economy work together to meet those needs. In particular, the current over reliance on the private car, in the absence of satisfactory alternatives, is part of a wider social policy issue in the Irish context, i.e. the historic neglect of public transport and its consequent underdevelopment. If this infrastructural deficit is addressed in the coming decade, as it must be in the interests of a sustainable economy and society, it is critical that the needs of people with disabilities are comprehensively integrated into all programmes and plans, such as the National Development Plan. This is beginning to happen through the work of the City and County Development Boards into which the NDA has an input (NDA, 2001b).

Conclusion

It is clear from both the overview of the mixed economy of welfare and the specific case study of transport, that the welfare needs of people with disabilities are not being adequately met by the Irish state. We have seen that Ireland can be classified in terms of the Drake typology as piecemeal, with slow movement towards the stated aspiration for a hybrid model. It is also clear that people with disabilities require full social citizenship of the rights-based model. The concluding part of this chapter will consider how the Irish state could move to bridge these gaps, between rhetoric and performance, between state commitments and the disability movement's aspirations, gaps which ensure that, despite legal and policy progress since 1996, the anger and frustration among people with disabilities and their families, described in the 1996 report, remains high in the disability sector.

In a paper prepared for the NDA and delivered to the Policy Institute in April 2002, social policy analyst Jane Pillinger outlined a series of measures which could be taken in order to transform the current unsatisfactory situation into one of quality service for people with disabilities. Pillinger argued that:

- Service improvements must be rooted in a more robust rights based and duty based approach;
- Services must be informed by a set of clear principles (recognition, voice, rights on the one hand, and attentiveness, responsibility, competence and responsiveness on the other hand) so that both working practices and organisational culture among service providers of all types change in step;
- Disability awareness in the broadest sense must permeate all processes of change though strategies such as staff training, institutional supports for development of expertise, a co-ordinated and integrated approach to service delivery, encouragement of partnership and participation among others.

(2002: 22)

The goal of these three sets of changes, argued Pillinger, has to be no less than a transformation of Irish society through placing equal value on the social citizenship of one of the most marginalised groups in Irish society: 'What is ultimately required is a massive cultural shift away from what is convenient for the organisation to one that focuses on the needs of the disabled service user.' (2002: 23).

The context and mechanisms for that shift already exist, within the Strategic Management Initiative and Quality Customer Service frameworks of the Irish public service, along with the equality laws and policy initiatives of the last three years (Pillinger, 2002: 1–4). Most importantly, these frameworks were reinforced in relation to services for people with disabilities, by the mandate accorded to the National Disability Authority when it was founded by the Act of 1999. The role of the National Disability Authority, according to Section 8 (2), is:

1 to advise the Minister on appropriate standards for programmes and services provided or to be provided for persons with disabilities . . .
2 to act as an advisory body with regard to the development of general and specific standards . . .
3 to monitor the implementation of standards and codes of practice in programmes and services provided to persons with disabilities and to report to the Minister thereon . . .
4 to recognise . . . good standards and quality . . . through the provision of a disability equality award system.

The NDA has investigated a broad range of examples of good practice internationally, as well as piloting quality assurance models in the Irish context. It has given a consistent message regarding service provision and the welfare of people with disabilities in all its submissions and recommendations to date. In practical terms, there are two specific generic strategies which have been demonstrated in other countries as effective in bringing positive change to service provision within a rights based framework. These are advocacy services for people with disabilities and independent and individualised needs assessment by a single agency with the power to interact across the range of services to ensure delivery of the services identified (Forum for People with Disabilities, 2001). These strategies are being researched by the NDA in order to identify appropriate models for the Irish context. Results of those research projects should be available in early 2003. Furthermore, research projects are being established which will examine service provision and gaps as well as international models of good practice, in the five priority policy areas of education, employment/training, health, income adequacy and transport.

Most importantly, in June 2002 the NDA began the process of developing national standards for services for people with disabilities by commencing an initiative in the health sector. In partnership with the Department of Health and Children, the NDA initiated the development of National Disability Services Standards applicable to all services for people with disabilities in Ireland funded through the health systems. These national standards will focus on the outcomes for people with disabilities with the goal of achieving excellence in service provision. The ultimate intention of the NDA is to develop similar national standards across all service provision for people with disabilities, whether these are mainstream or specialised, provided directly by the State or indirectly supported by the State within its mixed economy approach.

In this way, the National Disability Authority intends to play a key role in ensuring that the gap between rhetoric and practice, between aspiration and delivery, is closed. The ultimate aim is to ensure that the vision of full social citizenship for people with disabilities in Ireland, outlined so comprehensively in 1996 in *A Strategy for Equality*, is finally realised through real change in the lives and experiences of Irish citizens who happen to have physical, sensory, intellectual impairments or to experience mental distress. A more effective system of welfare for people with disabilities, along with comprehensive action to ensure that those who can and wish to move into paid work are enabled to do so, is the twin strategy required to make the vision of equality, citizenship and human rights, conceptualised in 1996, a concrete reality in the Ireland of the twenty-first century.

Chapter 11

Social policy, poverty and disability: A Northern Ireland perspective

Jeremy Harbison

Introduction

Whilst the purpose of this book is to consider the major areas of social policy in relation to disability in contemporary Ireland, it must be remembered that the island of Ireland is covered by two distinct jurisdictions. The 1.7 million people living in Northern Ireland (NI), including the more than 200,000 people with disabilities, experience many of the same challenges as their disabled fellow citizens in the Republic. There are, however, important differences in the policy framework within which disability issues and developments occur.

This chapter reviews policy developments of importance for disabled people against the position on disability policies existing elsewhere, and the situation of people with disabilities in NI is explored, particularly through their economic status and current levels of income.

International perspective

Elwan (1999) prepared a paper for the World Bank on the association between poverty and disability worldwide. Her conclusion was that across societies, in the developed as well as the developing world, disabled people were poorer as a group than the general population, and that people living in poverty were significantly more likely than others to be disabled. This review is valuable in extracting a number of key issues and factors in the association between disability and poverty. Such comparative analysis facilitates an understanding of how, on the one hand, there is a causal link between poverty leading to disability, and on the other, a link between disability leading to poverty.

The path from poverty to disability is especially clear in developing countries. Poor households do not have adequate food, basic sanitation, and access to preventive health care. Mothers have low birthweight babies who are more at risk of debilitating disease than healthy babies, and malnutrition is a cause of disability as well as a contributory factor in other ailments that increase susceptibility to other disabling diseases. Poor people live in lower quality housing and work more often in demanding and risky physical labour environments, with higher risks of contamination where environmental standards are likely to be lower than in developed countries.

The path and potential causal links from disability to poverty have been extensively studied in the more developed countries. Three types of factors have been identified which can make disabled people, or families with disabled members, worse off. The first set of factors links the lower education and employment levels to loss of income for disabled people. Neufeldt and Mathieson (1995), in reviewing the position relating to education, conclude that on average disabled people receive less education and are likely to leave school with fewer qualifications than others. Differences in educational level do not, however, completely explain differences in labour force participation. For example, analysis of UK, Canada and Hong Kong data showed (Neufeldt and Albright, 1998) that even when educational levels are equated between disabled and other groups, the probability of disabled people having jobs is significantly lower. For example, at grade nine educational level only 17 per cent of disabled people had jobs compared with 55 per cent of non-disabled.

An analysis of a wide range of studies leads Neufeldt and Albright (1998) to the conclusion that in high income countries employment of disabled people is roughly half the rate of non-disabled and at least twice as many disabled people compared with non-disabled are not in the labour force. Also, when disabled people are employed, there is a greater tendency for them to be under-employed relative to their levels of training and education.

On income, the evidence is clear that in developed countries disabled people have lower incomes than non-disabled, even when age is taken into account. The lower income observed during working years continues into old age, since higher rates of unemployment, interrupted employment and employment in low-paid jobs with poor prospects experienced by disabled people affect their income after retirement. Disabled people are less likely to have the kind of pension or level of provision that will adequately protect them from poverty in old age (La Plante *et al.*, 1996). Studies on the extent of disabled people experiencing poverty in a number of developed countries agree that, whilst official programmes vary in the amount and kind of assistance provided, persons with disabilities still face a substantially higher risk of falling below the poverty line than is the case for the rest of the population (e.g. Neufeldt and Albright, 1998, La Plante *et al.*, 1996).

A second set of factors identified as linking disability to poverty relates to the additional costs resulting from disability. These extra costs include such things as medical expenses, equipment and adaptations required to housing.

These can be considerable – in the US, for example, total per capita medical expenditures are over four times greater for people with activity limitation than those for people without (Trupin *et al.*, 1995).

The cost of providing care to a disabled person may be borne by the disabled person directly, may be met by the state, or may fall on relatives or friends providing the care. The costs to carers, particularly the loss of employment and earnings, as well as reductions in living standards of other family members because of the loss of the carer's earnings, are increasingly being recognised. For example, the cost of raising a severely disabled child has been estimated as three times that of a child without a disability (Burkhauser and Daly 1993). Mothers of disabled children are much less likely to be in paid work; as the children get older this difference increases, and people who have looked after disabled relatives or friends for at least ten years have lower average incomes, are more dependent on welfare benefits, have less invested in pension schemes and have less wealthy families (Barnes and Baldwin, 1999).

The third set of factors linking disability to poverty relates to the barriers experienced by people with disabilities including marginalisation or exclusion from services and community activities. In developing countries, disabled people are often perceived negatively and subject to stigmatisation and neglect which reduces the opportunities for them to contribute productively thus increasing the risk of falling into poverty. Neufeldt and Albright (1998) note the main kinds of barriers experienced by the disabled, including lack of adequate or appropriate transportation, physical inaccessibility, lack of learning opportunities and negative attitudinal barriers. Job discrimination is identified as one of the most persistent barriers to the increased employment of disabled people. These constraints affect access to education and employment opportunities and reduce the opportunities for income enhancement as well as social participation.

The position in the EU

The links between disability, employment status and low levels of income are equally powerful across Europe. Unemployment rates for people with disabilities in the countries of the EU are extremely high; according to the European Commission (1996: 4), 'people with disabilities are two or three times more likely to be unemployed, and to be so for longer periods, than the rest of the population.'

Similarly, data relating to levels of poverty in various EU countries indicate that, in the main, people with disabilities are more likely to fall under poverty levels. For example, a study of men with disabilities in Germany (Burkhauser and Daly, 1993) concluded that, even with substantial transfer and employment programmes, the population with disabilities still faced a substantially higher risk of poverty than the rest of the population.

The EU's engagement in the disability field has changed substantially over the last 30 years. For much of this time involvement was constrained by the EU's lack of legal 'competence' in social policy in general and in disability policy in particular. From the early 1980s until the mid-1990s the EU was primarily involved in disability issues through four successive action programmes which encouraged the exchange of experience, dissemination of innovations, ideas and information to promote good practice in the member states. In this period, the EU had a relatively cautious and non-directive role in the area.

Since the mid-1990s the EU has developed a new, broader disability strategy, together with a stronger ambition to change the policies and practice of the member states. This shift was signalled by a Communication from the Commission in 1996. The aims and principles of this policy document were endorsed by the Council of Ministers at the end of the same year in the form of a Resolution (European Commission, 1996). Key elements in these statements were the notions of equal opportunities for disabled people, non-discrimination, main-streaming, a rights-based approach, inclusion, full participation and the identification and removal of barriers to equal opportunities.

The Amsterdam Treaty of 1997 furnished the EU with a new basis for its policy development and engagement in relation to disability issues. Article 13 of the Treaty opened the way for Community action to combat discrimination on the grounds of sex, racial or ethnic origin, religion or belief, disability, age or sexual orientation. A significant next step in securing the EU with legal competence in this area was made with the Council Directive of November 2000 establishing a general framework for equal treatment in employment and occupation. This outlawed discrimination based on religious belief, disability, age and sexual orientation. Simultaneously the Council agreed on a Community Action Programme to combat a wider range of discrimination. The Action Programme covered treatment by Public Agencies and Services (for example, health, social security and education), the media, participation in decision making and access to goods and services including housing, transport, culture, leisure and sport.

Responsibility for implementing the new anti-discrimination policy will rest principally with the member states. No explicit definition of disability is provided in Article 13 of the Amsterdam Treaty, the Council Directive, or the Community Action Programme. The importance of this is that the implementation of the Equal Treatment Strategy in member states will be influenced by the understandings of disability as developed in each national policy context.

Parallel to these policy developments, the EU has included people with disabilities as one of the vulnerable groups that should be given special consideration in the yearly National Employment Action Plans for member states. Again, the guidelines do not provide any definitions of disability and reinforce the view that member states can implement the directive and the associated actions by fitting these around their existing policies, rather than undertaking major changes across EU in an agreed approach to disability policy (Mabbett and Bolderson, 2001).

Northern Ireland, social policy and social exclusion

The previous section has described how European action, through the implementation of the Equal Treatment Strategy in member states, is significantly influenced by the policies and understanding of disability as developed in each national policy context. Thus responsibility for implementing the new anti-discrimination policy will rest principally with the individual countries in the EU.

National Action Plans against poverty and social exclusion were produced by June 2001 in response to the common objectives on poverty and social exclusion agreed by the EU at Nice. In these plans each member state sets out major challenges it faces, the strategic approach, objectives and policy measures used to tackle these issues. The UK's National Action Plan on Social Inclusion (2001: 1) noted that:

> Following the Constitutional Reforms of 1999, many of the key areas of policy responsibility in the field of poverty and social exclusion rest with devolved administrations . . . therefore, joint and complementary working between the different tiers of government is key to the successful pursuit of policies across the UK.

Thus any discussion of social exclusion in general, including issues relating to disability, must recognise the interdependence of national and regional policies. This was recognised in respect of Northern Ireland (NI) by David Trimble who, referring to the launch of the New Targeting Social Need Action Plans (Executive Information Service, 2001), said 'A regional administration such as ours can only do so much and we must work within the national context set by tax and benefit rates among other things.'

The Northern Ireland Executive's approach to tackling social exclusion has been through the New Targeting Social Need Policy (New TSN) which aims to tackle social need and social exclusion by targeting efforts and available resources towards people, groups and areas in greatest need (Northern Ireland Executive, 2001). This involves using more resources to benefit the most disadvantaged people, groups and areas. It aims to change the way things are done so that programmes and services are provided in ways that are more helpful to disadvantaged people, including people with disabilities. New TSN is based on three components. First, there is a focus on tackling unemployment and increasing employability. Second, inequalities in other key areas such as health, housing and education are tackled, including the multiple problems of disadvantaged areas, and third, the Promoting Social Inclusion initiative involves departments working together with other partners to identify and tackle factors which can contribute to social exclusion and undertake initiatives to improve and enhance the life and circumstances of the most deprived and marginalised people in the community.

The New TSN approach has been heavily criticised by the Civic Forum (2002) as demonstrating 'problems of incoherence' at the heart of the policy, confusion as to whether the policy objective was to advance equality more generally or remove sectarian differentials, having no designated budget and doing nothing to bring about a 'joined-up' approach to work across departments to tackle exclusion or engage non-governmental action. The Civic Forum argues for the need to develop a distinct regional strategy for social inclusion, clearly led by the Northern Ireland Executive and committed seriously to a joined up approach to implementation.

Social policy and disability in Northern Ireland

New TSN (2001) sets the framework for government policy for people with disabilities. Critically, however, in relation to employment and income, policy is, like that of the rest of the UK, firmly set on the principles at UK level of 'work for those who can and security for those who cannot'. The 'Welfare to Work Reforms' introduced following the election of the new UK government in 1997 are based on a three-pronged approach to disability policy. First, access to social security has gradually been changed and, in certain areas, tightened. Second, a number of new work-related programmes for people with disabilities have been introduced, linked to benefit changes. Third, the recognition of barriers to equality of opportunity for people with disabilities has led to anti-discrimination and equality legislation and to the establishment (in Northern Ireland) of the Equality Commission to monitor and promote this legislation.

Social Security changes

The new approach has led to a significant change in the 'basket of benefits' relating to disability. Disability benefits in NI can be considered within four broad groupings, and policy has changed differentially in relation to each group. Detailed accounts of changes in benefits can be found in Burchardt (1999) and Yeates (2001). An indication of the caseloads on these four groups of benefits in Northern Ireland and changes to the caseloads over the last ten years can be seen in Figure 1.

The first group of benefits are *Compensatory* for individuals who have become sick or disabled as a result of serving their nation whether in a military or occupational capacity. These benefits are tax free and not means tested; because they were designed to compensate individuals for their disability, the benefits are payable in addition to any earnings or other income and are set at

Figure 1 **Sickness/Disability caseloads Northern Ireland 1990–2002**

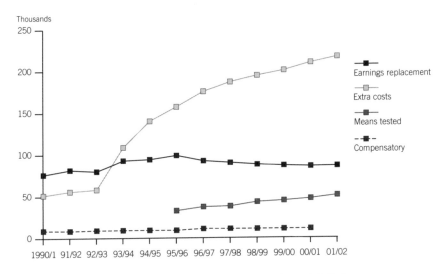

Source: Research and Statistics Branch, Department of Social Development, Belfast

a relatively generous level. Figure 1 indicates that levels of compensatory benefits have remained largely unchanged over the last decade.

The second set of benefits are *Earnings Replacement* which are paid on the basis of an assessment of incapacity for work. During the 1970s there was a period of expansion and improvement in the coverage of earnings replacement benefits, but more recently successive governments have attempted to control their expansion. Long-term benefits were linked to prices rather than earnings, short-term sickness benefits became flat rate rather than earnings related and attempts were made to toughen eligibility criteria.

The reform of benefits within the 'Welfare to Work' approach concentrated on reducing the tendency for non-employed claimants to be categorised as disabled rather than unemployed, and preventing the social security system from actively supporting the reporting of disability and the claiming of incapacity benefits. A range of changes to benefits ensued, designed to restrict access to Earnings Replacement benefits and to make these less generous than benefits available for genuine job seekers. A 'personal claimability assessment' was introduced to screen and assist personal advisers in developing a back-to-work plan for claimants. The changes were designed to prevent moves into Earnings Replacement benefits, to keep claimants in touch with the possibility of employment and to discourage early retirement (Yeates, 2001).

The development of benefits to recognise the *Extra Costs* of disability followed evidence from national surveys which demonstrated the additional costs incurred as a result of disability and how these were not being met by existing benefits. In particular, benefits for those with the most severe impairments were found to be inadequate and those with less severe impediments were often getting nothing at all. Extra Cost benefits were reformed in the early 1990s and the 'Welfare to Work Reforms' have further extended coverage of the benefits in respect of the most seriously disabled and in age. Figure 1 shows the rapid and continuing sharp increase year-on-year of claimants receiving these benefits in NI.

Finally, *Means Tested* benefits for the sick and disabled have mirrored the development of both Earnings Replacement and Extra Cost benefits. Initially sickness and disability benefits were not differentiated from other reasons for being out of work. Developments simplified the means testing and created premiums recognising additional disability costs through the payment of extra amounts for disability.

In conclusion, the reforms flowing from 'Welfare to Work' have focused social security benefits more narrowly on people with severe disabilities, older disabled people (over pensionable age) and disabled children. The Disability Income Guarantee was introduced in 2001, designed specifically to provide additional help to those severely disabled people on the lowest incomes for whom work is not an option. It provides a guaranteed level of income for those under sixty who are receiving an income-related benefit and who suffer from significant disability. The Disabled Child Premium is payable in respect of each child meeting qualifying conditions living in a household that is receiving income-related benefits.

The importance of benefit changes in NI can be seen in the fact that 37 per cent of total social security expenditure (which was around £3 billion) was spent on people in receipt of sickness and disability benefits in 1998–9 and 18 per cent on long-term sickness and disability benefits (Yeates, 2001). Figure 1 demonstrates how the fastest growing area has been Extra Cost benefits, with about half of this growth coming from claims from people over state pension age and a smaller amount from claims on behalf of children.

Job programmes

The impact of these social security reforms and the extent to which they achieve their policy aims remain to be established. The second major component of the new 'Welfare to Work' policy related to disabled people of working age. Here the changes in the social security system were made increasingly oriented towards entry or re-entry into the workforce. A set of policy initiatives to increase the opportunities for disabled people to enter or re-enter employment is simultaneously being put in place. These range from active labour market policies (New Deal for Disabled People), proposals to improve and modernise the services provided to the unemployed and economically inactive, and changes in the tax and benefit system.

The New Deal for Disabled People is a job brokerage programme designed for people who have a disability or a long-term illness. It emphasises the individual support available for each participant in his/her search for work. Access to Work Schemes further facilitate the opportunities for people with disabilities to work, by helping them overcome environmental barriers through funding special aids, adaptations to premises and equipment, funding a support worker or additional travel to work costs.

Employment Support Programmes provide opportunities for people with disabilities to work alongside non-disabled and to receive the full rate for the job. Finally, the Disabled Person's Tax Credit was introduced in 1999 to help people who have a disability move into work by ensuring that they receive a minimum level of income in work. These initiatives, associated with the changes to the benefit system outlined earlier through the increasing orientation of social security towards entry or re-entry into the workforce, have not to date been evaluated and their impact remains to be assessed. As a following section will make clear, a major problem of lack of employment for people with disabilities remains.

Anti-discrimination measures

The third plank of government action in Northern Ireland has been to tackle the barriers that impede people with disabilities in their search for work and in access to services and to promote equality of opportunity for people with disabilities, particularly through the public sector.

The Disability Discrimination Act (1995) recognises that some disabled people need practical help to enable them to get a job or to access services. In combination with the right of non-discrimination, the Act introduced a duty for providers to make 'reasonable adjustments' to help overcome the practical effects of a disability. The duty to make reasonable adjustments is a vital foundation of the legislation and distinguishes it from other areas of anti-discrimination legislation. The Act introduced new rights for disabled people in areas of employment and access to goods, facilities, services and premises. It also allows government to set minimum standards so that disabled people can use public transport easily.

The employment provisions of the act came into force at the end of 1996. These make it unlawful for employers with 15 or more employees to discriminate against disabled employees or disabled job applicants in any aspect of employment. It places a duty on employers to make reasonable adjustments if employment arrangements, or the workplace itself, place a disabled person at a substantial disadvantage compared to a non-disabled person. Reasonable adjustments have to be considered at every stage of employment.

The Act also makes it unlawful for service providers, landlords and other persons to discriminate against disabled people in certain circumstances. The duties on service providers are being introduced in three stages finishing in 2004.

The Disability Discrimination Act was an important step forward in disabled people's rights but when it was enacted was strongly criticised as not going far enough particularly through the lack of an enforcement body responsible for ensuring compliance with the legislation and the exclusion of education and the partial exclusion of transport from the rights of access provisions.

The lack of an enforcement body was subsequently addressed by the establishment of the Equality Commission for Northern Ireland. From April 2000 the Commission has had duties and powers in relation to disability matters. The Equality (Disability etc.) (Northern Ireland) Order 2000 made provision for the Equality Commission to work towards the elimination of discrimination against disabled people, to promote the equalisation of opportunities for people with disabilities and to take steps to encourage good practice in the treatment of disabled people. The Commission can assist disabled people by offering information, advice and support in taking cases forward, can provide information and advice to employers and service providers and can undertake formal investigations. Finally, the Commission can prepare statutory codes of practice providing practical guidance on how to comply with the law and arrange independent conciliation between service providers and disabled people in the area of access to goods, facilities and services.

The Belfast Agreement has also introduced major policy changes of specific relevance for people with disabilities. This Agreement, and the subsequent legislation enacting it (The Northern Ireland Act, 1998) mainstreamed equality considerations into all public policies. Within this legislation (Section 75) a statutory obligation is placed on all Public Authorities in NI in carrying out their functions to have due regard to the need to promote equality of opportunity 'between persons with a disability and persons without' as well as between other designated groups. Public Authorities have to each produce an Equality Scheme outlining how their policies take into consideration the need to promote equality of opportunity for people with disabilities (as well as other identified groupings) and have to carry out Equality Impact Assessments on new policies to establish whether or not they impact adversely on persons with a disability (as well as the other groupings). Equality Schemes have to be endorsed by the Equality Commission, and Annual Reports on the implementation of Equality Schemes and the outcome of Equality Impact Assessments have to be made to the Equality Commission.

This Statutory Duty arising from the legislation is unique to Northern Ireland; its objective is to strengthen the mainstreaming of equality and to make equality central to the whole range of public decision making. The impact and effectiveness of Section 75 remains to be assessed, but through the formal and comprehensive consultation required for Equality Schemes and Equality Impact Assessments, disabled groups and organisations have formal access to and involvement in public policy making.

This section has described the broad policy framework within Northern Ireland for people with disabilities. It has outlined the three-pronged attack to promote employment for those with disabilities who can work and security for those who cannot, based on a targeting and differentiation of social security benefits, the development of programmes geared to facilitate the entry or re-entry of people with disabilities into the labour market and actions to prevent discrimination against people with disabilities and to promote equality of opportunities for disabled people, particularly in the public sector.

Disability, employment and incomes in Northern Ireland

There are limited objective data on the employment and income status of people with disabilities in Northern Ireland. A recent review of data sources in relation to poverty in NI (Dignan and McLaughlin, 2002) has emphasised the lack of such information. When a specific group such as people with disabilities is considered, the position is even more unsatisfactory. The most comprehensive series of studies on disability was completed by government (Policy Planning and Research Unit – PPRU) between 1989 and 1990 and is now over ten years old (McCoy and Smith, 1992). More recent sources of data are the Labour Force Surveys (LFS) which are completed on a quarterly basis with around two thousand households in Northern Ireland. Information is currently available at both household and individual level for the Autumn 2001 sample (Equality Commission for Northern Ireland, 2002). Finally, the Statistics and Research Branch of the Department for Social Development make available comprehensive and timely statistics on a range of social security benefits. A recent spatial analysis of disadvantage in NI (Social Deprivation Research Group, 2001) provides some further analysis. As always, with such statistics, the definition of disability is a fraught issue. The PPRU suite of surveys used a definition based on the WHO's International Classification (ICIDH), while the LFS definition is derived from that used in the Disability Discrimination Act – a person has a disability if he or she has a physical or mental impairment which has a subsequent and long-term adverse effect on a person's ability to carry out normal day-to-day activities.

Incidence, age and severity
The various estimates agree that in Northern Ireland there are around 200,000 adults over 16 with physical or mental disabilities. The majority of people with disabilities are aged over 60 (around 60 per cent of all) and are female, although when only the population of working age is considered there are more males than females. In addition, the studies indicate that 14,600 children aged 0–15 are disabled.

The PPRU studies used a five-fold classification of the severity of disability. There were estimated to be 22,000 people in the most severe category and the rate of severe disability increased sharply with age – almost 60 per cent of people in this most severe category were over 60.

Comparisons of the rate of disability with equivalent figures for Great Britain (GB) showed that at all levels of disability the rate in NI was higher, with a rate of 174 per thousand in NI against just 142 per thousand in Great Britain. The Northern Ireland rate was higher than the worst region of GB (Wales). Similarly, on all disability benefits, NI claim rates are significantly higher than those in GB. For example, on Disability Living Allowance (the main 'extra cost' benefit), current (2001) rates in NI are 8.1 per cent of the total population, compared with 3.9 per cent in Great Britain, and this has been a continuing differential. Claimant rates are the result of a complex of factors of which actual levels of disability are but one component, but the picture across all disability benefits shows a similar and striking high level of claiming in Northern Ireland.

Disability and education

The important role of education in mediating employment and income has been identified earlier. Results show that people in Northern Ireland with disabilities have significantly lower educational qualifications than the population as a whole. Table 1 shows the position in 1989–90 and again in 2001. Whilst the position has improved over this time period, disabled people are still more than twice as likely as non-disabled to hold no qualifications, and half as likely to have a degree or other HE qualification, and this difference is consistent across all age groups.

Table 1 **Education levels of people with disabilities in Northern Ireland, 1989–90 and 2001**

		Total Population		Population aged 25–44	
		Disabled	All	Disabled	All
1989–90	Degree/HE	6%	13%	9%	19%
	Some	24%	38%	29%	41%
	None	70%	49%	64%	40%
2001	Degree/HE	10%	22%		
	Some	46%	58%		
	None	44%	21%		

Sources: McCoy and Smith (1992) and Equality Commission for Northern Ireland, (2001)

Disability and employment

Again the position of the employment status of people with disabilities in Northern Ireland confirms that in other countries. Only around one third (36 per cent) of disabled people of working age were in employment in 2001, compared to 75 per cent of non-disabled. Whilst disabled people account for around 20 per cent of the working-age population in NI, they account for only ten per cent of all those in employment.

Employment rates vary greatly between types of disability, being lowest for people with mental ill health and learning disabilities. Disabled people are three times more likely to be economically inactive than those who are not disabled.

A further measure of the impact of disability on households is to consider 'work-rich households', where all persons in the household are in employment, and 'work-less households' where no one is in employment. In households with no disabled member in 2001, 48 per cent were categorised as work-rich but this is the case in only 22 per cent of households with at least one person disabled, while 38 per cent of households with at least one person disabled were defined as 'workless', in contrast to 12 per cent of households with no disabled members.

Income levels

The most comprehensive data on the incomes of people with disabilities comes from the now somewhat dated PPRU studies covering 1989 and 1990 (Zarb and Maher, 1997). At a time when average gross weekly income for adults in the general population in Northern Ireland was around £170, that for disabled adults was £107, and almost 60 per cent of the disabled group had earnings of less than £100 per week. Overall, disabled adults' earnings were around 30 per cent lower than those of equivalent groups in the general population. For example, single disabled non-pensioner households average weekly income was 80 per cent that of equivalent non-pensioner households in the general population, disabled non-pensioner couples income was 62 per cent while disabled pensioners had more similar incomes – 94 per cent of equivalent groups in the general population.

The PPRU studies also considered the impact of disability on the financial circumstances and standards of living of people with disabilities. Half of all households containing disabled adults had no personal savings, and for those that did, the amount was generally less than £3000. Almost two thirds of disabled adults described their financial circumstances as 'just getting by', whilst a further six per cent reported they were 'getting into difficulties'. Around one third of disabled adults had experienced at least one of a range of financial problems, such as falling behind with rent, mortgages or other payments during the previous twelve months. A fifth reported that they regularly went without at least one basic item such as a daily cooked meal or a warm winter coat, while around 70 per cent were lacking one or more common consumer durables such as a washing machine or a television.

Benefit dependency
Dependency on social security benefits is a clear measure of low-income households. A previous section (and Figure 1) has established the importance of social security for people with disabilities in NI. In the 2001 figures, 69 per cent of the disabled population of working age were on some state benefits, compared with around 29 per cent of the non-disabled population. The earlier PPRU figures explored the issue in greater detail; for all disabled adults 66 per cent of total income came from such benefits compared with 21 per cent in the general population, and only 23 per cent of the income of disabled adults came from earnings. For those in the most severe category of disability, 88 per cent of income came from benefits and only nine per cent from earnings.

Disability-related expenditure
In the 1989–90 studies, the average amount of expenditure on disability related items (for example, aids, adaptations, extra expenditure on travel, fuel) for all disabled adults was £8.15 per week, equivalent to over £12 at 2002 prices or eight per cent of disposable income. There was a clear association with the severity of disability experienced, with those in the most severely disabled category spending an additional £14.46 per week on such items. An analysis of the group of disabled children estimated that an average amount of £20.86 per week was spent on such expenditure for all the children in the sample, rising to over £27 per week for the most severely disabled children.

Disability and multiple deprivation
A recent report (Social Deprivation Research Group, 2001) has analysed the spatial concentration of deprivation across NI. Seven 'domains' of deprivation were constructed from available up-to-date statistical indicators as well as an overall measure of multiple deprivation. One domain analysed the spatial concentration of 'Health Deprivation and Disability'; a second analysed income deprivation. The results confirmed the concentration of health and disability problems in highly deprived wards in Belfast, Derry, Newry and Mourne and Craigavon. The close link between health and disability measures and general measures of multiple disadvantage in areas was demonstrated, as was the clear and strong statistical association between health and disability and income deprivation (a highly significant correlation of +0.788).

Conclusions

This chapter has outlined the economic and financial position of people with disabilities in Northern Ireland. The 200,000-plus adults in the population are characterised by low levels of qualifications and under-employment, a heavy dependence on social security benefits and many people with disabilities are facing major problems coping with their financial circumstances. Rates of disability are higher than elsewhere in the UK and the concentration of people in areas of multiple deprivation and the contribution of disability to indices of poverty is clear.

The broad policy response by the Northern Ireland Executive to the problems of people with disabilities is encapsulated in the New TSN approach, and the specific thrust of policy in relation to economic well-being is contained in the 'Welfare to Work' reforms.

This is based on a three-pronged response for people with disabilities: a new package of measures to encourage entry or re-entry of people with disabilities into the labour market, a realignment of the basket of social security benefits designed to encourage movement into employment for those people with disabilities who can work and additional disability related support for those who cannot. Alongside these developments, anti-discrimination legislation is being implemented, a new Equality Commission has the remit to enforce the legislation and a Statutory Duty placed on all Public Authorities in Northern Ireland to strengthen the mainstreaming of equality and to make equality central to the whole range of public decision making, involving extensive formal consultation and completion of Equality Impact Assessments to establish the potential impact of new policies on people with disabilities.

Exciting and potentially critical policy developments are taking place, but many questions remain to be answered before it is possible to claim with conviction that the economic and financial position of persons with disabilities in Northern Ireland is improving. The New TSN approach is currently under review and has been fiercely criticised by, amongst others, the Civic Forum (2002). The package of employment-related initiatives is slowly being introduced and has been criticised as inadequate for the purpose. The major changes to the benefit regime remain to be monitored and evaluated to assess their impact on people with disabilities. It has, for example, been suggested (Burchardt, 2000) that the new 'basket of benefits' is neither sufficiently flexible nor responsive enough to cope with the dynamics of disability, where intermittent patterns of disability are common. Burchardt suggests that the assumption that 'once disabled, always disabled' has led to disability benefits being seen as a one way street, an outcome which marginalises disabled people and is costly for the benefit system. Further evidence (e.g., Yeates, 2001) suggests that perverse incentives may remain within the new benefit system particularly in respect to people with disabilities.

The effectiveness of the new disability legislation remains to be established. The Equality Commission for Northern Ireland has recently announced a range of disability settlements (2002) for compensation to people with disabilities. These settlements were achieved during the first year in which the Equality Commission assisted complainants in resolving cases brought under the legislation. More detailed study is needed of the operation and effectiveness of both the legislation and the enforcement approach.

The Statutory Duty introduced as part of the Belfast Agreement enables people with disabilities, along with other key groups extensive participation in the process of policy making. This is designed to build equality issues into the very core of public policy making and to involve extensive consultation with disability groups and a requirement to assess formally the impact of new policies on people with disabilities; again the impact and effectiveness of this legislation and its implementation remain to be evaluated.

Significant changes in policy in NI are under way, but the true measure of their impact and effectiveness will be the demonstration of improvements in the current income levels, employment status, access to services and full participation in the life of NI by people with disabilities.

Recommended Reading

Civic Forum (2002) *A Regional Strategy for Social Inclusion*. Belfast: Civic Forum.
Critical Social Policy (2000) Disability and the restructuring of welfare. Special Issue (20: 4).
Department for Social Development (2001) *Joblessness and Poverty*.
Belfast: DSD.
Drake, R. (1999) *Understanding Disability Policies*. London: Macmillan.
Northern Ireland Executive (2001) *Programme for Government: Making a Difference 2002–2005*.
    Belfast: OFMDFM.

Acknowledgements: Particular thanks are due to the Northern Ireland Statistics and Research Agency for provision of additional figures and analysis on social security benefits, Labour Force Survey and multiple deprivation.

Chapter 12

An emerging rights perspective for disabled people in Ireland: An activist's view

Donal Toolan

Cultural influences form a backdrop to current attitudes and values that flavour the policy responses to disabled people and their families. These are important to our understanding of the increased and focused demand for rights-based responses to disabled people in Ireland. These rights-based responses connect to a global movement (Driedger, 1989) which for five decades have sought to counter the deep layers of prejudice and influences that historically normalised the segregation, sterilisation and extermination of disabled people. This chapter looks, from an activist's perspective, at how the development of a rights-based response to disability challenges traditional, 'charity-focused' approaches to people with disabilities. It also examines the social, economic and cultural factors that have limited the recognition of the rights of disabled people.

Historical overview

Disabled people have historically been problematised through medicalisation or criminalisation so that they might be detained or confined away from society. An example of this has been the experience of those with mental health issues, who filled the vacated leprosariums (Foucault, 1989) of the middle ages until the medical model kicked in with drugs that resulted in greater shifts to move people back to their communities. A lack of adequate social supports led to many people with mental health issues finding themselves contributing to the numbers profiled as homeless or located within prison systems in the United States and increasingly here in Ireland (Bresnihan, 2001).

Some of the cruelties visited on disabled people in the past are only beginning to be acknowledged. Examples of these are disabled children taken from, or sometimes left by, families in a diversity of orphanages, schools or the care of others who did not have the same view of their humanity. Medical experiments were carried out on people with learning disabilities in the 1950s and 1960s. The huge physical, sexual, emotional and psychological scarring which the State legitimised, or at minimum remained actively indifferent to, can be seen in the harrowing narrative of Paddy Doyle's *The God Squad* (Doyle, 1990).

In May 1999 the Irish Government was embarrassed into some accountability following a series of documentaries resulting in the establishment of the Laffoy Commission to investigate the abuses against children including those with disabilities sent to various institutions (Raftery and O'Sullivan, 1999). Considerable focus in recent years has rightly emphasised rights violations experienced within religious institutions involved in the provision of services and the role of the state in abnegation of any responsibility of care. However, less emphasis or scrutiny has focused upon the secular charitable organisations to emanate from this 'culture of care'. Their role as interpreters of what disabled people want and need has also provided obstacles for the development of income support responses. These are directly linked to the needs and desires of disabled people (Cantillon *et al.*, 2001) and may explain the minimal progression of recommendations within A Strategy For Equality (1996) regarding disabled people's income support. Currently, an estimated 3,000 disabled people living in closed residential spaces receive no income support in their own name with little outrage from those delivering services and interpreting people's needs.

Historically, the medical model operated from a perception in which the infantilising of disabled people ensured that power rarely left the professionals who sought to administer care and cure. Its practitioners engaged in a form of medical imperialism which Oliver (1990) noted focused upon definitions of cure with scant regard for people's social realities. More recently, having embraced the language of the market place to demonstrate economic transparency, the person with disability has become a 'customer', a 'consumer', a 'service user' or a 'client'. However, this status has little connection to a world dominated by labels of clinical conditions where choice or rights are few and, if not curable, then destined for the arena of rehabilitation. The concept of rehabilitation is problematic for advocates of a rights model. This is primarily because of its close connection with a medical construct that defines people's experiences before trying to wedge them into some neat pocket of normality. This implicitly suggests that perceived imperfections need to be reoriented into the society – a concept that seriously demeans the lives of disabled people.

The historical perception of disabled people in terms of their medical impairments is evident from the number of organisations that provide services or represent the interests of people with any number of medical labels. The medicalisation of disabled people's lives in GPs' surgeries, hospitals and special education facilities have been dominated by processes that have sought care rather than to cure. This has been the cause of significant damage, not just in how society comes to perceive disabled people but also in disempowering people of their own autonomy and self-determination.

Images of disability

A significant element that characterises the power of the charitable model is the developed relationship between charity and advertising – a relationship that has provided an emotive and exploitive imagery of disability throughout history. *Fake Beggar*, a film by Thomas Edison made in 1898, is probably the first cinematic portrayal of disability (Norden, 1994). The opening scene portrayed a 'legless beggar' leading a man with a sign on his chest reading 'Help the Blind'. As filmmakers have done throughout the decades since, Edison was picking up on a popular theme to engage with society's perceptions about a group that could use a particular trait to evoke ridicule or pity as was required. At the time, the authorities on both sides of the Atlantic were concerned about the numbers mimicking people with disabilities in order to receive alms. Other filmmakers quick to pick up on a popular theme followed with titles such as the *Fraudulent Beggar* and *Blind Man's Bluff*, and were developing a cinematic narrative that would help locate disabled people as buffoon, idiot, deviant, rarely real and always 'other'.

More provocative realities were reflected decades later in Todd Browning's classic *Freaks*, which exploited a reality and time, when people once paid to see disabled people perform their otherness for entertainment. Those who have been to a *Snow White* pantomime with her seven friends of short stature might not regard such a reality as either extraordinary or distant. Indeed Fiedler (1978) contends that 'human freaks have been manufactured for ritualistic aesthetic and commercial purposes ever since history began'. Shakespeare had, centuries earlier, relied on inaccurate sources to disable Richard III to aid his depiction as a treacherous villain, while Dickens gave us Tiny Tim, the pathetic cherub from *A Christmas Carol* to encourage tears as we salute his bravery.

The media continue to communicate a view that reinforces or, at a minimum, encourages prejudice about disabled people and their marginal place in society by using well-honed fears. Road safety campaigns that use images of a victim using a wheelchair to deter people from driving too fast do not provide the best affirmation for the identity of those who chose to use a wheelchair as an efficient way of getting from A to B. Charities have encouraged similar messaging that feeds on our mortal and aesthetic fears and urges us to dig deeper so we can distance such images, diseases or imperfections from our realities. This message is accompanied by media pressure to spend time and resources in the pursuance of physical perfection that the right diet, clothes and plastic surgery can achieve.

Such media-fuelled responses have been challenged in Ireland by alternative perspectives emanating from programmes produced by disabled broadcasters. Offering direct access to disabled people to produce programming goes some way towards challenging the clappy-happy charities who suggest everything in life can be sorted by a cup of tea and a Telethon where publicity shy celebrities can demonstrate their compassion towards others. The establishment of the Disability Programmes Unit by the BBC in the UK and the commissioning of programmes like *In From the Margins* by RTÉ in 1992 demonstrate just some examples over the past decade of how the media can be used to articulate a rights perspective.

The economic implications of developing a rights perspective took an interesting twist when an insulting and offensive article by Mary Ellen Synon appeared in the Irish *Sunday Independent* in October 2001, questioning the validity of the athleticism of disabled participants in the Paralympics. The widespread public anger that followed the publication of this article provided a significant insight into the cultural perceptions of disability. This was coupled with the threat by disability charities to withdraw lucrative recruitment and other advertising campaigns from the paper. It was forced to publish a number of apologies and its editorial judgement received considerable censure as having strayed way beyond a certain line. This accidental insight into a relationship between rights and revenue demonstrates how the charitable model has had to box clever to align itself with particular issues of concern in order to gain legitimacy whilst capitalising on any resultant exposure. The charity message becomes dominant because of economic considerations. A current powerful media campaign around the Special Olympics clearly creates positive conditions for the participation of people with learning disabilities in sport, but how much of the messaging is designed to make non-disabled people feel good about their capacity to care?

At the same time as disabled rights groups are looking for the enactment of disability rights legislation, charities under a 'not for profit' banner are projecting demeaning and dehumanising messaging in order to attract resources for their services. If such demeaning messaging were being used by development agencies seeking aid for people in impoverished societies they might be publicly challenged as racist or exploitative. Such messaging by charities remains virtually unchallenged and is normalised by an increasingly compliant media. Some sections of the media may be forced, for economic reasoning, to question the practices of their own (as was the case of the Synon case in the *Sunday Independent*), but those who are paying for such advertising rarely enjoy the same scrutiny. The failure to introduce long stated regulation of so called charities called for in the Costello Report in 1989 demonstrates how the status quo has served the ambiguous political relationship between those who make up our legislature and those who provide charitable responses.

The impact of such influences may, in part, explain some of the findings in the research commissioned by the National Disability Authority in 2002 to determine social attitudes towards disability. The research has looked at those influences with which disabled people and their families have had to contend while they seek to negotiate a rights position in society. The research clearly indicates a perception of disability that relates only to physical impairment (80 per cent of respondents). Fifty per cent of those questioned believed that 'people with disabilities are those who are not able to participate fully in life because of a physical, hearing, visual, learning, mental health or emotional impairment'. Thirty-one per cent believed that disabled people were 'the victims of some personal tragic happening' while just 25 per cent had an understanding that 'it is society that disables people'.

This research represents an effort to determine how to strategically develop a societal response that would allow disabled people the same opportunities as other citizens. It also revealed strong support for greater recognition of disabled people's rights. But perhaps Irish people are no different from those in other cultures in their recognition of disabled people's rights? In order to understand the rights of disabled people, a society has to have to have a developed understanding of rights in general. In Ireland our articulation of such an understanding is both complex and contradictory. Our geo-political experience has historically been dominated by the need to develop the right to become independent of our colonising neighbour. Social history suggests that this has produced a society that is far from comfortable with individual rights, particularly if the individual cannot conform to a code normally associated with a particularly oppressive brand of Catholicism within the evolution of our state.

The development of a rights culture in Ireland

Modern Ireland's engagement with the concepts of rights seems at best uncomfortable. Any resolution of that discomfort seems to have been arrived at though the efforts of a perceived minority and their capacities to ultimately rely upon external forces to vindicate their lonely position. The experience of women and their struggle against a male Catholic order which sought, through the agents of the state, to regulate and restrict their lives, is probably the clearest expression of how our legislature historically engaged with concepts of individual rights. Even with our accession to the European Union politicians felt confident to argue that we should hold on to powers allowing us to maintain unequal pay and conditions for women. Similarly homosexuals, who remained criminalised up to 1993 in Ireland, also depended on the European courts to direct the Irish Government into a process of equal recognition. Travellers' cultural traditions have been treated with absolute disdain. MacGreil (1996) notes the deteriorating position of Travellers as meriting attention at all levels. The emergence of anti-racism campaigns and strategies to challenge discrimination in recent years indicates how previously perceived external realities and their economic implications in the use of migrant labour to feed the demands of economic growth now force our engagement with rights.

As demonstrated above, these social movements in Ireland have developed significant voices from our economic and judicial engagement with the institutions of the European Union. A vocabulary that references pluralism, civil liberties and, more recently, human rights has gained a certain currency as we increasingly become committed, on paper at least, to UN and other international agreements that focus on the centrality of a rights perspective. This change of perspective mirrors a decline of the dominant religious position in Irish life.

Another significant reality that has informed a shift in our perceptions of rights has come about from the changing dynamic around the territory of the island of Ireland. The Belfast or Good Friday Agreement references our need to value rights and provides the establishment of a Human Rights Commission in Northern Ireland and in the Republic. However, it is interesting to note the almost casual approach of the Government of the Irish Republic in relation to this significant agreement. We have failed to incorporate the European Convention of Human Rights into Irish law and have failed to recognise the social implications for the southern part of the island. Our reluctance to incorporate and to recognise this and other treaties such as the UN Convention on Social, Economic and Cultural Rights provides evidence of caution and sometimes outright fear as to the relevance of giving meaningful effect to people's rights. We are told frequently that our Constitution provides adequate protection to treat all peoples equally. However, it seems, to borrow from Orwell, that those with property are in practice treated a little *more* equally.

However, there is no doubt that clear shifts have taken place in terms of how a rights perspective has been interpreted in our varying institutions and, indeed, how our society sometimes struggles with the need to recognise the diversity of its citizens. This emerging rights culture may not be one with which we are instinctively familiar or comfortable. There are significant national and global pressure points to threaten its progress which brings with it serious challenges to those advancing civil and political liberties. For those with limited capacity to produce or consume, such as the majority of disabled people living in developing economies, or those constrained by impoverishing structures in rich economies such as Ireland, taking up the protection provided in international law will prove increasingly relevant.

Disabled people's rights movement and its impact on policy

The significance of a rights culture in Ireland has, as yet, not had the same impact for disabled people as it has for other groups. This is because, historically, European judicial instruments, such as those that have aided women's equality, have not provided sufficient basis to challenge discrimination on grounds of disability. Emerging directives could potentially alter that position, provided Ireland does not seek to derogate responsibilities – a characteristic of our engagement with international agreements. We do not, of course, need to wait for European direction (as with any area of social reform) on what is the right thing to do for all our citizens. The Report of the Commission on the Status of People with Disabilities (1996), which clearly established the need to move from charitable and medical models to a rights-based model, demonstrates a clear attempt in this respect. It is significant in that the Commission evolved in 1993 from negotiations with the Forum of People with Disabilities. The Forum is one of a number of emerging groupings of disabled people in Ireland benefiting from the influences and experiences of similar groupings in the EU and elsewhere as well as the growth in a diversity of representative social movements in Ireland.

This influence helped the developments of different groups such as those concerned with independent living. Based on a movement that began in Berkeley California some twenty years earlier, the first Irish Centre for Independent Living promoted the provision of independent living supports that allowed disabled people to live in their communities rather than institutions. Self-advocacy groups of people with learning disabilities drew their inspiration from an international movement called People First. The Irish Deaf Society promoted deaf culture to challenge those who historically spoke on their behalf. Similarly, survivors of mental health services worked to repeal the antiquated laws of containment which assisted in developing the Mental Health Act, 2001. The National League of the Blind is but a rare example of a disabled group in Ireland who organised themselves into a union early in the last century.

The early models of organisations that represented the interests of disabled people fell into a number of distinct categories. Organisations that were of religious origin provided specific responses for disabled people such as training, education and shelter. They tended to be impairment specific in focus with schools for children who were blind or deaf. In later decades those with learning or physical disabilities or people with mental illness were historically incarcerated in a diversity of institutions. Other organisations to emerge were those founded by civic minded individuals with resources and a 'desire to do good' (Ryan, 1999), who established different charities which were impairment specific and driven by medical experts eager to try out new models of care and rehabilitation. Some evolved in response to emerging health issues such as polio. Some forty years ago a broad number of parent organisations with a focus on their child's impairment also emerged. Many of these organisations were seeking disabled people's rights to services. However, many found themselves as providers of specific services, a position encouraged by the state which welcomed this separate layer as a mechanism for distancing itself from service provision to people with special needs.

In the 1960s and early 1970s, groups of disabled people became involved with impairment-specific responses with an increased self-representation model focused upon rights. Liam McGuire, a disabled activist and trade unionist, was involved with the Irish Wheelchair Association and was one of the early organisers of Disabled Peoples International (Moore, 1990). Such groups joined the emerging layer of organisations delivering separate accessible responses alongside an increasingly excluding mainstream society. Disillusioned with the slow pace of change, organisations of disabled people such as DAM (Disability Awareness Movement) began advocating access to the same rights and opportunities as other citizens in the 1980s and 1990s in Ireland. The focus was more on collectivism than impairment and drew upon the recently introduced Americans with Disabilities Act (1990). This legislation provided a significant impetus to campaigns for effective disability rights legislation in countries throughout the world.

In launching the Commission on the Status of People with Disabilities in 1993, the Minister for Equality and Law Reform acknowledged *that a serious injection of political will* might be required to create the conditions which would enable disabled people to access the same opportunities as other citizens. This Commission was heralded as the most extensive exploration of disability in the history of the state. Disabled people and their families speculated that the legislation and other policies likely to emanate from the Commission would provide a model for other European member states. Those involved in the disability rights movement in the UK at the time were envious of their neighbours' success in influencing Government policy in this way. Disability rights were longer being advanced in the UK and there had been successive attempts by the Conservative Government to stall the enactment of anti-discrimination legislation similar to that which had been obtained in the United States in 1990 with the enactment of the Americans with Disabilities Act.

The legislative guidelines necessary to fulfil the Irish Government's ambition to be model Europeans was a core element of the recommendations contained within the Report of the Commission on the Status of People with

Disabilities, *A Strategy for Equality*, published in 1996. The stated intention to implement this report formed the basis for the Irish Government receiving the prestigious UN Roosevelt Award, which recognises the efforts of countries to further the participation of disabled people.

While the UK Government has now introduced discrimination rights legislation, the Irish Government's commitment remains only partially unfulfilled. Following the Report of the Commission on the Status of People with Disabilities in 1996, the then Government sought to introduce equality legislation which would protect people against discrimination on nine grounds which included disability. The Irish Supreme Court rejected this legislation in relation to disability, on the grounds that it was unfair to require an employer to do more than was reasonable to accommodate disabled employees.

The subsequent enactment of employment equality and equal status legislation laid down the requirement that employers and service providers should do all that is reasonable to accommodate disabled people. Burnt by the experience, the Government concentrated on other aspects of the report of the Commission on the Status of People with Disabilities. They began working to ensure that key statutory services would be provided to disabled people – thus starting to dismantle the existing separate provision of training and information services.

The Taoiseach heralded the resultant ethos of 'mainstreaming' in 2000, suggesting that disabled people would have access the same services and opportunities as other citizens. Gone were the historic medical and charitable models; disability rights and mainstreaming were the new order of the day. Absent from these statements, however, were the practicalities of incorporating existing, separate provisions into the mainstream. The question remained as to whether specific supports, such as personal assistance, sign interpretation, accessible information, advocacy supports, needs assessments, would be incorporated into the mainstream framework. The numbers of unemployed disabled people, currently suggested by the Government to be in the region of 70 per cent as compared to 4.7 per cent within the non-disabled population, suggest that the supports offered to disabled people up to now have been less than effective.

The report of the Commission on the Status of People with Disabilities (1996) advocated that disabled people should be free to access the same opportunities as other citizens. This was to be within a context where people would have access to effective legal mechanisms to ensure equality of opportunity. Two years later, the Government responded by taking a young man with autism and his mother to the Supreme Court to overturn an earlier ruling that recognised that the state had a duty to provide for his educational and developmental needs. This move created a public outcry at the state's callousness in seeking to judicially restrict a perceived constitutional right. The state was successful in illustrating how our learned judges understand or interpret equality and the extent the legislature will go to restrict opportunity. However, an interesting aspect to this has been the reaction of the general public into this glimpse of the reality of being disabled in Ireland. It is such positive public support that will ultimately contribute to the legislature's provision of the political will necessary to give rights meaning for disabled people.

In December 2002, the Government were publicly forced into withdrawing the Disabilities Bill that was almost unanimously regarded as flawed and ineffective legislation. The recommendations regarding necessary legislation, signalled in the Commission's Report, was ignored by Government. The Disabilities Bill appeared to be an attempt to restrict the use of the courts system to vindicate rights where agreed actions were not forthcoming. However, the proposed legislation has proved important in mobilising disabled people and their families as to what they understand they are entitled as citizens in a democracy, even if the state is, as yet, unconvinced by their claim.

Significantly, in some emerging disability rights movements, disabled people have been able to draw on the experience of other groups in their fight for equal rights. In such incidences an important factor is that legislation has already been put in place to ensure people can access the same opportunities as other citizens. In the United States, many of those disabled people who use the courts to gain access to education have used the racial equality arguments of civil rights legislation as a guide to their bid for educational participation. Such countries have developed disability rights legislation after years of engagement on the broader issues of rights culture and identity. Ireland is still at the early stages of that particular debate.

Looking towards the future

For much of the last century, the dominant Irish identity, promoted and presented in public policy, was drawn historically from a narrow canvas that was Catholic and non- British. It was not until the last decade of the twentieth century that a range of legislation was enacted that opened up greater possibilities for diverse interpretations of what is an Irish identity. Equality legislation, in particular, has provided an opportunity for multiple identities to be explored. The realisation that full participation in areas such as health and social services, education, housing and income maintenance needs to be underpinned by law is growing in Ireland. Some 30 non-governmental organisations presented reports to the UN committee examining Ireland's compliance with the UN Convention on Social Economic and Cultural

Rights. Those involved in negotiating national agreements on behalf of rights-based groups, including disability interest groups, are increasingly prioritising a rights dimension in their negotiations.

A characteristic feature of the Irish Government's arguments against affording rights to disabled people is the suggestion that giving disabled people access to education and other support services as a basic entitlement would create inequity in the delivery of such services to others. The state's response to disabled people and their advocates has been to suggest that their demands, i.e. rights enshrined in law, would deny the needs of others, for example, the effective treatment of the acutely ill. Apart from the disturbing resonance with the eugenic argument that it is unproductive and uneconomic to waste resources upon disabled people, such a stance also puts in doubt the Government's commitment to seek out the full participation of disabled people in service planning and delivery.

A stratagem to postpone deliverance of rights appears to involve an increased appetite for definitions and number crunching before actual solutions to address the inequality can be considered. Facts and evidence are absolutely critical for planning, but their gathering and formulation cannot or should not postpone actions to prohibit standards and practices that violate basic human rights which must be immediately acted upon (Oliver, 2002). The state cannot continue to invest taxes in a range of service responses that do not contain independent advocacy systems (Bermingham, 2001). Independent advocacy would ensure that real standards exist to protect people against violation of their rights. It would also offer meaningful support in negotiating within a social ethos that excludes and discriminates. As we incorporate global solutions in our information and infrastructural development, why should we not use our best international practice to make services such as education inclusive, accessible and responsive to the diversity of all our children's needs?

How far Irish society will go in the development of law and policy responses that demonstrate more than a rhetorical commitment to the equality of disabled people remains to be seen. Much will depend on fundamental and radical shifts taking place from where power currently lies in frequently unaccountable entities to one that locates the desires and needs of disabled people at the centre. The direct involvement of disabled people and the extent of their involvement in that power shift will fundamentally inform the nature of which rights are articulated and given effect.

Chapter 13

Towards free and inclusive societies for people with disabilities

Gerard Quinn with Anna Bruce

Introduction

The application of the general human rights framework of reference in the field of disability is relatively new. This is curious to say the least. One of the main attractions of human rights is its supposedly universal quality. Yet it seems that nearly every culture has no-go areas where logic and the rule of law do not apply and are not even expected to apply. The truly interesting thing is that most cultures experience no contradiction – no cognitive dissonance – in subscribing to high principle on the one hand and yet in denying the benefits of these principles to particular groups or sections of the population on the other. In its essence therefore, the human rights revolution in the context of disability has to do with making the human being visible (the so-called 'visibility project' of human rights) and with making the benefits of the rule of law, human rights and democracy available to all.

The application of human rights in the context of disability is not merely new – it is profoundly interesting. This is because it offers tangible proof of the much vaunted but little understood thesis concerning the interdependence and indivisibility of sets of human rights (civil and political as well as economic, social and cultural). These rights are not merely about honouring human dignity in a static way. Primed properly, they help to forge pathways into inclusive societies and economies. They help set the terms of access, entry and participation in the mainstream. In other words, they help secure a system of freedom. In this way, key goals of the disability rights movement are peculiarly modern and exemplify a new kind of human rights agenda.

Historical overview

For quite a long time the most important human rights issue affecting persons with disabilities was deemed to be the reform of anachronistic civil commitment laws. This was and is important; but note what it misses. It misses substantive rights such as the right to health and the positive right to treatment. It misses the question of the status of persons with mental disabilities in society as distinct from the incarceration context. To this day, the reform of civil commitment laws tends to be inadequately tied to the more general rights revolution in the context of disability.

Human rights are not just about protection against power – they are also crucially about restoring power to the person. This holds the key to the disability rights revolution. It entails a new orientation toward difference, in this case the human difference of disability. It views disability as something that complicates but does not ruin human existence or the basic incommensurable value of each human being. Set against the backdrop of using rights to restore power to people, economic, social and cultural rights have an enabling function; they provide a bridge whereby persons with disabilities can take their place as valued and often highly productive citizens. That is, such rights are not defendable (or not merely defendable) because they represent the least a state can do for the welfare of the individual. They are defendable because they facilitate freedom, because they enable people to take charge of their own lives. It is in this sense that economic, social and cultural rights enhance freedom.

At the heart of this rights-based perspective lies a revolutionary new approach to human difference or the so-called 'social construct' idea. According to the 'social construct' idea people are not born different. Difference is not inherent in a human being. It comes into existence – or is socially constructed – when one person is compared to another or to an average or benchmark. The real problem is not the difference of disability but the way in which that difference is constructed. Obviously, the benchmark or average against which the difference of disability is created and measured is that of the able-bodied person. But the real question is why that average was selected in the first place.

The point about averages or benchmarks is that they are not merely used to *mark* people apart but also to *keep* people apart. This is so because the life world – the economy, culture, the provision of goods and services and the structure of public services – is created to cater only for those who conform to the average. Thus, anyone who fails to conform is marked and kept apart. The real problem from the 'social construct' perspective lies not in the person but in the way society treats the difference of disability.

From this perspective the main 'problem' in the disability field is not the disability itself but the way society treats the human difference of disability. In other words, the real problem is located outside the person and in the receptiveness of otherwise of society to the difference presented by disability. Hence, the disability rights movement is part of a much broader movement that aims at the development of inclusive societies where all persons are deemed entitled to play their part and assume their civil responsibilities like everyone else.

The point about such implicit social exclusion is that it amounts to a lack of respect for difference. While all people are different they are all equal in the eyes of the law. It follows that the core human right implicated by the civil rights perspective is equality. Creating a society that values difference and that does not use difference as an excuse for marginalisation or social exclusion is not easy. It means evaluating current programmes for their compatibility with respect for equality. It means undoing the inequalities inherited from the past. It means a sustained effort at ensuring genuine equal access to the life world for all.

International human rights law rests essentially on four connected basic human values: dignity, autonomy, equality and social solidarity. These values lie at the vary basis of the legitimacy of this state. They animate a system of freedom – a system that provides protection against power but also space to assume power over one's own life. Human dignity means that people are to be valued because they are people. Autonomy means creating space for the flourishing of the human spirit. This spirit lies within *all* of us regardless of the difference of disability. Equality means creating a society that treats all equally and makes due and positive allowance for difference including the difference of disability. Solidarity means helping those who cannot help themselves or whose capacity to do so is greatly diminished. Solidarity exists not to make us feel good – still yet to dispense charity without any actual involvement. It exists because the system of freedom needs a substantive underpinning to allow people to use their capacities

Putting these values together in the context of disability leads to a connected agenda. Saying that equality provides the core right is but the start of analysis. Equality can be rendered in three very different ways. At one extreme, equality is merely a formal right to exactly the same treatment as all others. This is of little avail to people with disabilities for it fails to adequately take account of the difference of disability. For example, to formally require that all persons would be admitted to a restaurant on exactly the same terms would be of little use to someone who requires a ramp to gain access. At the other extreme, an insistence of exact equality of results for all regardless of ability or contribution would not appear to fit with the claim that people with disabilities should be treated on the individual merits. In between those two extremes lies the equal opportunities model.

The equal opportunities model insists that all persons be treated on their merits and that the task of law and policy is to open up opportunities to all on an equal basis. It rejects the formal equality model and instead insists that actors (employers, shopkeepers) take account of disability and 'reasonably accommodate' it in order to achieve genuine equality. A comprehensive equal opportunities model is one that tracks the typical life cycle of an individual. Its focus points can be clustered as follows:

Preparing people with disabilities for participation
Equal access to in the preparatory processes for participation (inclusive education, vocational education and training)

Guaranteeing access to the environment
Equal access *within* the Built Environment (e.g., effective building regulations)
Equal access to the built environment (e.g., accessible public transportation).
Equal access to the communications medium (telecommunications policy)

Non-discrimination law
Clear and regularly enforced anti-discrimination law in the fields of employment and in the provision of goods and services (e.g., restaurant)

Mainstreaming disability in the policy process
Removing disability policy from specialist health and welfare ministries and mainstreaming responsibility into all general ministries (e.g., employment, training, civil rights)

Re-styling welfare and social supports to achieve
the goals of independence and participation
Ensuring that welfare and other supports do not hinder participation but actively support it.

A comprehensive equal opportunities programme does not rest exclusively on formal law. In the context of disability, it requires extensive economic and social supports in order to prime people to become productive citizens and assume control over their own lives. These supports need to be through and integrated and tied to a model that sees the participation of the disabled person as a social and economic asset. Such support will need to be provided in the mainstream so as not to initiate or perpetuate a cycle of wasteful exclusion. The economic and social exclusion felt by all women is felt particularly by women with disabilities. In turn, their overall status tends to be lower than that even of their disabled male peers. The application of economic, social and cultural rights for such women is therefore particularly important.

The evolution of UN human rights law and disability

The United Nations has contributed much to the evolution of human rights in the context of disability. Its contribution can be gauged along several interconnected axes:

1   various non-binding UN declarations and resolutions as well as UN
     sponsored studies in the area of disability,
2   general UN human rights treaties with at least inferential application in
     the context of disability,
3   thematic UN human rights treaties that have some specific reference in the
     area of disability,
4   work programmes and other pronouncements and efforts of the various
     UN Specialised Agencies (ILO, WHO, UNESCO, etc.).

Non-binding UN declarations and resolutions and UN sponsored studies in the area of disability

The United Nations has promulgated a wide variety of resolutions,
recommendations and other forms of soft law (e.g., influential studies) in
relation to disability. These instruments are important as they influence the
agenda of various UN specialised agencies and also influence the way various
monitoring bodies interpret existing treaty law. They can also embolden
elements of civil society to agitate for even 'harder' forms of law.

Many of the earlier resolutions, focused exclusively on rehabilitation and
vocational services (e.g., ECOSOC resolution of 1950 dealing with the 'Social
and Physical Rehabilitation of the Physically Handicapped'). Two resolutions
of the 1970s are particularly revealing in that they indicated a shift from
'caring' to 'rights' in the context of disability. In 1971, the General Assembly
passed a resolution entitled 'Declaration on the Rights of Mentally Retarded
Persons'. Significantly, this resolution starts by pointing out that persons with
disabilities enjoy a parity of human rights protection with all other persons.

The General Assembly passed another milestone resolution in 1975 entitled
'Declaration on the Rights of Disabled Persons'. Among other things, the
Declaration specifies a number of economic, social and cultural rights of importance to the development of capacities and social integration. It declared a right
to have special needs taken into account at all stages of economic and social
planning, protection against exploitation and treatment of an abusive nature.
An innovation was its insistence that organisations of persons with disabilities
'may be consulted in all matters regarding the rights of disabled persons'.

In 1982 the General Assembly marked an irreversible shift away from
'caring' to 'rights' by promulgating a World Programme of Action (WPA).
The Programme was no longer concerned merely with 'caring' but also with
'equalisation of opportunities'. The Programme states [para. 45]:

> The consequences of deficiencies and disablement are particularly serious for
> women. There are a great many countries where women are subjected to social,
> cultural and economic disadvantages which impede their access to, for example,

health care, education, vocational training and employment. If, in addition they are physically or mentally disabled their chances of overcoming their disablement are diminished, which makes it all the more difficult for them to take part in community life. In families, the responsibility for caring for a disabled parent often lies with women, which considerably limits their possibilities of taking part in other activities.

The WPA ushered in the International Decade of the Disabled.

During the 1980s an influential study was published under the auspices of the UN entitled *Principles, Guidelines and Guarantees for the Protection of Persons Detained on Grounds of Mental Ill-Health or Suffering from Mental Disorder* (Erica Irene-Daes, 1986). The eventual political reaction was the adoption by the General Assembly in 1993 of the 'Principles for the Protection of Persons with Mental Illness and the Improvement of Mental Health Care'.

The then UN Centre for Social Development and Humanitarian Affairs Division for the Advancement of Women held a major conference on disabled women in 1990. A major reference document was produced for the event entitled *Women and Disability: Some Issues.* Problems relating to the delivery of such public services as health care, social security, education, vocational training and rehabilitation and employment were singled out in the report.

The implementation of the WPA was monitored in 1987 and 1992. Not much progress could be reported. Pressure was growing for an extra thematic human rights treaty on the rights of persons with disabilities. This pressure was helped by the publication of an even more influential report under the auspices of the UN in 1993 entitled *Human Rights and Disabled Persons* (Leandro Despouy). This Report stated (paras 140–5):

> It has been proven that women in many countries are disadvantaged with respect to men from the social, cultural and economic point of view, which makes it very difficult for them to have access to health services, education, vocational training, employment, etc. This statement, which is valid for women in general, also applies to disabled women. For the latter, however, the lack of access to health services will certainly aggravate their disability or make it difficult for them to be rehabilitated quickly by making their participation in community life even more problematic.

Instead of moving towards drafting a treaty the General Assembly opted to issue a special resolution entitled the UN Standard Rules for the Equalisation of Opportunities for Persons with Disabilities (1993). The Standard Rules fixate on the last element of the WPA, namely equalisation of opportunities. It contains four parts:

1   *Preconditions for Equal Opportunities*
    [most of which directly implicate economic and social rights and
    programmes, e.g., medical care, rehabilitation, support services].

2   *Target areas for Equal Participation*
    [most of which directly implicate economic and social rights and
    programmes, e.g., education, employment, income maintenance, family
    life and personal integrity, culture, recreation and sports].

3   *National Implementation Measures*
    [most of which directly implicate economic and social rights/programmes,
    e.g., information and research, policy making and planning, economic
    policies]

4   *International Monitoring*
    [UN Special Rapporteur on the Standard Rules].

The UN Secretariat organised a major conference on the effectiveness of
the Rules in 1998. One of the chief conclusions was the need to move toward
a convention in the field. The Organisation of American States (OAS) has
now formally adopted a full convention on the rights of disabled persons
(1999). Many of the provisions in this convention cover economic, social
and cultural rights.

Thematic human rights treaty law: disability perspective
Mention should be made of certain thematic human rights treaties that
are not central but touch on disability. The most obvious of these is the
Convention for the Elimination of all Forms of Discrimination Against
Women. The relevant non-discrimination norms span both civil and political
rights as well as economic, social and cultural rights. The CEDAW Committee
has stated (General Recommendation 18, 1991) that states which are parties to
the Convention must include information on the status of women with
disabilities in their periodic reports. The Convention:

> *Recommends* that States Parties provide information in disabled women in their
> periodic reports, and on measures taken to deal with their particular situation,
> including special measures to ensure that they have equal access to education and
> employment, health services, social security and to ensure that they can partici-
> pate in all areas of social and cultural life.

The Rights of the Child Convention also has direct application in the context
of disability. Article 23 of the Convention deals specifically with the situation
of disabled children.

World conferences: disability perspective
The status of people with disabilities – including women with disabilities – has been specifically noted with concern in the proceedings and conclusions of many UN World Conferences.

The Vienna Declaration and Programme of Action adopted by the World Conference on Human Rights in 1993 specifically mentions disability. It re-asserts that people with disabilities have the same human rights as everyone. Para 64 states:

> The place of disabled persons is everywhere. Persons with disabilities should be guaranteed equal opportunity through the elimination of all socially determined barriers, be they physical, financial, social or psychological, which exclude or restrict full participation in society.

Remarkably, the situation concerning disabled women does not appear to have received much attention at the World Conference to Review and Appraise the Achievements of the United Nations Decade for Women, Equality and Development out of which was issued the *Nairobi Forward Looking Strategies for the Advancement of Women* (1985). Para 296 of the Nairobi Strategy states that:

> It is generally accepted that women constitute a significant number of the estimated 500 million who are disabled as a consequence of mental, physical or sensory impairment. Many factors contribute to the rising numbers of disabled persons, including war and other forms of violence, poverty, hunger, nutritional deficiencies, epidemics and work-related accidents. The recognition of their human dignity and human rights and the full participation by disabled persons in society is still limited, and thus presents additional problems for women who may have domestic and other responsibilities.

The Nairobi Strategy went on to exhort states to adopt the WPA (1982) and adhere to the principles set out in the 1975 Declaration on the Rights of Disabled Persons.

In addition to re-affirming the human rights of all women, the Beijing Declaration (Fourth World Conference on Women, 1995) contained an explicit commitment [para 32] to

> Intensify efforts to ensure equal enjoyment of all human rights and fundamental freedoms for all women and girls who face multiple barriers to their empowerment and advancement because of such factors as . . . disability.

Elsewhere the Declaration speaks in terms of the fact that

> Many women face particular barriers because of various diverse factors in addition to their gender. Often these diverse factors isolate or marginalise such women. They are, inter alia, denied their human rights, they lack access to or are denied access to education and vocational training, employment, housing and economic self-sufficiency and they are excluded from decision-making processes. Such women are often denied the opportunity to contribute to their communities as part of the mainstream. [Global Framework, para 31].

Strategic Objective F.5 (j) of the Declaration exhorts states to

> Ensure access to and develop special programmes to enable women with disabilities to obtain employment and retain employment, and ensure access to education and training at all proper levels, in accordance with the Standard Rules on the Equalisation of Opportunities for People with Disabilities; adjust working conditions, to the extent possible, in order to suit the needs of women with disabilities, who should be assured legal protection against unfounded job loss on account of their disabilities.

The status of disabled persons figures prominently in the Copenhagen Declaration on Social Development and Programme of Action (World Summit for Social Development, 1995). Commitment 4 contained therein refers to the social integration on a non-discriminatory basis of vulnerable groups. Governments should

> Work towards the equalisation of opportunities so that people with disabilities can contribute to and benefit from full participation in society. Policies concerning people with disabilities should focus on their abilities rather than their disabilities and should ensure their dignity as citizens. [para 75.k].

Many of the Copenhagen Commitments have application to the situation of persons with disabilities and specific mention of their plight is made in many parts of the Resolution and Report of the Summit. The objective of ending gender-based discrimination is prominent although the connection between gender and disability is not directly drawn.

The status of disabled people figured similarly in the deliberations and final pronouncements of the HABITAT II (Istanbul Declaration, 1996). Chapter III D of the Declaration refers explicitly to gender equality. The accompanying Global Plan of Action refers explicitly to the housing needs of persons with disabilities.

General human rights treaty law: disability perspective

The foundation document is the Universal Declaration on Human Rights which does not specifically mention disability. The original intention was to craft one composite Bill of Rights. What eventuated were two separate conventions corresponding to the two sets of rights: International Covenant on Civil and Political Rights (ICCPR) and the International Covenant on Economic, Social and Cultural Rights (ICESCR).

Both conventions contain a number of provisions of direct relevance to disability and some specifically to women with disabilities.

ICCPR and disability.
The ICCPR contains the familiar continuum of civil and political rights including

- the *right to life* (Art. 6). This has especial relevance in the context of disability in relation to the selective abortion of disabled foetuses.
- the *right to non-discrimination* (Art. 2.1.). This is central to the disability debate since the claim is not so much for more resources but for genuinely equal access to all the processes of society (economic, social and political).
- the right to have 'equal access, on general terms of equality, to *public services* in one's country' (Art. 25(c)).
- the right to *liberty, due process of law and fair trial* (Art. 14). This has especial relevance in the context of mental disability and civil commitment law.
- rights to and within the *family* (Art. 23). This has relevance in the context of the right of disabled persons to found a family and disabled women to bear children.
- right against *involuntary servitude* (Art. 8.3). This may have relevance in the context of work schemes which involve the disabled.
- right to take part in *public affairs and to vote* (Art. 25).

The ICCPR does not specifically mention disability. Nonetheless the concept of non-discrimination espoused by the Committee of Civil and Political Rights is easily capable of sweeping disability into the coverage of the convention. General Commentary No. 18 to the ICCPR states:

> The enjoyment of rights and freedoms on an equal footing . . . does not mean identical treatment in every instance . . . the principle of equality sometimes requires States Parties to take affirmative action in order to diminish or eliminate conditions which cause of help to perpetuate discrimination prohibited by the Convention.

Clearly, civil and political rights may not be cost free. Clearly also, people with disabilities constitute one of those groups for whom extra effort is needed in order to bring an end to discrimination.

The UN Covenant on Economic, Social and
Cultural Rights (ICESCR) and disability

General Commentary No. 5 to the ICESCR is very forthcoming on the issue
of disability. It starts by insisting that disability discrimination is prohibited
by the terms of the covenant even though the covenant does not specifically
mention disability. It also states that the obligations of the States Parties are
firm and perhaps firmer that usual in the context of disability.

> [The general obligations under Article 2] . . . requires Governments to do much
> more than merely abstain from taking measures which might have a negative
> impact on persons with disabilities. The obligation in the case of such a vulnerable
> and disadvantaged group is to take positive action to reduce structural disadvantages
> and to give appropriate preferential treatment to people with disabilities in order
> to achieve the objectives of full participation and equality within society for all
> persons with disabilities. This almost invariably means that additional resources
> will need to be made available for this purpose and that a wide range of specially
> tailored measures will be required.

The Commentary emphasises that the responsibilities of States Parties extend
to encompass the structuring of the private sector. This has especial relevance
in the context of the privatisation of public utilities and resources including
health resources. To confine regulation and intervention to the public sector
would mean, in the words of the Commentary,

> [that] the ability of persons with disabilities to participate in the mainstream of
> community activities and to realise their potential as active members of society
> will be severely and often arbitrarily constrained.

State side intervention might be needed to 'temper, complement, compensate
for, or override the results produced by market forces'. Furthermore, reliance
on private voluntary groups to assist persons with disabilities can never, in
itself, 'absolve Governments from their duty to ensure full compliance with
their obligations under the Covenant'.

General Comment No 5 to the ICESCR also makes specific mention of
the equal rights of disabled women in the context of economic, social and
cultural rights. It states (para 19)

> Persons with disabilities are often seen as genderless human beings. As a result, the
> double discrimination suffered by disabled women is often neglected . . . Despite
> frequent calls by the international community for particular emphasis to be placed
> upon their situation, very few efforts have been undertaken during the Decade.
> The neglect of disabled women is mentioned several times in the Secretary-
> General Report on the implementation of the WPA. The Committee therefore

urges States Parties to address the situation of disabled women with high priority in future implementation of economic, social and cultural rights-related programmes.

In sum, both UN Covenants are now viewed as applying with special force in the context of disability and particularly with respect to disabled women. For example, the Committee on Economic, Social and Cultural Rights was recently quite critical of the pace of change in Ireland with respect to the rights of persons with disabilities.

A Draft Optional Protocol to the ICESCR has been proposed which would permit the right of individuals or groups to submit communications (complaints) concerning non-compliance with the covenant. This would be of great use to the people with disabilities.

In General Comment 5, dealing exclusively with disability, the Committee notes that 'States parties have devoted very little attention to this issue [disability] in their reports.'[1] While General Comment 5 does not provide any further guidelines regarding specific reporting obligations regarding persons with a disability, the general reporting obligations suggests that the following elements would be included:

> States should, have they not already done so, review national legislation, admini-strative rules and procedures, and practices and report how these conform to the realisation of the economic, social and cultural rights of persons with a disability.
>
> State reports should also contain a comprehensive policy or programme of action envisaging how the rights of persons with a disability are to be realised, as well as identification of difficulties and obstacles to such realisation. The actual situation of persons with a disability regarding each right should be monitored in each report, and the progressive realisation of their rights should be evaluated against national goals and benchmarks. States should take help of representatives of persons with a disability in the creation of reports and should make the report available to the public, especially to persons with a disability.

A snapshot of 19 state reports under the ICESCR on the issue of disability (1993–2000)

Employment

In the overwhelming majority of the reports analysed, the issue of disability discrimination is not mentioned. Only one report mentions the creation of a law specifically targeting disability discrimination[2] (in the field of employment), another report states disability as a prohibited ground for discrimination in Labour Law,[3] and another country mentions the insertion of disability as a prohibited ground for discrimination in the Constitution (Basic Law-Constitution?).[4] Yet another report mentions an entitlement to sheltered work and special training in the section on article 2.[5]

The issue of and equal participation and elimination of prejudice as a goal is explicitly stated in only two reports.[6] There is no clearly detectable progress over time, although one country improves on its third report by presenting a non-discrimination law in employment in its fourth report.[7]

The aspect of the right to work which is most instrumental in the paradigm shift in disability is access to mainstream employment for persons with a disability. In addition to the two reports mentioning non-discrimination laws in the employment area, about one half of the reports (eight countries) mention special efforts to increase employment opportunities for persons with a disability.[8] The most commonly reported measures are vocational training and placement or creation of work opportunities (open market as well as sheltered), and five reports (four countries) actually mention the need for the elimination of societal barriers in the area of employment.[9] Three of these reports (two countries) convey measures of financial assistance to persons with a disability to make a certain workplace accessible to him/her.[10]

Generally, the right to rehabilitation and finding suitable work almost exclusively belongs to persons with a disability who have previously worked. Similarly, most of the reports analysed mention the right to social security for workers who attain a disability. This right is most often an individual, enforceable right described in considerable detail. The right to social assistance for persons with a disability who have never worked is almost always described in a more general and imprecise manner, and does not seem to be an individual and enforceable right, but rather a policy statement.

Three reports give statistics of unemployed persons with a disability.[11] While these are informative as to what percentage of registered unemployed have a disability, and how many persons with a disability are registered as unemployed, they do not answer the question what percentage of persons with a disability are unemployed.

Education

The most important aspect of the right to education in the context of promoting a paradigm shift in disability is the inclusion of persons with a disability in the general educational system. While almost all reports refer to the education of persons with a disability in some manner,[12] in the overwhelming majority of reports special educational facilities are the only context in which the education of persons with a disability is mentioned. Three reports explicitly mention the importance and active pursuance of a policy of inclusion of persons with a disability in the general educational system.[13]

One report mentions the provision of transport according to individual need as a means to equalise opportunities between children with a disability and able-bodied children.[14] In two other cases, persons with a visual and hearing impairment are singled out as educated together with or in special units connected to classes with able-bodied students.[15] The approach of special units connected to general schools is reported in three cases as an alternative to special schools for persons with a disability in general.[16] One report mentions personal educational assistants for children with disabilities, but does not tell if this is in special or general schools.[17] Four reports provide statistics on the number of special schools and students,[18] while only one report makes an estimation of the percentage of children with a disability covered by primary education.[19] One report mentions a legal right for everyone to primary education, regardless *inter alia* of health, but does not explicitly mention disability.[20]

Cultural participation
The right to cultural participation covers both the enjoyment and the creation of culture. The creation of culture is the sharing of a perception of reality, a specific point of view. In addition to the general value of cultural expression, there is a particular value in the cultural expression of a person with a disability, as this is a (or rather many) previously silenced perspectives. The right to take part in cultural life is instrumental to a changed perception of disability as it multiplies the visibility of persons with a disability, seeing that they are not only present in the enjoyment of culture but also creators of culture which is disseminated in society at large.

Only one report mentions persons with a disability in the context of Article 15.[21] This report gives information both regarding the participation in culture and the creation of culture by persons with a disability. As regards participation, the report mentions theatre groups with persons with a disability, as well as 'social groups' belonging to organisations for persons with a disability. Some of these organisations receive minor government grants. According to the report, most mainstream cultural venues are still inaccessible for persons with a disability. Regarding the creation of culture, the report mentions the publishing by organisations of persons with a disability of magazines of superior quality, the creation of a separate school of poetry written by persons with a disability and fashion design for persons with a disability.

Overall approach to the disability policy
A comprehensive account of the situation of persons with a disability in the context of the ICESCR would include:

1   a general policy statement based on an approach of equality, inclusion, participation, rights and a social definition of disability;
2   how this perspective is applied and realised in the context of each right;
3   the extent to which these rights are presently enjoyed by persons with a disability.[22]

No report analysed comes close to fulfilling these requirements. Coverage of persons with a disability is, at best, piecemeal, and more often than not it is not explicitly, if at all, based on a policy such as the one described above. Less than half of the reports analysed explicitly mention either a policy or a specific measure with inclusion and participation as its aim in the context of any right.[23] Three reports mention a policy/law[24] or a measure/recognition[25] regarding the elimination of societal barriers in the form of buildings etc. One report explicitly mentions equal opportunities as a goal in the context of persons with a disability[26] and another mentions the need for elimination of prejudice against persons with a disability.[27]

The majority of reports mention persons with a disability in the same breath as other groups of persons perceived as 'innocent, vulnerable or dependent',[28] such as 'orphans, helpless women, the aged, the disabled and incapacitated persons'.[29] By doing this, the specific discrimination and lack of enjoyment of rights facing each of these groups is obscured by an image of inherent helplessness, calling for charity rather than empowerment and justice. Similarly, more often than not, the word 'right' is not used in the description of measures to fulfil the needs of persons with a disability

In the majority of cases, the terms disability and handicap are used interchangeably,[30] and offensive terminology[31] such as 'mentally retarded'[32] is commonplace. These two aspects seem to show improvement over time as they are less frequent in the reports submitted in the year 2000.

In the reports analysed, there are no references to the Standard Rules or General Comment 5, one reference to the International Year of the Disabled[33] and one to the World Programme of Action.[34] One report mentions the creation of national institutions to further the rights of persons with a disability.[35]

Conclusions: The effectiveness of the system so far and implications for the future
On the basis of the analysis, certain conclusions can be drawn. First of all, the move to the human rights framework of reference in the disability field is long overdue and is here to stay. But it is still misunderstood both by human rights organisations as well as by disability NGOs.

Secondly, the essence of this revolution has to do with breaking down barriers to the mainstream of life for excluded groups. Human rights are about giving power to people and not just about protecting people against power.

Thirdly, economic, social and cultural rights can play an enormously important role in enabling people with disabilities to take charge of their own lives. It follows that social supports should always be geared towards increasing choice and enabling people to participate in the life of the polity, in the social sphere and also in the productive labour market.

Fourthly, General Comment No 5 is quite far seeing and revolutionary. However, States Parties have not generally responded well. They generally treat disability as a welfare or health care issue. A lot more work needs to be done by the INGOs as well as by the Committee to educate States Parties.

The main goal: Towards a UN convention on the rights of persons with disabilities

An event of historic proportions took place in 2002 at the United Nations in New York. A special Ad Hoc Committee of Member States of the UN began the process of drafting a legally binding treaty on the rights of persons with disabilities. The process is expected to take anywhere up to five years to complete. While the ultimate shape of the treaty is unpredictable, the very fact that the process is under way is testament to the power of the rights-based model of disability at least at the international level.

The treaty-drafting process did not have auspicious beginnings. It can trace its roots back to the World Programme of Action in favour of Disabled People (WPA) of 1982. The WPA ushered in the Decade of People with Disabilities – a decade during which little was achieved. It was that lack of achievement that led an Independent Expert Group which set up to review the WPA in 1987 to recommend that a legally binding treaty should be adopted on the subject. Indeed, Italy and Sweden proposed drafts of such an instrument at the time. While the UN General Assembly rejected the arguments for a treaty, it did not do so on the merits. Rather, it declined to initiate a new drafting exercise after having done so in a number of other fields. In any event, it wished to give the existing web of six human rights treaties enough time to prove their worth in the context of disability. Two of these treaties cover general civil, political, economic social and cultural rights. Three of them cover the thematic application of these rights to groups such as women, children and racial minorities and the last covers torture. The rationale for thematic treaties is to clarify the application of the general standards in the context of a particular group. The disability treaty would add a new thematic treaty to this body of law.

However, rather than leave the disabled community empty handed, the General Assembly adopted a new instrument in 1993 which went half way between an ordinary Resolution of the General Assembly and a treaty, the UN Standard Rules on the Equalisation of Opportunities for People with Disabilities (SRE). The SRE did not contain legally binding rules. Yet it did contain a monitoring mechanism that is more usually to be found in a treaty. Interestingly, the special rapporteur charged with this monitoring responsibility was Bengt Lindqvist who had earlier produced the Swedish draft treaty.

The tide had swung fairly decisively in favour of a binding treaty by the late 1990s. The enactment by the US of a civil rights statute in the context of disability – the Americans with Disabilities Act or ADA of 1990 – underscored the power of the shift from welfare to rights. The ADA has inspired many parliaments around the world to follow suit, despite some recent setbacks in the US Supreme Court. Closer to home, the unprecedented inclusion of disability as a ground for prohibited discrimination in Article 13 of the Treaty of Amsterdam pegged Europe to the rights-based model. The SRE, though a useful policy instrument, lacked the power of a treaty to drive reform forward.

This shift of international opinion was bound to be reflected, sooner or later, in the UN system. It was reflected first in the workings of the UN Commission on Human Rights which has traditionally passed a non-contentious biannual resolution on human rights and disability. In fact, Ireland has been the main sponsor of this resolution since the late 1990s. In 2000, Ireland tried to get the concept of a treaty back onto the agenda through this resolution. At that time, Ireland was apparently thwarted by some of its EU partners. It nevertheless deserves great credit for its diplomatic efforts.

In anticipation of the issue coming before the UN Human Rights Commission in 2002, the Office of the UN High Commissioner for Human Rights under Mary Robinson commissioned Professor Theresia Degener (Germany) and the author (Gerard Quinn) to direct research on the current use and future potential of the six UN treaties on human rights in the context of disability. The study, which was published in February 2002, found that although the six existing treaties had considerable relevance in the abstract, this relevance was not likely to be realised under the existing system (study to be found at www.unhchr.ch). We added to the arguments for a thematic treaty on disability, not as a way of creating and adding new law but more as a way of drawing out and making explicit the relevance of the general standards in the specific context of disability.

However, before the study was completed and before the UN Commission on Human Rights had an opportunity to look again at the issue, the Mexican Government surprised everyone by getting a Resolution passed by the General Assembly in New York in December 2001 to the effect that an Ad Hoc Committee of interested states would begin the process of 'considering proposals' for the drafting of a treaty on disability. Before the Ad Hoc Committee could meet, the Mexican Government organised a high level seminar on the topic of a treaty in Mexico City in June 2002. It unveiled its own draft text at the seminar which has been much improved since then (see www.sre.gob.mx/discapacidad). That seminar produced two important 'Outcome Documents' – one of which was a set of principles according to which the treaty should be drafted and the other was an indicative outline of what the treaty might contain. Among other things, the principles emphasised the need to make sure that the new treaty built on the existing general human rights standards and the importance of NGO participation.

The Ad Hoc Committee met over a two-week period and was scheduled to meet again in late Spring 2003. It was innovative from a procedural point of view. NGOs that have consultative status with ECOSOC were admitted to the proceedings as a matter of right. This includes only very few large global disability NGOs (e.g., World Blind Union). However, a momentous decision was taken at the Ad Hoc Committee to admit ordinary disability NGOs to all future sessions under certain conditions. That would include, for example, groups such as the Forum of People with Disabilities in Ireland. An important procedural decision was also taken to invite Human Rights Commissions to all future sessions. It is looking increasingly likely that Human Rights Commissions from around the world will not only participate but also coordinate their participation. Indeed, the Ad Hoc Committee recommended to States that persons with disabilities and other experts in the field of disability rights should be included on their delegations for coming sessions. The Committee also recommended that there should be a series of Regional meetings on the treaty. One is likely to be held for Europe over the coming months.

From a substantive point of view, the first session of the Ad Hoc Committee achieved very little which is not surprising at this stage in the process. Many states and some groups of states (e.g., the EU) outlined their initial positions on the substance of any new instrument. The EU, for example, issued important and generally positive statements in plenary on the arguments for a treaty, on the possible content of a treaty and on the enforcement mechanism that might be adopted. The EU grouping was no doubt aware of the resonance of the issue given that next year is the European Year of People with Disabilities. The next session of the Ad Hoc Committee should see the commencement of the drafting process in earnest.

It is worth bearing in mind that about four fifths of the world's 600 million people with disabilities live in developing countries. This process is as vital to them as it is to us. It is important that Irish NGOs should learn about the UN process and the role they can play in it. Though seemingly remote, what happens at the next session of the Ad Hoc Committee will ultimately have a powerful bearing on the enjoyment of rights by Irish people with disabilities.

In sum, the current consultation exercise on the Disabilities Bill at home has a broader context. That context is the worldwide acceptance of the rights-based approach to disability. The challenge now is to translate that into something concrete at home and, by so doing, to recapture some of the high ground Ireland had already won for itself on the international stage until recently.

Notes

Chapter Four: Social Security and disability

1   Social Insurance payments are currently fully financed by contributions; this reflects high employment levels and a relatively young population, so the ratio of contributors to beneficiaries is currently high; it is envisaged that as demands on the Fund grow, the Exchequer contribution will resume.

2   The National Anti-Poverty Strategy Income Adequacy Working Group commented on the fact that the Living in Ireland survey does not specifically identify households headed by people with disabilities; nor does the data identify people with disabilities within households, making it impossible to identify the number of people with disabilities living in poverty.

3   Consistent poverty here is defined as being in a household with less than 70 per cent of median income and also experiencing basic deprivation; for fuller definition and a discussion of the various measures of poverty, see Nolan *et al.* (2002)

4   An exception to this general rule is Disablement Pension under the Occupational Injuries scheme.

5   Under the Rules of Behaviour, a person is generally precluded from carrying out any work while in receipt of contributory illness and disability payments. However, with the prior approval of the Department, a person may be exempted from the operation of these Rules so as to engage in employment or training which is considered to be rehabilitative or therapeutic. Certain other types of employment are also exempted, such as charitable work and light work which is not normally remunerated.

Chapter Eight: Ethnicity and disability

1   The European Economic Area (EEA) includes the 15 EU member states as well as Norway, Liechtenstein and Iceland.

2   Council Resolution of 20 December 1996 on Equality of Opportunity for People with Disabilities, OJ L 186 of 2 July 1999, p. 3.

3   Council Directive 2000/43/EC of 29 June 2000 implementing the principle of equal treatment between persons irrespective of racial or ethnic origin, OJ L 180 of the 19.7.2000, p. 22.

4   Council Directive 2000/78/EC of 17 November 2000 establishing a general framework for equal treatment in employment and occupation, OJ L 303 of 2.12.2000, p. 16.

5   Council Decision of 27 November 2000 establishing a Community action programme to combat discrimination (2001 to 2006), OJ L 303 of the 2.12.2000, p. 23.

6   Yorkshire Forward is the Regional Development Agency for Yorkshire, Humberside and North and Northeast Lincolnshire.

7   International Labour Organisation Convention C097 concerning Migration for Employment (Revised), 1949.

8   International Labour Organisation Convention C159 concerning Vocational Rehabilitation and Employment (Disabled Persons), 1983.

9   In the UK the groups most at risk of SCD are of African Caribbean and West African origin.

10   The Working Group identified refugees who are older people, unaccompanied young children and young adults, victims of extreme violence, and people with pre-existing mental health problems as psychologically and emotionally vulnerable groups.

11   The other grounds are age, family status, gender, marital status, sexual orientation and religion.

12   The members of the Forum are the Equality Authority (Republic of Ireland), the Commission for Racial Equality (GB), the Disability Rights Commission (GB), the Equal Opportunities Commission (GB), the Northern Ireland Human Rights Commission, the Equality Commission for Northern Ireland and the Human Rights Commission (Republic of Ireland).

Chapter Nine: Ageing and disability

1   Phase 1 areas include the North Eastern Health Board, South Easter Health Board, South West Area Health Board and Western Health Board.

Chapter Ten: The mixed economy of welfare and disability

1   There are no reliable statistics yet available on the numbers of people with disabilities in Ireland. This situation is due to change when the results of the census 2002 become available in 2003. It will be further developed with the National Disability Study planned by the National Disability Authority for 2003–6.

2   As exemplified by the withdrawal of the Government's Disability Bill in January 2002 in the face of widespread opposition across the disability sector, by the increasing numbers of individual legal cases being taken against the state by parents of children with disabilities and by the unprecedented number of independent disability candidates standing in the recent parliamentary elections.

3   A national study was commissioned by the Department of Transport in July 2002 and will be finalised in early 2003. A review of transport services and gaps in provision is also being carried out for the NDA and will be concluded in early 2003.

4   Information on developments during 2002 supplied by the Department of Transport in a verbal communication.

Chapter Thirteen: Towards free and inclusive societies for individuals

1   ICESCR Committee, General Comment 5, Persons with Disabilities, Eleventh session, 1994, UN Doc. E/1995/22, para. 2.

2   Sweden 4 (2000).

3   Cayman Islands (UK) 4 (2000).

4   Germany 3 (1996), 4 (2000).

5   Algeria 1(1994).

6   Germany 3 (1996), Korea 1 (1994).

7   Sweden 3 (1994), 4 (2000).

8   Sweden 3 (1994), 4 (2000), Germany 4 (2000), Korea 1(1994), Algeria 1(1994), 2 (2000), Guatemala 1 (1995), Zimbabwe 1 (1995), Ukraine 3 (1994), Iraq 2 (1993).

9   Sweden 3 (1994), 4 (2000), Germany 4 (2000), Korea 1(1994), Ukraine 3 (1994).

10   Sweden 3 (1994), 4 (2000), Germany 4 (2000).

11   Sweden 3 (1994), Germany 3 (1996), Ukraine 4 (2000).

12   Except for Germany 4 (2000), Ukraine 3 (1994) Nigeria 1 (1996), Guatemala 1 (1995).

13   Isle of Man (UK) 4 (2000), Zimbabwe 1 (1995), Panama 2 (2000). Falkland Islands (UK) 4 (2000) mentions a new secondary school accessible for persons with a disability.

14   Germany 3 (1996).

15   Isle of Man (UK) 4 (2000), Cayman Islands (UK) 4 (2000).

16   Isle of Man (UK) 4, Yugoslavia 2 (1999), Gibraltar (UK) 4 (2000).

17   St Helena (UK) 4 (2000).

18   Yugoslavia 2 (1999), Korea 1 (1994), Ukraine 3 (1994), Iraq 2 (1993).

19   Yugoslavia 2 (1999).

20   Ukraine 4 (2000).

21   Yugoslavia 2 (1999). In addition (St Helena (UK) 4 (2000) mentions Handicapped Persons Aid Society as one out of 11 local bodies receiving small government grants.

22   Link to reporting obligations.

23   Germany 3 (1996), 4 (2000), Panama 2 (2000), Yugoslavia 2 (1999), Zimbabwe 1 (1995), Algeria 1 (1994), Sweden 3 (1994), Ukraine 3 (1994), Isle of Man (UK) 2 (1993).

24   Korea 1 (1994).

25   The Falkland Islands (UK) 4 (2000), Yugoslavia 2 (1999).

26   Germany 3 (1996).

27   Korea 1 (1994).

28   Nigeria 1(1996).

29   Nepal 1(2000).

30   But see Sweden 4 (2000), correcting use of the term handicap in Sweden 3 (1994), Gibraltar (UK) 4 (2000), St Helena (UK) 4 (2000), Yugoslavia 2 (1999), Guatemala 1 (1995), Korea 1 (1994), Ukraine 3 (1994), Sweden 3 (1994), Isle of Man (UK) 2 (1993), Turk and Caicos Islands (UK) 2 (1993).

31   Algeria 2 (2000) (Disabled and maladjusted persons), Nepal 1 (2000) (the disabled and incapacitated persons). Zimbabwe 1 (1995) (natural deformity), Ukraine 3 (1994) (children with defects in their physical development), Iraq 2 (1993) (totally disabled/totally handicapped).

32   Panama 2 (2000), Zimbabwe 1(1995), Ukraine 3 (1994), Sweden 3 (1994), Isle of Man (UK) 2 (1993), Gibraltar (UK) 2 (1993) (retarded), Iraq 2 (1993) (mentally, psychologically and physically retarded).

33   Korea 1 (1994).

34   Algeria 1 (1994).

35   Guatemala 1 (1995), (Office for the Rights of the Disabled, National Commission for the Disabled).

References

Abberley, P. (1987) 'The concept of oppression and the development of a social theory of disability', *Disability, Handicap and Society* 2 (1): 5–19.

Abberley, P. (1992) 'Counting us out: a discussion of the OPCS disability surveys', *Disability, Handicap and Society*, 7 (2): 139–55.

Abu-Habib, L. (1997) *Gender and Disability: Women's Experiences in the Middle East.* Oxford: Oxfam.

ADM (2000) *Going the Extra Mile: Meath Accessible Transport Project Community Action Plan Summary report.* Dublin: ADM.

AHEAD (Association for Higher Education Access and Disability) (1994) Committee on Access and Participation of Students with Disabilities in Higher Education, *Report to the Higher Education Authority*, Dublin: AHEAD.

AHEAD (1995) *Legislation, Disability and Higher Education.* Dublin: AHEAD.

Ahmad, W. I. U., Darr A. and Jones, L. (2000) '"I send my child to school and he comes back an Englishman": minority ethnic deaf people, identity politics and services' in Ahmad W. I. U. (ed.), *Ethnicity, Disability and Chronic Illness.* Buckingham: Open University Press, pp. 67–84.

Albrecht, G. L., Seelman, K. D. and Bury, M. (2001) 'Introduction: The formation of disability studies', in Albrecht, G. L., Seelman, K. D. and Bury, M. (eds) *Handbook of Disability Studies.* London: Sage: 1–10.

Allan, J. (1999) *Actively Seeking Inclusion: Pupils with Special Needs in Mainstream Schools.* London: Falmer Press.

Alvarez, J. (1999) *Reflections on an Agequake.* New York: NGO Committee on Aging.

Armstrong, F., Armstrong, D. and Barton, L. (eds) (2000) *Inclusive Education: Policy, Contexts and Comparative Perspectives.* London: David Fulton.

Armstrong, F., Belmont, B. and Verillon, A. (2000) 'Vive le différence? Exploring context, policy and change in special education in France: Developing cross-cultural collaboration', in Armstrong, F., Armstrong, D. and Barton, L. (eds), *Inclusive Education: Policy, Contexts and Comparative Perspectives.* London: David Fulton.

Atkin, K. and Ahmad. W. I. U. (2000) 'Living with sickle cell disorder: how young people negotiate their care and treatment' in Ahmad W. I. U. (ed.), *Ethnicity, Disability and Chronic Illness.* Buckingham: Open University Press, pp. 45–66.

Atkin, K., Ahmad, W. I. U. and Anionwu, E. N. (2000) 'Service support to families caring for a child with sickle cell disorder or beta thalassaemia major: parents' perspectives' in Ahmad W. I. U. (ed.), *Ethnicity, Disability and Chronic Illness.* Buckingham: Open University Press, pp. 103–22.

Bailey, J. (ed.) (1992) *Social Europe.* London: Longman.

Ballard, K. (ed.) (1999) *Inclusive Education: International Voices on Disability and Justice.* London: Falmer.

Barbotte, E., Guillemin, F. and Chau, N. (2001) 'Prevalence of impairments, disabilities, handicaps and quality of life in the general population: a review of recent literature', *Bulletin of the World Health Organisation* 79 (11): 1047–55.

Barnes, C. (1991) *Disabled People in Britain: A Case for Anti-Discrimination Legislation.* London: Hurst.

Barnes, C. (1993) 'Participation and control in day centres for young disabled people aged 16 to 30 years', in Swain, J., Finkelstein, V., French, S. and Oliver, M. (eds), *Disabling Barriers—Enabling Environments.* London: Sage, pp. 169–77.

Barnes, C. and Mercer, G. (1996) *Exploring the Divide: Illness and Disability.* Leeds: The Disability Press.

Barnes, C., Mercer, G. and Shakespeare, T. (1999) *Exploring Disability: A Sociological Introduction.* Cambridge: Polity.

Barnes, H. and Baldwin, S. (1999) 'Social security, poverty and disability', in Ditch, J. (ed.), *Introduction to Social Security.* London: Routledge, pp. 156–76.

Barton, L. (1988) 'Research and practice: the need for alternative perspectives', in Barton, L. (ed.), *The Politics of Special Educational Needs.* Lewes: Falmer.

Barton, L. (1996) 'Sociology and disability: some emerging issues', in Barton, L. (ed.), *Disability and Society: Emerging Issues and Insights.* Essex: Addison Wesley Longman, pp. 3–17.

Bau, A.M. (1999) 'Providing culturally competent services to visually impaired persons' *Journal of Visual Impairment and Blindness,* May: 291–7.

Baxter (1995) 'Confronting colour blindness: Developing better services for people with learning difficulties from Black and ethnic minority communities' in Philpot, T. and Ward, L. (eds.) *Values and Visions: Changing Ideas in Services for People with Learning Difficulties.* Oxford: Butterworth-Heinemann, Oxford, pp. 203–17.

Begley, M., Garavan, C., Condon, M., Kelly, I., Holland, K. and Staines, A. (1999) *Asylum in Ireland: A Public Health Perspective.* Dublin: University College Dublin.

Begum, N. (1992) 'Disabled women and the feminist agenda' *Feminist Review,* 40 (1992): 70–84.

Begum, N. (1996) 'Doctor, doctor . . . disabled women's experience of general practitioners', in Morris, J. (ed.), *Encounters with Strangers: Feminism and Disability.* London: The Women's Press, pp. 168–93.

Beresford, P. (1996) 'Poverty and disabled people: Challenging dominant debates and policies', *Disability and Society,* 11 (4): 553–67.

Bergeskog, A. (2001) *Labour Market Policies, Strategies and Statistics for People with Disabilities: A Cross National Comparison.* Uppsala: IFAU – Office of Labour Market Policy Evaluation.

Bermingham, D. (2001) *Advocacy A Rights Issue,* Dublin: Forum of People with Disabilities.

Berthoud, R. and Nazroo, J. (1997) 'The mental health of ethnic minorities', *New Community,* 2 (3): 309–24.

Bhakta, P, Katbamna, S. and Parker, G. (2000) 'South Asian carers' experiences of primary care teams', in Waqar, I. U. (ed.), *Ethnicity, Disability and Chronic Illness.* Buckingham: Open University Press, pp. 123–41.

Bickenbach, J. E., Chatterji, S., Badley, E. M. and Ustun, T. B. (1999) 'Models of disablement, universalism and the international classification of impairments, disabilities and handicaps', *Social Science and Medicine* 48 (9): 1173–87.

Birenbaum, A. (2002) 'Poverty, welfare reform, and disproportionate rates of disability among children', *Mental Retardation* 40 (3): 212–18.

Blacher, J. (2001) 'Transition to adulthood: mental retardation, families, and culture', *American Journal on Mental Retardation* 106 (2): 173–88.

Bogdan, R., Brown, M. A. and Bannerman Foster, S. (1992) 'Be honest but not cruel: Staff/parent communication on a neonatal unit', in Ferguson, P. M., Ferguson, D. L. and Taylor, S. J. (eds), *Interpreting Disability: A Qualitative Reader.* New York: Teachers College Press, Columbia University, pp. 19–37.

Bollini, P. and Siem, H. (1995) 'No real progress towards equity: health of migrants and ethnic minorities on the eve of the year 2000', *Social Science and Medicine* 41 (6): 819–28.

Booth, T. and Ainscow, M. (eds) (1998) *From Them to Us: An International Study of Inclusion in Education.* London: Routledge.

Borsay, A. (1986) 'Personal trouble or public issue? Towards a model for people with physical and mental disabilities', *Disability, Handicap and Society* I (2): 171–95.

Borsay, A. (1998) 'Returning patients to the community: disability, medicine and economic rationality before the industrial revolution', *Disability and Society* 13 (5): 645–63.

Braddock, D., Emerson, E., Felce, D. and Stancliffe, R. J. (2001) 'Living circumstances of children and adults with mental retardation or developmental disabilities in the United States, Canada, England and Wales and Australia', *Mental Retardation And Developmental Disabilities Research Reviews* 7 (2): 115–21.

Bresnihan, V. (2001) *Out of Mind, Out of Sight: Report on Confinement of Mentally Ill Prisoners in Ireland,* Dublin: Irish Penal Reform Trust.

Bricher, G. (2000) 'Disabled people, health professionals and the social model of disability: Can there be a research relationship?', *Disability and Society* 15 (5): 781–93.

Building Regulations (Amendment) Regulations, (2000), S.I. No. 179 of 2000. Dublin: Stationery Office.

Burchardt, T. (1999) *The Evolution of Disability Benefits in the UK: Re-Weighting the Basket.* London: London School of Economics, Centre for Analysis of Social Exclusion.

Burchardt, T. (2000) 'The dynamics of being disabled', *Journal of Social Policy* 29 (4): 645–68.

Burke, H. (1987) *The People and the Poor Law in Nineteenth Century Ireland.* Dublin: Women's Education Bureau.

Burkhauser, R. and Daly, M. (1993) 'A comparison of German and American people with disabilities: Results from the German socio-economic panel', *DIW-Vierteljahreshefte zur Wirtschaftforschung* I/2: 17–26

Butler, R.N. (1969) 'Age-ism: another form of bigotry', *The Gerontologist* 9: 243–6.

Buzzi, I. (1995) 'A critical view of integration in Italy', in O'Hanlon, C. (ed.), *Inclusive Education in Europe.* London: David Fulton, pp. 75–81.

Bytheway, B. (1995) *Ageism.* Buckingham: Open University Press.

Calderbank, R. (2000) 'Abuse and disabled people: vulnerability or social indifference?', *Disability and Society* 15 (3): 521–34.

Cantillon, S., Corrigan, C., Kirby, P. and O'Flynn, J. (eds) (2001) *Rich and Poor: Perspectives on Tackling Inequality in Ireland.* Dublin: Oak Tree Press.

Census of Ireland 1851 (1854). Dublin: Alexander Thom.

Census of Ireland 1871 (1873). Dublin: Alexander Thom.

Central Statistics Office (2001) Quarterly National Household Surveys, Quarter 2, March–May, CSO, Dublin.

Central Statistics Office (2002a) Quarterly National Household Surveys, Quarter 1, CSO, Dublin.

Central Statistics Office (2002b) Disability in the Labour Force, Quarterly National Household Survey, Quarter 2, CSO, Dublin.

Central Statistics Office (2002c) Statistical Release: Quarterly National Household Survey. CSO: Dublin

Centre for Independent Living (2000) *Independent Living: Towards the New Millennium.* Dublin: Centre for Independent Living.

Civic Forum (2002) *A Regional Strategy for Social Inclusion.* Belfast: Civic Forum.

Clancy, P. (1990) 'Socio-economic group, gender and regional inequalities in student participation in higher education', in Fennell, C. and Mulcahy, M. (eds) *Equality of Opportunity in Irish Third Level Institutions: Proceedings of a Forum.* Cork: University College Cork.

Clough, P. and Barton, L. (eds) (1995) *Making Difficulties: Research and Constructions of SEN.* London: Paul Chapman.

Colgan, A. (1997) 'People with disabilities in the health services', in Robins, J. (ed.), *Reflections on Health, Commemorating Fifty Years of the Department of Health, 1947–1997.* Dublin: Stationery Office: 11–25.

Commission of Inquiry on Mental Handicap (1965) *Report.* Dublin: Stationery Office.

Commission of the European Communities (1997) *Employment in Europe.* EC Directorate-General for Employment, Industrial Relations and Social Affairs Unit V/A.1. Luxembourg: Commission of the European Communities.

Commission of the European Communities (1998) *A New European Community Disability Strategy.* Document 98/0216 (CNS). Brussels: Commission of the European Communities.

Commission on Social Welfare (1986) *Report of the Commission on Social Welfare.* Dublin: Stationery Office.

Commission on the Status of People with Disabilities (1996) *A Strategy for Equality.* Dublin: Stationery Office.

Conference of Religious of Ireland (CORI) (1998) *Inequality in Education: The Role of Assessment and Certification.* Dublin: CORI.

Conroy, P. (1994) 'Income maintenance and social protection' in *Disability Exclusion and Poverty, Papers from the National Conference on Disability Exclusion and Poverty – A Policy Conference 1993.* Dublin: Combat Poverty Agency, pp. 75–110.

Conroy, P. (2002) 'Towards a disabilities act', in *Get Your Act Together: Conference Report and Tool Kit,* 3 December 2001, Dublin, pp. 12–14.

Conroy, P. and Fanagan, S. (2001a) *Research Project on the Effective Recruitment of People with Disabilities into the Public Service, 2000.* Dublin: Employment Equality Authority.

Conroy, P. and Fanagan, S. (2001b) *The Costs of Disability,* Working Paper. Dublin: Forum of People with Disabilities.

Constitution Review Group (1996) *Report.* Dublin: Stationery Office.

Coolahan, J. (1981) *Irish Education: Its History and Structure.* Dublin: Institute of Public Administration.

Coolahan, J. (1989) 'Educational policy for National Schools, 1960–1985', in Mulcahy, D. and O'Sullivan, D. (eds), *Irish Educational Policy: Process and Substance.* Dublin: Institute of Public Administration.

Coolahan, J. (ed.) (1994) *Report on the National Education Convention.* Dublin: The National Education Convention Secretariat.

Council Decision of 27 November 2000 establishing a Community action programme to combat discrimination (2001 to 2006), OJ L 303 of the 2.12.2000, p. 23.

Council Directive 2000/43/EC of 29 June 2000 implementing the principle of equal treatment between persons irrespective of racial or ethnic origin, OJ L 180 of the 19.7.2000, p. 22.

Council Directive 2000/78/EC of 17 November 2000 establishing a general framework for equal treatment in employment and occupation, OJ L 303 of 2.12.2000, p. 16.

Council of Europe (1992) *Recommendation No. R(92)6 of the Committee of Ministers to Member States on a Coherent Policy for People with Disabilities.* Strasbourg: Council of Europe.

Council Resolution of 20 December 1996 on Equality of Opportunity for People with Disabilities, OJ L 186 of the 2.7.1999, p. 3.

Crewe, N. M. and Zola, I. K. (eds) (1983) *Independent Living for Physically Disabled People.* San Francisco: Josey-Bass.

Crowley, N. (1999) 'Travellers and social policy' in Quin, S., Kennedy, P., O'Donnell, A. and Kiely, G. (eds.), *Contemporary Irish Social Policy.* Dublin: UCD Press, pp. 243–63.

Curry, J. (1993) *Irish Social Services* (2nd edition). Dublin: Institute of Public Administration.

Dáil Éireann (1998) Committee of Public Accounts, *First Interim Report on the Appropriation Accounts 1996.* Dublin: Government of Ireland.

Dalton, A. J. and Janicki, M. P. (1999) 'Ageing and dementia', in Janicki. M. P. and Dalton, A. J. (eds), *Dementia, Ageing and Intellectual Disabilities: A Handbook,* Philadelphia: Brunner/Makel, pp. 5–31.

Dalton, B. (1996) 'The Provision of Services for Blind and Visually Impaired Students in Second and Third Level Education'. Unpublished Master of Equality Studies thesis, National University of Ireland, Dublin.

Daly, M. (2002) 'Access to Social Rights in Europe' unpublished paper, Institute of European Affairs Seminar.

Daniels, H. and Gartner, P. (1999) *Inclusive Education: World Yearbook of Education.* London: Kogan Page.

Dant, T. and Gregory, S. (1991) *The Social Construction of Deafness, Block 3, Unit 8, Issues in Deafness.* Milton Keynes: Open University.

Daunt, P. (1990) *Age and Disability: A Challenge for Europe.* Final Report of the Eurolink Seminar on Age and Disability incorporating a European Code of Good Practice. London: Eurolink Age.

Daunt, P. (1993) 'Western Europe', in Mittler, P., Brouillette, R. and Harris, D. (eds), *Special Needs Education.* London: Kogan Page.

Davis, K (1993) 'On the movement', in Swain, J., Finkelstein, F., French, S. and Oliver, M. (eds.), *Disabling Barriers: Enabling Environments.* London: Sage, pp. 285–92.

DeJong, G. (1979) 'Independent living: From social movement to analytic paradigm', *Archives of Physical Medicine and Rehabilitation* 60: 436–46.

Deloitte and Touche (2001) *Audit of the Irish Health System for Value for Money,* Vol. 1: *Executive Summary.* Dublin: Deloitte & Touche.

Department of Education (1992) *Education for a Changing World.* Green Paper on Education. Dublin: Stationery Office.

Department of Education (1993) *Report of the Special Education Review Committee.* Dublin: Stationery Office.

Department of Education (1995) *Charting Our Education Future,* White Paper on Education. Dublin: Stationery Office.

Department of Education and Science (1998) *Education Act.* Dublin: Stationery Office.

Department of Education and Science (1999) *Arrangements for the Assessment of Candidates with Special Needs: Discussion Paper.* Dublin: Stationery Office.

Department of Education and Science (2000) *Arrangements for the Assessment of Candidates with Special Educational Needs in Certificate Examinations: Report to the Minister for Education and Science.* Dublin: Stationery Office.

Department of Education and Science (2001) *Statistical Report 1999/2000.* Dublin: Stationery Office.

Department of the Environment and Local Government (2000) *Part M Technical Guidance Document to the Building Regulations.* Dublin: Stationery Office.

Department of Equality and Law Reform (1999) *Towards Equal Citizenship: Progress Report on the Implementation of the Recommendations of the Commission on the Status of People with Disabilities.* Dublin: Stationery Office.

Department of Health (1986) *Health: The Wider Dimensions.* Dublin: Stationery Office.

Department of Health (1991) *Needs and Abilities: A Policy for the Intellectually Disabled.* Dublin: Stationery Office.

Department of Health (1993) *Report of the Inspector of Mental Hospitals.* Dublin: Government Publications.

Department of Health (1997a) A Plan for Women's Health. Dublin: Stationery Office.

Department of Health (1997b) Report of the Working Group on the Implementation of the Health Strategy in Relation to Persons with a Mental Handicap: Enhancing the Partnership. Dublin: Stationery Office.

Department of Health and Children (1998) *Working for Health and Well-Being: Strategy Statement 1998-2001.* Dublin: Stationery Office.

Department of Health and Children (2000) *The National Children's Strategy: Our Children – Their Lives.* Dublin: Stationery Office.

Department of Health and Children (2001a) *Primary Care: A New Direction,* Dublin: Stationery Office

Department of Health and Children (2001b) *Towards Quality and Fairness: A Health System For You.* Dublin: Stationery Office.

Department of Health and Children (2001c) *Mental Health Act.* Dublin: Stationery Office.

Department of Health and Children (2002a) *Traveller Health: A National Strategy 2002–2005.* Dublin: Department of Health and Children.

Department of Health and Children, Ireland (2002b) Dublin: Press Release supplied by Department of Health, 5 March 2002: http://www.doh.ie/pressroom/pt20020305.html.

Department of Health and Social Welfare (1984) *Towards A Full Life: Green Paper on Services for Disabled People.* Dublin: Stationery Office.

Department of Health (United Kingdom) (2001) *Valuing People: A New Strategy for Learning Disability for the 21st Century.* London: HMSO.

Department of Justice, Equality and Law Reform (1998) *Building a Future Together: Report of the Establishment Group for the National Disability Authority and Disability Support Service.* Dublin: Stationery Office.

Department of Justice, Equality and Law Reform (1999a) *Towards Equal Citizenship: Progress Report on the Implementation of the Recommendations of the Commission on the Status of People with Disabilities.* Dublin: Stationery Office.

Department of Justice, Equality and Law Reform, Ireland (1999b) *National Disability Authority Act.* Dublin: Stationery Office.

Department of Social and Family Affairs (2000) *Comhairle Act.* Dublin: Stationery Office.

Department of Social and Family Affairs (2002) *Building an Inclusive Society: Review of the National Anti-Poverty Strategy under the Programme for Prosperity and Fairness.* Dublin: Stationery Office.

Department of the Taoiseach (1999a) *Implementing the Information Society: An Action Plan.* Dublin: Stationery Office.

Department of the Taoiseach (1999b) *Report of the Interdepartmental Working Group on Web Publication Guidelines for Public Sector Organisations* www.taoiseach.gov.ie/upload/publications/29/.pdf (1999).

Department of the Taoiseach (2003) *Developing Irish Social and Equality Statistics to Meet Policy Needs: Report of the Steering Group on Social and Equality Standards.* Unpublished.

Dignan, T. and McLaughlin, E. (2002) *New TSN Research: Poverty in Northern Ireland.* Belfast: Office of the First Minister and Deputy First Minister (OFMDFM).

Disability Federation of Ireland – Mid West Platform. (2001) *Transport Needs and Provision in Limerick City for Disabled People.* Limerick: DFI

Disability Federation of Ireland (2002) *Submission to Department of the Environment and Local Government: proposals for qualitative improvements in taxi services and the future regulation of those services.* Dublin: DFI.

Disability Rights Commission (DRC) (2002) *Yorkshire RDA Pilot Partnership Project.* Manchester: DRC.

Disabled Peoples' International (1991), *Vox Nostra,* 1 (1).

Dolsen, R. L. (1992) 'Community based services for older persons', in Orr, A. L. (ed.), *Vision and Ageing: Crossroads for Service Delivery.* New York: American Foundation for the Blind, pp. 185–208.

Doyle, P. (1990) *The God Squad.* London: Corgi.

Drake, R. F. (1996a) 'A critique of the role of the traditional charities', in Barton, L. (ed.), *Disability and Society: Emerging Issues and Insights.* London: Longman, pp. 146–66.

Drake, R. F. (1996b) 'Charities, authority and disabled people: A qualitative study,' *Disability and Society* 11 (1): 5–23.

Drake, R.F. (1999) *Understanding Disability Politics.* London: Macmillan.

Driedger, D. (1989) *The Last Civil Rights Movement.* London: Hurst.

Drudy, S. (1991) 'Developments in the sociology of education in Ireland, 1966–1991', *Irish Journal of Sociology* 1: 107–27.

Drudy, S. and Lynch, K. (1993) *Schools and Society in Ireland.* Dublin: Gill & Macmillan.

Duffy, M. (1993) 'Integration or Segregation: Does it Make a Difference?'. Unpublished Master of Equality Studies theis, National University of Ireland, Dublin

Dunn, P.A. (1990) 'The impact of the housing environment upon the ability of disabled people to living independently', *Disability, Handicap and Society* 5 (1): 37–51.

Dyson, A. and Millward, A. (1997) 'The reform of special education or the transformation of mainstream schools', in Pijl, S., Meijer, C. and Hegarty, S. (eds), *Inclusive Education: A Global Agenda.* London: Routledge.

Eagly, A. H. and Wood, W. (1999) 'The origins of sex differences in human behavior: evolved dispositions versus social roles', *American Psychologist* 54 (6): 408–23.

Egan, J. and Walsh, P. N. (2001) 'Sources of stress among adult siblings of Irish people with intellectual disabilities', *Irish Journal of Psychology* 22 (1): 28–38.

Eisenberg, M. G. (1982) 'Disability as stigma', in Eisenberg, M.G., Griggins, C. and Duval, R.J. (eds), *Disabled People as Second Class Citizens*. New York: Springer, pp. 3–12.

Elwan, A. (1999) *Poverty and Disability. A Survey of the Literature*. Washington DC: World Bank.

Emerson, E., Hatton, C., Bauer, I., Bjorgvinsdottir, S., Brak, W., Firkovska-Mankiewicz, A., Haroardottir, H., Kavaliunaite, A., Kebbon, L., Kristofferson, E., Saloviita, T., Schippers, H., Timmons, B., Timcev, L., Tossebro, J., and Wiit, U. (1996) 'Patterns of institutionalisation in 15 European countries', *European Journal on Mental Disability* 3 (11): 29–32.

Employment Equality Act, 1998.

Epstein, S. (1997) *We Can Make It: Stories of Disabled Women in Developing Countries*. Geneva: International Labor Organisation.

Equal Status Act, 2000.

Equality Authority (2000) *An Introduction to the Equal Status Act*. Dublin: Equality Authority.

Equality Authority (2002) *Annual Report 2001*. Dublin: Equality Authority.

Equality Commission for Northern Ireland (2001) *Disabled People in the Labour Market*. Disability Briefing (3). Belfast: ECNI.

Equality Commission for Northern Ireland (2002) *News Archive: Disability Settlements August*. Belfast: ECNI.

Establishment Group for the National Disability Authority and Disability Support Service, Ireland (1998) *Building a Future Together*. Dublin: Stationery Office.

European Commission (1996) *Equality of Opportunity for People with Disabilities*. COM (96) 406, Brussels: European Commission.

European Commission (2000a) *Communication from the Commission to the Council, the European Parliament, the Economic and Social Committee and the Committee of the Regions: Towards a Barrier Free Europe for People with Disabilities*, COM (2000) 284 final of 12.05.02. Brussels: Commission for the European Communities.

European Commission (2000b) *eEurope 2002: An Information Society for All: An Action Plan*. Brussels: European Commission.

European Commission (2001) *Communication of the Commission: eEurope 2002 – Accessibility of Public Websites and their Content*, COM (2001) 529 final of 25.09.2001. Brussels: European Commission

European Commission (2002) *eEurope 2005: An Information Society for All*. http://europa.eu.int/information_society/newsroom/library/referencedoc/doc_en.pdf.

European Conference of Ministers of Transport (1999) *COST 335: Passengers' Accessibility of Heavy Rail Systems*. http://www.cordis.lu/cost-transport/src/cost-335.htm.

European Council of Ministers (1992) Council Directive 92/85/EEC of 19 October 1992, concerning the implementation of measures to improve the health and safety for pregnant women, women who have recently given birth or are breastfeeding at work, *Official Journal of the European Communities*, L 348/1 of 28.11.1992.

European Council of Ministers (2000) Council Directive 2000/43/EC establishing a general framework for Equal Treatment in employment and occupation, *Official Journal of the European Communities*, L 303/16 of 2000.

European Parliament (2002) *Disability Intergroup Newsletter*, Issue 8, March–April.

European Social Fund (ESF) Evaluation Unit (1996) *Summary Report: Training for People with Disabilities*. Dublin: Department of Enterprise and Employment.

Eurostat (2001) *Disability and Social Participation in Europe*, Luxembourg: Office of Official Publications of the European Union.

Fahey, T. (1997) 'The Elderly, the family and the state in Ireland', in House of the Oireachtas (1997) *Interim Report of the Joint Oireachtas Committee on the Family: The Elderly, the Family and the State in Ireland*. Dublin: Stationery Office.

Fahey, T. and Fitzgerald, J. (1997) *Welfare Implications in Demographic Trends*. Dublin: Combat Poverty Agency and Oak Tree Press.

Fanning, B., Loyal, S. and Staunton, C. (2000) *Asylum Seekers and the Right to Work in Ireland*. Dublin: Irish Refugee Council.

Fanning, B., Veale, A. and O'Connor, D. (2001) *Beyond the Pale: Asylum-seeking Children and Social Exclusion in Ireland*. Dublin: Irish Refugee Council.

Faughnan, P. and Kelleher, P. (1993) *The Voluntary Sector and the State: A Study of Organisations in One Region*. Dublin: CMRS..

Faughnan, P. and O'Donovan, A. (2002) *A Changing Voluntary Sector: Working with New Minority Communities in 2001*. Dublin: Social Science Research Centre, University College Dublin.

Fawcett, B. (2000) *Feminist Perspectives on Disability*. Harlow: Prentice Hall.

Fazil, Q., Bywaters, P., Ali, Z, Wallace, L. and Singh, G. (2002) 'Disadvantage and discrimination compounded: the experience of Pakistani and Bangladeshi parents of disabled children in the UK', *Disability and Society* 17 (3): 237–53.

Felce, D. (1997) 'Defining and applying the concept of quality of life' *Journal of Intellectual Disability Research* 41 (2): 126–35.

Fianna Fáil and Labour (1993) *Programme for a Partnership Government 1993–97*. Dublin: Stationery Office.

Fianna Fáil and the Progressive Democrats (1997) *Action Programme for the Millennium*. Dublin: Stationery Office.

Fianna Fáil and the Progressive Democrats (2002) *An Agreed Programme for Government Between Fianna Fáil and the Progressive Democrats*. Dublin: Stationery Office.

Fiedler, Leslie (1978) *Freaks, Myths and Images of the Secret Self*. New York: Simon & Schuster.

Finkelstein, V. (1993) 'Disability: A social challenge or an administrative responsibility?', in Swain, J., Finkelstein, V., French, S. and Oliver, M. (eds), *Disabling Barriers – Enabling Environments*. London: Sage, pp. 34–43.

Finklestein, V., French, S. and Oliver, M. (eds) (1993) *Disabling Barriers – Enabling Environment*. London: Sage, pp. 61–8.

Finlay, F., Boyd, M., Hallahan, M. and Kennedy, M. (1994) 'Integration: pipe-dream or possibility?' *Reach* 7 (2): 85–8.

Finnane, M. (1981) *Insanity and the Insane in Post-Famine Ireland*. London: Croom Helm.

Forum for People with Disabilities (2001) *Advocacy: A Rights Issue*. Dublin: Forum for People with Disabilities.

Foucault, M. (1989) *Madness And Civilization : A History of Insanity in the Age Of Reason*, London: Tavistock Routledge.

Foucault, M. (2002) *Power: Essential Works of Foucault*, vol. 3, edited by J. D. Faubion. London: Penguin.

Fraser, N. (1995) 'From redistribution to recognition? dilemmas of justice in a "post-structuralist" age', *New Left Review* 212: 68–93.

French, S. (1994) 'Disabled people and professional practice', in French, S. (ed.), *On Equal Terms: Working with Disabled People*. Oxford: Butterworth Heinemann.

French, S. (1996) 'The Attitudes of Health Professionals towards Disabled People', in Hales, G. (ed.), *Beyond Disability: Towards an Enabling Society*. London: Sage

Friedlander, H. (1995) *The Origins of Nazi Genocide*. Chapel Hill NC: University of North Carolina Press.

Fry, C. L., Dickerson-Putman, J., Draper, P., Ikels, C., Keith, J., Glascock, A. P., and Harpending, H. C. (1997) 'Culture and the meaning of a good old age', in Sokolovsky, J. (ed.), *The Cultural Context of Aging: Worldwide Perspectives* (2nd edition) Westport, CT: Bergin & Garvey, pp. 99–123.

Fujiura, G. T. and Rutkowski-Kmitta, V. (2001) 'Counting disability', in Albrecht, G. L., Seelman, K. D. and Bury, M. (eds) *Handbook of Disability Studies*. London: Sage, pp. 69–93.

Gallagher, P. (2001) *Report of the National Physical and Sensory Disability Database*. Dublin: Health Research Board.

Gallagher, P. (2002) *Report of the National Physical and Sensory Disability Database Development Committee 2001*. Dublin: Health Research Board.

Giddens, A. (1993) *Sociology*. Cambridge: Polity.

Gill, C. J. and Brown, A.A. (2002) 'Health and ageing issues for women in their own voices', in Walsh, P. N. and Heller, T. (eds), *Health of Women with Intellectual Disabilities*. Oxford: Blackwell, pp. 139–53.

Goffmann, E. (1961) *Asylums*. New York: Doubleday.

Goffman, E. (1990) *Stigma: Notes on the Management of Spoiled Identity*. Harmondsworth: Penguin.

Good, A. (2000) 'European Union Supra State Feminism: Redistributional Gender Equality Policy and Training in Ireland and Europe, 1971–97'. Unpublished PhD thesis, Trinity College, Dublin.

Goodbody Economic Consultants (forthcoming) *Disability and the Labour Market: An Analysis of Data on the Labour Market Situation of People with Disabilities*. Unpublished draft report. Dublin: Goodbody Economic Consultants.

Government of Ireland (1965) *Report of the Commission of Inquiry on Mental Handicap*. Dublin: Stationery Office.

Government of Ireland (1995) *Report of the Task Force on the Travelling Community*. Dublin: Stationary Office.

Government of Ireland (1996) Report of the Review Group on Health and Personal Social Services for People with Physical and Sensory Disabilities, *Towards an Independent Future*. Dublin: Stationery Office.

Government of Ireland. (1999) *National Development Plan 2000–2006*. Dublin: Stationery Office.

Government of Ireland (2000) *Programme for Prosperity and Fairness*. Dublin: Stationery Office.

Grant, G. (2000) 'Older family carers: Challenges, coping strategies and support', in May, D., (ed.), *Transitions and Change in the Lives of People with Learning Disabilities*. London: Jessica Kingsley, pp. 177–93.

Greaney, V. and Kellaghan, T. (1984) *Equality of Opportunity in Irish Schools: A Longitudinal Study of 500 Students.* Dublin: Educational Company.

Guralnick, M. J. (1998) 'Effectiveness of early intervention for vulnerable children: A developmental perspective. *American Journal on Mental Retardation* 102 (4): 319–45.

Harper, D.C. and Wadsworth, J. S. (1993) 'Grief in adults with mental retardation: preliminary findings', *Research in Developmental Disabilities,* 14: 313–30.

Hawkins, B. A. (1999) 'Rights, place of residence and retirement: Lessons from case studies on ageing', in Herr, S. and Weber, G. (eds), *Ageing, Rights and Quality of Life: Prospects for Older People with Developmental Disabilities.* Baltimore: Paul H. Brooks, pp. 93–108.

Health Research Board (2000) *Irish Psychiatric Services Activities 1998.* Dublin: Health Research Board.

Heller, T. (1999) 'Emerging models', in Herr, S. and Weber, G. (eds) *Ageing, Rights and Quality of Life: Prospects for Older People with Developmental Disabilities.* Baltimore: Paul H. Brooks, pp. 149–66.

Hendricks, J. (1992) 'Social aspects of ageing and visual impairment', in Orr, A. L. (ed.), *Vision and Ageing: Crossroads for Service Delivery.* New York: American Foundation for the Blind, pp. 69–92.

Hockey, J. and James, A. (1993) *Growing Up and Growing Old.* London: Sage.

Hurst, A. (ed.) (1998) *Higher Education and Disabilities: International Approaches.* Aldershot: Ashgate.

Imrie, R. (1996) *Disability and the City: International Perspectives.* London: Paul Chapman.

Imrie, R. and Kumar, M. (1998) 'Focusing on disability and access in the built environment', *Disability and Society* 13 (3): 357–74.

Institute for Design and Disability (2002) *The Barcelona Declaration Project 2002–2004.* Dublin: Institute for Design and Disability/National Disability Authority.

Interdepartmental Working Group on the Integration of Refugees in Ireland (1999) *Integration: A Two Way Process.* Dublin: Department of Justice, Equality and Law Reform.

International Labour Office (ILO) (1958) *Discrimination (Employment and Occupation) Convention,* 1958 (No. 111).

International Labour Organisation Convention (1949) C097 concerning Migration for Employment (Revised).

International Labour Organisation Convention (1983) C159 concerning Vocational Rehabilitation and Employment (Disabled Persons).

Irish Deaf Society (1993) *Understanding Human Rights of Deaf People.* Dublin: Irish Deaf Society.

Irish Deaf Society (1997) *Bilingual Education for Deaf Children: Best Option for the Future?* Dublin: Author.

Irish National Teachers Organisation (INTO) (1996) *Providing Education for Pupils with Severe and Profound Handicap.* Dublin: INTO.

Irish Refugee Council (IRC) (2002) *Submission to the Working Group on NAPS and Health* (unpublished).

Janicki, M. (1999) 'Public policy and service design', in Herr, S. and Weber, G. (eds), *Ageing, Rights and Quality of Life: Prospects for Older People with Developmental Disabilities.* Baltimore: Paul H. Brooks, pp. 289–310.

Janicki, M. (2001) 'Toward a rational strategy for promoting healthy ageing amongst people with intellectual disabilities' *Journal of Applied Research in Intellectual Disabilities* 14 (3): 171–4.

Jette, A. M. (1995) 'Disability trends and transitions', in Binstock, R. H. and George, L. K. (eds) *Handbook of Ageing and the Social Sciences* (4th edn). San Diego CA: Academic Press, pp. 94–116.

Jones, L., Atkin, K., and Ahmad, W. I. U. (2001) 'Supporting Asian deaf young people and their families: The role of professionals and services', *Disability and Society* 16 (1): 51–70.

Kallianes, V. and Rubenfeld, P. (1997) 'Disabled women and reproductive rights', *Disability and Society* 12 (2): 203–21.

Kalyanpur, M. (1996) 'The influence of western special education on community-based services in India', *Disability and Society* 11 (2): 249–70.

Katbamna, S. Bhakta, P. and Parker, G. (2000) 'Perceptions of disability and care-giving relationships in South Asian communities', in Waqar, I. U. (ed.), *Ethnicity, Disability and Chronic Illness*. Milton Keynes: Open University Press, pp. 12–27.

Katz, S. J., Kabeto, M. and Langa, K. (2000) 'Gender disparities in the receipt of home care for elderly people with disability in the United States', *Journal of the American Medical Association* 284 (23): 3022–7

Kearns, P. and Lynch, Y. (2002) *It's Normal to be Different: A Report to Inform a Disability Employment Strategy for the Northside of Dublin*. Dublin: The Workhouse.

Kellaghan, T., Weir, S., O'hUallacháin, S. and Morgan, M. (1995) *Educational Disadvantage in Ireland*. Dublin: Department of Education, Combat Poverty Agency, Educational Research Centre.

Kennedy, F. (2001) *From Cottage to Creche: Family Change in Ireland*. Dublin: Institute of Public Administration.

Kerry Network of People with Disabilities (2001) *Visualising Inclusion*. Tralee: Kerry Network of People with Disabilities.

King, D. and Hansen, R. (1999) 'Experts at work: state autonomy, Social learning and eugenic sterilization in 1930s Britain', *British Journal of Political Science* 29 (3): 77–114.

Kirk, S., Gallagher, J. and Anastasiou, N. (1997) *Educating Exceptional Children* (8th edition). Boston: Houghton Mifflin.

Kitchin, R., Shirlow, P. and Shuttleworth, I. (1998) 'On the margins: disabled people's experience of employment in Donegal, West Ireland', *Disability and Society* 13 (5): 785–806.

Kloeppel, D. and Hollins, S. (1989) 'Double handicap: Mental retardation and death in the family', *Death Studies*, 13: 31–8.

Koop, C. E. (1999) 'The top ten issues in health care today', in Grossman, D. C. and Valtin, H. (eds), *Great Issues for Medicine in the Twenty-first Century*, New York: Annals of the New York Academy of Sciences (882): 137–41.

Koornneef, E. (2000) 'Retirement in Menni services: From project to programme' *Frontline* 43: 18.

Kwiotek, R. (1999) 'The Need for a Disability Equality Model: A New Critical Theoretical Approach to Disability' Unpublished thesis, Master of Equality Studies, National University of Ireland, Dublin.

Lambert, J. (1994) *Solidarity and Survival: A Vision for Europe*. Aldershot: Avebury.

Lane, H. (1993) *The Mask of Benevolence: Disabling the Deaf Community*. New York: Vintage Books.

La Plante, M. P., Carlson, D., Kaye, H. S. and Bradshaw, J .E. (1996) 'Families with disabilities in the United States', *Disability Statistics Report* (8). Washington DC: US Department of Education.

Laughlin, C. and Cotten, P. D. (1994). 'Efficacy of a pre-retirement planning intervention for aging individuals with mental retardation', *Journal of Intellectual Disability Research* 38: 317–28.

Linehan, T. P. (1991) 'History and Development of Irish Population Censuses', *Journal of the Statistical and Social Inquiry Society of Ireland*, XXVI (iv): 91–120.

Lister, R. (1997) *Citizenship: Feminist Perspectives*. Houndsmills: Macmillan.

Lonsdale, S. (1990) *Women and Disability*. London: Macmillan.

Loprest, P., Rupp, K., and Sandell, S. H. (1995) 'Gender, disabilities, and employment in the health and retirement study', *Journal of Human Resources* 30 (S293–S318): Supplement.

Ludlow, B. L. (1999) 'Life after loss: Legal, ethical and practical issues', in Herr, S. and Weber, G. (eds) *Ageing, Rights and Quality of Life: Prospects for Older People with Developmental Disabilities*. Baltimore: Paul H. Brooks, pp. 189–222.

Lundstrom, F. *et al.* (2000) 'The changing face of disability legislation, policy and practice in Ireland', *European Journal of Social Security* 2 (4): 379–97.

Lunsky, Y. and Havercamp, S. (2002) 'Women's mental health', in Walsh, P. N. and Heller, T. (eds) *Health of Women with Intellectual Disabilities*. Oxford: Blackwell, pp. 59–75.

Lunt, I. and Evans, J. (1994) 'Dilemmas in special education: Some effects of local management of schools', in S. Riddell and S. Brown (eds), *Special Educational Needs Policy in the 1990s: Warnock in the Market Place*. London: Routledge.

Lynch, K. and McLaughlin, E. (1995) 'Caring labour and love labour', in P. Clancy *et al.* (eds), *Irish Society: Sociological Perspectives*. Dublin: Institute of Public Administration.

Lynch, P. (1995) 'Integration in Ireland: Policy and practice', in O'Hanlon, C. (ed.) *Inclusive Education in Europe*. London: David Fulton, pp. 61–74.

Mabbett, D. and Bolderson, H. (2001) 'A significant step forward? EU social policy and the development of a rights-based strategy for disabled people', Paper given at the Social Policy Conference, Belfast 24–26 July.

MacGreil, M. (1996) *Prejudice in Ireland Revisited*. Maynooth: Survey and Research Unit, Department of Social Studies, St Patrick's College.

Marshall, T. H. (1952) *Citizenship and Social Class*, Cambridge: Cambridge University Press.

Martz, E. (2001) 'Acceptance of imperfection', *Disability Studies Quarterly* 2 (3): 160–5.

McCarthy, M. (2002). 'Sexuality', in Walsh, P. N. and Heller, T. (eds), *Health of Women with Intellectual Disabilities*. Oxford: Blackwell, pp. 90–102.

McCoy, D. and Smith, M. (1992) *The Prevalence of Disability among Adults in Northern Ireland*. Belfast: PPRU.

McDonagh, R. (2002) 'The web of self-identity: Racism, sexism and disablism' in Lentin, R. and McVeigh, R. (eds), *Racism and Anti-Racism in Ireland*. Belfast: Beyond the Pale, pp. 129–35.

McDonnell, P. (1992) 'Vested interests in the development of special education in Ireland', *Reach* 5 (2): 97–106.

McDonnell, P. (1993) 'Access and equal opportunity for the Irish deaf community', *Proceedings of the Second Congress of the Irish Deaf Society: Understanding Human Rights of Irish Deaf People*. Dublin: Irish Deaf Society, pp. 23–5.

McDonnell, P. (1997) 'Access to further education and training and the role of Irish sign language' *Proceedings of the Third Congress of the Irish Deaf Society: Deaf Access—Towards the Year 2000*, Dublin: Irish Deaf Society, pp. 15–18.

McDonnell, P. (2000) 'Integration in education in Ireland: Rhetoric and reality', in Armstrong, F., Armstrong, D. and Barton, L. (eds), *Inclusive Education: Policy, Contexts and Comparative Perspectives.* London: David Fulton, pp. 12–26.

McDonnell, P. (2001) 'Deep structures in deaf education: Implications for policy', in Leeson, L. (ed.), *Looking Forward: European Union of the Deaf in the Third Millennium: The Deaf Citizen in the 21st Century.* Coleford, Glos: Forest Books.

McDonnell, P. (forthcoming) 'Developments in special education in Ireland', *International Journal of Inclusive Education*

McGee, P. (1990) 'Special education in Ireland', *European Journal of Special Needs Education* 5 (1): 48–63.

McGlone, F. (1992) *Disability and Dependency in Old Age: A Demographic and Social Audit.* Dublin: Family Policy Studies Centre/Help the Aged.

McPherson, C. (1991) 'Violence as it affects disabled women: A view from Canada', in Boylan, E. (ed.), *Women and Disability.* London: Zed Books, pp. 54–5.

Meijer, C., Pijl, S. and Hegarty, S. (eds) (1994) *New Perspectives in Special Education: A Six Country Study of Integration.* London: Routledge.

Miltiades, H., and Pruchno, R. (2001) 'Mothers of adults with developmental disability: Change over time', *American Journal on Mental Retardation* 106 (6): 548-61.

Mittler, P., Brouillette, R. and Harris, D. (eds) (1993) *Special Needs Education.* London: Kogan Page.

Moore, M., Beazley, S. and Maelzer, J. (1998) *Researching Disability Issues.* Buckingham: Open University Press.

Moore, P. (1990) *Rebel on Wheels: A Biography of Liam Maguire.* Dublin: Poolbeg

Mordal, K. and Strømstad, M. (1998) 'Norway: Adapted education for all?', in Booth, T. and Ainscow, M. (eds) (1998*) From Them to Us: An International Study of Inclusion in Education.* London: Routledge, pp. 101–17.

Morris, J. (1991) *Pride Against Prejudice.* London: Women's Press.

Morris, J. (1993) *Independent Living or Community Care.* York: Joseph Rowntree Foundation.

Mulcahy, D. and O'Sullivan, D. (eds) (1989) *Irish Educational Policy: Process and Substance.* Dublin: Institute of Public Administration.

Mulcahy, M. (1976) *Census of the Mentally Handicapped in the Republic of Ireland 1974: Non-Residential.* Dublin: The Medico-Social Research Board.

Mulcahy, M. and Ennis, B. (1976) *Census of the Mentally Handicapped in the Republic of Ireland 1974: Residential.* Dublin: Medico-Social Research Board.

Mulcahy, M. and Reynolds, A. (1984) *Census of Mental Handicap in the Republic of Ireland 1981.* Dublin: The Medico-Social Research Board.

Mulvany, F. (2000) Annual Report of the National Intellectual Disability Database 1998/1999. Dublin: Health Research Board.

Mulvany, F. (2001) Annual Report of the National Intellectual Disability Database Committee 2000. Dublin: Health Research Board.

National Advisory Committee on Training and Employment (NACTE) Steering Group on Sheltered and Supported Work and Employment (1997) *Employment Challenges for the Millennium,* Dublin: National Rehabilitation Board.

National Consultative Committee on Racism and Interculturalism (2001) *Racism as a Cause of Poverty: A Submission to the Review of the National Anti-Poverty Strategy* (unpublished).

National Council for Curriculum and Assessment (1999) *Special Educational Needs: Curriculum Issues, Discussion Paper.* Dublin: NCCA.

National Council on Ageing and Older People (2001) *Demography – Ageing in Ireland Fact File no. 1.* www.ncaop.ie/FF1demography.pdf.

National Council on Disability (2002) *White Paper: Understanding the Role of an International Convention on the Human Rights of People with Disabilities.* Washington DC: National Council on Disability.

National Disability Authority (2001a) *A Matter of Rights: Strategic Plan 2001–2003.* Dublin: National Disability Authority.

National Disability Authority (2001b) *Submission to County Development Boards.* Dublin: NDA.

National Disability Authority (2001c) *Submission to the Department of Public Enterprise on the Establishment of a new Regulatory Framework for Railway Safety.* Dublin: NDA

National Disability Authority (2001d) *Submission to the Department of Public Enterprise on the Public Consultation Document on the Railway Transport Initiative.* Dublin: NDA.

National Disability Authority (2002a) *Irish National Disability Authority IT Accessibility Guidelines.* Dublin: National Disability Authority. www.accessit.nda.ie

National Disability Authority (2002b) *Submission to the Department of Environment and Local Government on Proposal for Qualitative Improvements in Taxi Services and the Future Regulation of those Services.* Dublin: NDA.

National Disability Authority (2002c) *Proposals for Core Elements of Disability Legislation Paper for Consultation.* Unpublished.

National Disability Authority. (2002d) *Report on Disability Research in Ireland, 1996–2001.* Dublin: NDA.

National Economic and Social Council (1999) *Opportunities, Challenges and Capacities for Choice,* Report no. 105. Dublin: National Economic and Social Council.

National Economic and Social Council (2002) *An Investment in Quality: Services, Inclusion and Enterprise,* Report No. 110. Dublin: National Economic and Social Council.

National Economic and Social Forum (2002) *A Strategic Policy Framework for Equality Issues: Forum Report No. 23.* Dublin: Stationery Office.

National Pensions Board (1998) *Report on the Extension of Social Insurance to the Self-Employed.* Dublin: Stationery Office.

National Radio Cabs (2002). *Submission to the Department of the Environment and Local Government on Qualitative Improvements in Taxi Services and Future Regulation.* Dublin: National Radio Cabs.

National Rehabilitation Board (1992) *Report: The Journal of the National Rehabilitation Board: 25th Anniversary.* Dublin: National Rehabilitation Board.

National Rehabilitation Board (1994) *Equal Status: Submission to the Commission on the Status of People with Disabilities.* Dublin: NRB.

National Rehabilitation Board (1998) *Buildings for Everyone: Access and Use for All Citizens.* Dublin: NRB.

Neufeldt, A. H. and Albright, A. (1998) *Disability and Self-Directed Employment.* Ontario: Caftus University Publications.

Neufeldt, A. H. and Mathieson, R. (1996) 'Enforced dimensions of discrimination against disabled people', *Health and Human Rights* 1: 174–89.

New TSN Unit (2001) *New TSN: Making it Work*. Belfast: Office of the First Minister and Deputy First Minister (OFMDFM).

Nic Ghiolla Phádraig, M. (1995) 'The power of the Catholic Church in the Republic of Ireland', in Clancy, P. *et al.* (eds), *Irish Society: Sociological Perspectives*. Dublin: Institute of Public Administration.

Nolan, A. (2002) *Making the Case for Direct Payments*. Bray: Bray Partnership.

Nolan, B. *et al.* (2002) *Monitoring Poverty Trends in Ireland: Results from the 2000 Living in Ireland Survey*. Dublin: ESRI.

Norden, M. (1994) *The Cinema Of Isolation: A History of Physical Disability in the Movies*, New Brunswick, NJ: Rutgers University Press

Northern Ireland Executive (2001) *Programme for Government: Making a Difference 2002–2005*. Belfast: Office of the First Minister and Deputy First Minister (OFMDFM).

O'Brien, V. and Richardson, V. (1999) *Towards a Standardised Framework for Inter-County Adoption Assessment Procedures: A Study of Assessment Procedures in Inter-Country Adoption*. Dublin: Stationery Office.

O'Buachalla, S. (1988) *Education Policy in Twentieth Century Ireland*. Dublin: Wolfhound Press.

O'Connell, D. (2000) 'Equality legislation for people with disabilities: The broader regulatory context', *Proceedings of the Part M Regulations Seminar*. Dublin: Royal Institute of Architects in Ireland, 7 November 2000.

O'Connor, P. (1998) *Emerging Voices: Women in Contemporary Irish Society*. Dublin: Institute of Public Administration.

O'Donevan, D. (2002) *Statement from the Irish Delegation,* Second World Assembly on Ageing UN Programme on Ageing, New York: United Nations Secretariat.

O'Donoghue *v* Minister for Health (1993) High Court, 27 May.

OECD (1994) *The Integration of Disabled Children into Mainstream Education: Ambitions, Theories and Practices*. Paris: OECD.

OECD (1995) *Integrating Students with Special Needs into Mainstream Schools*. Paris: OECD.

OECD (1997a) *Implementing Inclusive Education*. Paris: OECD.

OECD (1997b) *Post Compulsory Education for Disabled People*. Paris: OECD.

OECD (1999) *Inclusive Education at Work: Students with Disabilities in Mainstream Schools*. Paris: OECD.

OECD (2000) *Special Needs Education: Statistics and Indicators*. Paris: OECD.

O'Farrell, F. (2000) *Citizenship and Public Service: Voluntary and Statutory Relationships in Irish Healthcare*. Dublin: The Adelaide Hospital Society.

Office of Director of Equality Investigations (2002) Cases DEC–E2002–004, DEC–E2002–001, DEC–2001–034. Dublin.

Office of the Director of Equality Investigations, Ireland (1998) *Employment Equality Act.* Dublin: Office of the Director of Equality Investigations.

Office of the Director of Equality Investigations, Ireland (2000) *Equal Status Act.* Dublin: Office of the Director of Equality Investigations.

Office of the High Commissioner for Human Rights and the International Centre of the ILO (1988) *Basic Human Rights Instruments,* Third Edition. Geneva.

O'Hanlon, C. (1994) 'SERC: An outsider's view', in Spelman, B. and Griffin, S. (eds), *Special Educational Needs—Issues for the White Paper*. Dublin: Education Department, University College Dublin and The Educational Studies Association of Ireland.

O'Hanlon, C. (ed.) (1995) *Inclusive Education in Europe.* London: David Fulton.

Oliver, M. (1990) *The Politics of Disablement.* London: Macmillan.

Oliver, M. (1992) 'Changing the social relations of research production?', *Disability, Handicap and Society* 7 (2): 101–14.

Oliver, M. (1993) 'Re-defining disability: a challenge to research', in Swain, J., Finklestein, V., French, S. and Oliver, M. (eds) (1993) *Disabling Barriers: Enabling Environment.* London: Sage, pp. 61–8.

Oliver, M. (1996) *Understanding Disability: From Theory to Practice.* London: Macmillan.

Oliver, M. (2002) 'Emancipatory Methodologies in disability research: a methodology for social transformation', Paper given at National Disability Authority Conference, Dublin, 3 December

Oliver, M. and Barnes, C. (1993) 'Discrimination, disability and welfare: From needs to rights', in Swain, J., Finkelstein, V., French, S. and Oliver, M. (eds), *Disabling Barriers: Enabling Environments.* London: Sage, pp. 267–77.

Oliver, M. and Sapey, B. (1999) *Social Work with Disabled People.* London: Macmillan.

O'Shea, E. (2000) *The Cost of Caring for People with Dementia and Related Cognitive Impairments.* Dublin: National Council on Ageing and Older People.

Parilla, A. (1999) 'Spain: Responses to Inclusion in Autonomous Regions', in Daniels, H. and Garner, P. (EDS), *Inclusive Education.* London: Kogan Page, pp. 107–14.

Parish, S. L. (2001) 'Parenting', in Walsh, P. N. and Heller, T. (eds) *Health of Women with Intellectual Disabilities.* Oxford: Blackwell, pp. 103–20.

Partnership 2000 (1996) Dublin: Stationery Office.

PDFORRA (1998) *Hearing Damage to Members of the Defence Forces,* Submission to the Public Accounts Committee, Dublin: PDFORRA.

Persson, B. (1998) 'Who needs special education?', *International Journal of Educational Research* 29: 107–17.

Persson, B. (2000) 'Special education in today's Sweden: A struggle between the Swedish model and the market', in Armstrong, F., Armstrong, D. and Barton, L. (eds), *Inclusive Education: Policy, Contexts and Comparative Perspectives.* London: David Fulton, pp. 117–32.

Phtiaka, H. (1997) *Special Kids for Special Treatment? or How Special Do You Need to Be to Find Yourself in a Special School?* London: Falmer Press.

Pierce, M. (forthcoming) *Issues of Multiple Identities for Black and Ethnic Minority People with Disabilities and Their Implications for Service Provision and Employment Strategies.* Dublin: Equality Authority.

Pijl, S. and Meijer, C. (1999) 'The Netherlands: Supporting integration by re-directing cash flows', in Daniels, H. and Garner, P. (eds), *Inclusive Education.* London: Kogan Page, pp. 82–91.

Pillinger, J. (2002) *Disability and Quality of Services: Irish and European Perspectives.* Policy Institute Working Paper PIWP04. Dublin: Policy Institute.

Porrell, F. W. and Miltiades, H. B. (2002) 'Regional differences in functional status among the aged', *Social Science and Medicine* 54 (8): 1181–98.

Programme for Prosperity and Fairness (2000) Dublin: Stationery Office.

Quin, S. (1999) 'Improving health care: Health policy in Ireland', in Quin, S., Kennedy, P., O'Donnell, A. and Kiely, G. (eds), *Contemporary Irish Social Policy.* Dublin: University College Dublin Press, pp. 27–48.

Quin, S. and B. Redmond (1999) 'Moving from needs to rights: Social policy for people with disability in Ireland', in Quin, S., Kennedy, P., O'Donnell, A. and Kiely, G. (eds), *Contemporary Irish Social Policy*. Dublin: University College Dublin Press, pp. 147–69.

Quinn, G. (1999) 'The human rights of people with disabilities under EU law', in Alston, P., Bustelo, M. R. and Heenan, J. (eds), *The EU and Human Rights*. Oxford: Oxford University Press.

Race, D. (1995) 'Historical development of service provision', in Malin, N. (Ed.) *Services for People with Learning Disabilities*. London and New York: Routledge, pp. 46–78.

Radio Telefís Éireann (RTÉ) (1999) Television report of 7 December 1999.

Raftery, M and O'Sullivan, E. (1999) *Suffer the Little Children: The Inside Story of Ireland's Industrial Schools*. Dublin: New Island.

Ralaheen Ltd. and Forum for People with Disabilities (2001) *A Reflection Document on the Cost of Disability Payment*. Dublin: Forum for People with Disabilities.

Randoll, D. (1995) 'A view of integration in Germany', in O' Hanlon, C. (ed.), *Inclusive Education in Europe*. London: David Fulton, pp. 39–48.

Redmond, B. (1996) *Listening to Parents*. Dublin: Family Studies Centre, University College Dublin.

Reinach, E. (ed) (1987) *Normalisation*. Aberdeen: Department of Social Work, University of Aberdeen.

Report of the Commission on the Status of People with Disabilities (1996) *A Strategy for Equality*. Dublin: Stationery Office.

Review Group on Health and Personal Social Services for People with Physical and Sensory Disabilities (1996) *Towards an Independent Future*, Dublin: Stationery Office.

Review Group on Mental Handicap Services (1991) *Needs and Abilities: A Policy for the Intellectually Doisabled*. Dublin: Stationery Office.

Riddell, S. (2000) 'Inclusion and choice: Mutually exclusive principles in special educational needs?', in Armstrong, F., Armstrong, D. and Barton, L. (eds), *Inclusive Education: Policy, Contexts and Comparative Perspectives*. London: David Fulton, pp. 99–116.

Rioux, M. and Bach, M. (eds) (1994) *Disability is Not Measles: New Research Paradigms in Disability*. Ontario: Roeher Institute.

Rispens, J. (1994) 'Rethinking integration: what can we learn from the past?' in Meijer, C., Pijl, S. and Hegarty, S. (eds), *New Perspectives in Special Education: A Six Country Study of Integration*. London: Routledge, pp. 133–40.

Roberts, K. (2000) 'Lost in the system? Disabled refugees and asylum seekers in Britain'. *Disability and Society*, 15 (6): 943–8.

Robine, J-M. (1999) 'Longevity and health: Relationship and changes over time', Plenary lecture at the British Society for Population Studies Conference, Dublin, 6–8 September 1999.

Robins, J. (1986) *Fools and Mad: A History of the Insane in Ireland*. Dublin: Institute of Public Administration.

Rock, P. J. (1996) 'Eugenics and euthanasia: A cause for concern for disabled people, particularly disabled women', *Disability and Society* 11 (1): 121–7.

Rose, N. (1996) *Inventing Our Selves: Psychology, Power and Personhood*. Cambridge: Cambridge University Press.

Ryan, A. (1999) *Walls of Silence: Ireland's policy Towards People with a Mental Disability* Callan, County Kilkenny: Red Lion Press

Samoradov, A. (1996) *Indicators of Cost-effectiveness of Policy Options for Workers with Disabilities*, Labour Market Papers No. 11. Geneva: International Labour Office.

Santrock, J., (1995) *Life-Span Development*. Iowa, USA: WC Brown.

Schalock, R. and Verdugo, M-A. (2002) *Handbook on Quality of Life for Human Service Practitioners*. Washington DC: American Association on Mental Retardation.

Schrojenstein Lantman-de Valk, H. M. J. van, Schupf, N. and Patja K. (2001) 'Reproductive and physical health', in Walsh, P. N. and Heller, T. (eds) *Health of Women with Intellectual Disabilities*. Oxford: Blackwell, pp. 22–36.

Scrutton, S. (1990) 'The foundation of age discrimination', in McEwen, E. (ed.), *The Unrecognised Discrimination*. UK: Age Concern, pp. 12–27. Place?

Scull, A. (1993) *The Most Solitary of Afflictions: Madness and Society in Britain 1700–1900*. New Haven, CT: Yale University Press.

Seanad Éireann Debates (1998), Vol. 154, 26 February. Dublin: Stationery Office.

Seltzer, M. M., Krauss, M. W., Hong, J. and Orsmond, G. I. (2001) 'Continuity or discontinuity of family involvement following residential transitions of adults who have mental retardation', *Mental Retardation* 39 (3): 191–4.

Shah, S. and Priestley, M. (2001) *Better Services, Better Health: The Healthcare Experiences of Black and Minority Ethnic Disabled People*. Leeds: Leeds Involvement Project.

Shakespeare, T. (1996a) 'Disability, identity, difference', in Barnes, C. and Mercer, G. (eds), *Exploring the Divide: Illness and Disability*. Leeds: Disability Press, pp. 94–113.

Shakespeare, T. (1996b), 'Power and prejudice: Issues of gender, sexuality and disability' in Barton, L. (ed), *Disability and Society: Emerging Issues and Insights*. London: Longman, pp. 191–214.

Shakespeare, T. (1998) 'Choices and rights: eugenics, genetics and disability equality', *Disability and Society* 13 (5): 665–81.

Sinnott *v* Minister for Education and Science (2001) Supreme Court, 12 July.

Skrtic, T. (ed.) (1995) *Disability and Democracy: Reconstructing (Special) Education for Postmodernity*. New York: Teachers College Press.

Smith, M., Robinson, P. and Duffy, B. (1992) *The Prevalence of Disability Among Children in Northern Ireland*. Belfast: Policy Planning and Research Unit (PPRU).

Social Deprivation Research Group (2001) *Measure of Deprivation in Northern Ireland*. Belfast: Northern Ireland Statistics and Research Agency (NISRA).

South West Mayo Development Company (1999) *Going the Extra Mile: A Community Action Plan for the Provision of Accessible Transport in County Mayo*. Mayo: SWMDC

Southwest Dublin Accessible Transport Steering Committee (2001) *Accessible Transport Service for People with Disabilities in Southwest Dublin: A Feasibility Study*. Dublin: SDATSC

(SPIRASI) Spiritan Asylum Services Initiative (2001) *Submission to the Working Group on NAPS and Health*.

St Michael's House (2002) *Submission to the Working Group on NAPS and Health* (unpublished).

Stienstra, D. (2002) *Intersections: Disability and Race/Ethnicity/Heritage/Language/ Religion*, [http://www.disabiltiy studies.ca/intersections.htm] [Accessed 10/06/02].

Stoker, C. (1863) 'On the necessity of a state provision for the education of the deaf and dumb of Ireland', *Journal of the Statistical and Social Inquiry Society of Ireland* December: 456–60.

Stuart, O. (1993) 'Double oppression: an appropriate starting point?', in Swain, J., Finkelstein, V., French, S. and Oliver, M. (eds.) *Disabling Barriers: Enabling Environments*. London: Sage, pp. 93–100.

Supreme Court (1997) *Article 26 and the Employment Equality Bill, 1996*, Case No. 118/97.

Supreme Court (2001a) *Sinnott* v. *Minister for Education*, Case No. 326 & 327/00.

Supreme Court (2001b) *T.D.* v *Minister for Education*, Case No. 203/00.

Sustaining Progress: Social Partnership Agreement 2003–2005 (2003) Dublin: Stationery Office.

Sutton, E., Sterns, H. L. and Schwartz-Park, L.S.(1993) 'Realities of retirement planning', in Sutton, E., Factor, A. R., Hawkins, B. A., Heller, T. and Seltzer, G. B., *Older Adults with Developmental Disabilities*. Baltimore: Paul H. Brookes, pp. 95–106.

Swain, J., Finkelstein, V., French, S. and Oliver, M. (eds) (1993) *Disabling Barriers: Enabling Environments*. London: Sage.

Swann, W. (1985) 'Is the integration of children with special educational needs happening?' *Oxford Review of Education* 11 (1): 3–18.

Tetler, S. (1995) 'Danish efforts in integration', in O'Hanlon, C. (ed.), *Inclusive Education in Europe*. London: David Fulton, pp. 9–23.

Thorpe, L., Davidson, P. and Janicki, M. (2001) 'Health ageing: adults with intellectual disabilities: bio-behavioural issues', *Journal of Applied Research in Intellectual Disabilities* 14 (3): 218–28.

Tighe, C. A. (2001) '"Working at disability": A qualitative study of the meaning of health and disability for women with physical impairments', *Disability and Society* 16 (4): 511–29.

Tøssebro, J., Aalto, M. and Brusen, P. (1996) 'Changing ideologies and patterns of services', in Tøssebro, J., Gustavsson, A. and Dyrendahl, G. (eds), *Intellectual Disabilities in the Nordic Welfare States*. Kristiansand: Norwegian Academic Press, pp. 45–66.

Tovey, H. and Share, P. (2000). *A Sociology of Ireland*. Dublin: Gill & Macmillan.

Traxler, A. J. (1980) *Let's Get Gerontologized: Developing a Sensitivity to Ageing: The Multi-purpose Senior Centre Concept: A Training Manual for Practitioners Working with the Ageing*. Springfield, Ill: Department of Ageing.

Troyna, B. and Vincent, C. (1996) 'The ideology of expertism: The framing of special education and racial equality policies in the local state', in Christensen, C. and Rizvi, F. (eds), *Disability and the Dilemmas of Education and Justice*. Buckingham: Open University Press, pp. 131–44.

Trupin, L., Rice, D. and Max, W. (1995) *Medical expenditures for people with disabilities in the US, 1987. Disability Statistics Report*, (5). Washington, DC: US Department of Education.

Tubridy, J. (1996) *Pegged Down: Experiences of People with Disabilities in Ireland with Significant Physical Disabilities*. Dublin: Institute of Public Administration.

UK Action Plan on Social Inclusion 2001–2003, www.scotland.gov.uk/library3/society/uk.

United Nations (1994) *Standard Rules for the Equalisation of Opportunities for Persons with Disabilities*. New York: United Nations.

United Nations (2002a) *Human Rights and Disability: The Current Use and Future Potential of United Nations Human Rights Instruments in the Context of Disability*. New York and Geneva: United Nations.

United Nations (2002b) Population Division Department of Economic and Social Affairs, *Figures on Population Ageing*. New York: United Nations.

United Nations (2002c) *Report of the Ad Hoc Committee on a Comprehensive and Integral International Convention on the Protection and Promotion of the Rights and Dignity of Persons with Disabilities, A/57/357*. New York: United Nations.

United Nations Development Programme (2000) *Human Development Report 2000: Human Rights and Human Development*. New York and Oxford: Oxford University Press.

United Nations General Assembly (1992) *Principles for Older Persons* (adopted on 16 December 1991) (Resolution NO. 46/91). New York: United Nations.

United Nations High Commissioner for Refugees (1999) 'Doubly disadvantaged and dispossessed' in Reid, G. (ed.), *The World Disability Report: Disability '99*, pp. 100–3. Geneva: International Disability Federation and London: The Winchester Group.

United Nations High Commissioner for Refugees (2002) *UNHCR Resettlement Handbook*. Geneva: UNHCR. [http://www.unhcr.ch]

US Congress (1990) *The Americans with Disabilities Act*, 42.U.S.C.§ 12101 and 47 U.S.C.§§ 225 and 611.

Varela, R. (1983) 'Changing social attitudes and legislation regarding disability', in Crewe, N. M. and Zola, I. K. (eds), *Independent Living for Physically Disabled People*. San Francisco: Josey-Bass, pp. 28–49.

Vernon, A. (1998) 'Multiple oppression and the disabled people's movement' in Shakespeare, T. (ed.), *The Disability Reader: Social Science Perspectives*. London: Cassell, pp. 201–10.

Vlachou, A. (1997) *Struggles for Inclusive Education: An Ethnographic Study*. Buckingham: Open University Press.

Vlachou-Balafouti, A. and Zoniou-Sideris, A. (2000) 'Greek policy practices in the area of special/inclusive education', in Armstrong, F., Armstrong, D. and Barton, L. (eds), *Inclusive Education: Policy, Contexts and Comparative Perspectives*. London: David Fulton, pp. 27–41.

Waddington, L. and Bell, M. (2001) 'More equal than others: distinguishing European Union equality directives', *Common Market Law Review* 38: 587–611.

Walker, A., Walker, C. and Gosling, V. (1999) 'Quality of life as a matter of human rights', in Herr, S. and Weber, G. (eds), *Ageing, Rights and Quality of Life: Prospects for Older People with Developmental Disabilities*. Baltimore, Paul H. Brooks, pp. 109–32.

Walmsley, J. (1996) 'Doing what mum wants me to do: looking at family relationships from the point of view of adults with intellectual disabilities', *Journal of Applied Research in Intellectual Disability* 9 (4): 324–41.

Walsh, P. N. (2002) 'Ageing and mental retardation', *Current Opinion in Psychiatry* 15 (5): 509–14.

Walsh, P. N. (2002) 'Women's health: a contextual approach', in Walsh, P. N. and Heller, T. (eds), *Health of Women with Intellectual Disabilities*. Oxford: Blackwell, pp. 7–21.

Walsh, P. N., Heller, T., Schupf, N. and van Schrojenstein Lantman-de Valk, H. (2000) *Healthy Ageing: Adults with Intellectual Disabilities: Women's Health Issues*. Geneva: World Health Organisation.

Walsh, P. N., Heller, T., Schupf, N. and van Schrojenstein Lantman-de Valk, H. (2001) 'Healthy ageing – adults with intellectual disabilities: women's health and related issues', *Journal of Applied Research in Intellectual Disabilities* 14 (3): 195–217.

Walsh, P. N. and Murphy, G. H. (2002) 'Risk and vulnerability: dilemmas for women', in Walsh, P. N. and Heller, T. (eds), *Health of Women with Intellectual Disabilities*. Oxford: Blackwell, pp. 154–69.

Wehman, P. and Walsh, P. N. (1999) 'Transitions from school to adulthood: a look at the United States and Europe', in Retish, P. and Shunit, R. (eds), *Adults with Disabilities: International Perspectives in the Community*. New Jersey: Lawrence Erlbaum.

Wendell, S. (1996) *The Rejected Body: Feminist Philosophical Reflections on Disability.* London: Routledge.

Western Health Board (2000) *Us Men, Our Health: Men's Health Strategy.* Galway: Western Health Board.

Whyte, C. (1994), 'Disability and poverty: Training and employment policy implications', in Combat Poverty Agency, *Papers from the National Conference: Disability, Exclusion and Poverty – A Policy Conference.* Dublin: Combat Poverty Agency, pp. 111–31

Williams, F. (2000) 'Principles of recognition and respect on welfare' in Lewis, G., Gewirtz, S. and Clarke, J. (eds), *Rethinking Social Policy.* London: Sage.

Winzer, M. (1993) *The History of Special Education: From Isolation to Integration.* Washington DC: Gallaudet University Press.

Winzer, M. A. (1997) 'Disability and society before the eighteenth century: dread and despair', in Davis, L. J. (ed.), *The Disability Studies Reader.* London: Routledge, pp. 75–109.

Wolfensberger, W. (1972) *The Principle of Normalisation in Human Services.* Toronto: National Institute on Mental Retardation.

Woods, M. and Humphries, N. (2001) *Seeking Asylum in Ireland: Statistical Update: Comparative Figures for Asylum Seekers and Refugees in Ireland and Europe in 2000 and 2001,* Dublin: Social Science Research Centre, University College Dublin.

Woods, R. (2002) *Building Partnerships: Supplementary Report and Stakeholder Analysis,* prepared for the Disability Rights Commission, Manchester.

Working Group on the Implementation of the Health Strategy in Relation to Persons with a Mental Handicap, Ireland (1997) *Enhancing the Partnership.* Dublin: Department of Health.

World Health Organisation (1997) 'Gender as determinant of health', in: *The World Health Report 1997.* Geneva: World Health Organisation, p. 83

World Health Organisation (2000a) *World Health Report 2000,* Geneva: World Health Organisation.

World Health Organisation (2000b) *Ageing and Intellectual Disabilities: Improving Longevity and Promoting Health Ageing: Summative Report.* Geneva: World Health Organisation.

World Health Organisation (2000c) *Healthy Ageing: Adults with Intellectual Disabilities.* http://www.who.int/mental_health and http:/www.iassid.org

World Health Organisation (2001a) *ICF – International Classification of Functioning, Disability and Health.* Geneva: World Health Organisation.

World Health Organisation (2001b) *Gender and Women's Mental Health: Gender Disparities and Mental Health.* http://www.who.int/mental

World Health Organisation (2001c) *The World Health Report 2001: Mental Health.* Geneva: World Health Organisation.

World Wide Web Consortium Web Accessibility Initiative Web Content Accessibility Guidelines version 1.0. http://www.w3.org/TR/WCAG10

Yeates, P. (2001) 'The disabled jobless and the receipt of Incapacity Benefit in Northern Ireland', in *Joblessness and Poverty.* Belfast: Department for Social Development

Young, I. (1990) *Justice and the Politics of Difference.* New Jersey: Princeton University Press.

Zappone, K. (2001) *Charting the Equality Agenda: A Coherent Framework for Equality Strategies in Ireland North and South.* Dublin: Equality Authority, and Belfast: Equality Commission for Northern Ireland.

Zappone, K. (ed.) (forthcoming) *Rethinking Identity: Implications for Equality and Human Rights Strategies*. Dublin: Joint Equality and Human Rights Forum.

Zarb, G. and Maher, L. (1997) *The Financial Circumstances of Disabled People in Northern Ireland*. Belfast: Northern Ireland Statistics and Research Agency (NISRA).

Zarb, G. and Oliver, M. (1993) *Ageing with a Disability: What do they Expect after All These Years*. London: University of Greenwich.

Index

abortion, 96–7
abuse, 94–5, 106, 172
accessibility, 157
access,
    to built environment, 5, 14, 17, 21, 24,
        26–7, 68, 69, 70, 72–3, 74, 79–80,
        81, 119, 185
    to employment, 14, 65–6
    environmental, 68, 69, 70, 74–5, 79, 80,
        81
    and independent living, 68, 71–2
    to IT, 17–19, 185
    and the law, 14, 75–6
    linguistic, 38
    to media, 174
    public services, 21, 73–4, 146
    services, 98
    to transport, 14, 17, 27, 68, 80, 145, 146,
        148, 185
    wheelchair, 27, 76, 85, 149
    and UN Standard Rules, 71
    universal, 17, 26, 27, 74, 77 (*see also*
        universal design)
accommodation, 129, 135–6, 137
accountability, 40
advocacy, 136, 154, 179, 181
    discourse of, 78
    independent, 181
    and older people, 136
    services, 22, 154, 179
age,
    differences, 86, 99
    and income, 156
    old, 111
    segregation, 100
    and severity of disability, 165–6
ageing, 112
    and disability, 6–7, 129–38
    and ethnicity, 127
    and gender, 107–8

and health, 104–5, 110, 133–4
    healthy, 7, 110, 133–6
    and inclusion, 136
    population, 6, 107–8, 129, 130–2, 137, 138
ageism, 129, 132–2
Alzheimer's disease, 7
Americans with Disabilities Act (1990),
        54–5, 70–1, 178, 197–8
anti-discrimination, 24, 163–5, 169
    legislation, 10, 26, 80
assistive technology, 68
assumptions,
    medical, 83
    philosophical, 83
    moral, 83
    underlying education system, 35, 37, 39
asylum seekers, 7, 115, 116, 122, 123, 128
    with disabilities, 116, 119, 122, 126, 127,
attitudes to disability
    discriminatory, 6, 56, 80, 140, 147, 149,
        157, 175
    professionals and, 85, 96
Australia, 119, 139, 142
autonomy, 135, 173

Barnes, 84, 85, 133
barrier free design (*see* universal design)
Begum, 93, 114
Belfast Agreement, 164, 170, 176
belonging, 129, 134–6
built environment,
    access to, 5–6, 17, 21, 24, 26–7, 68, 69,
        70, 72–3, 79–80, 81, 119, 185
    Barcelona Declaration, 27, 74–5
    Building Regulations, 6, 27, 72–3, 76
BUPA, 89

Canada, 119, 156
capacity to work, 57, 59, 60, 66, 67, 161

carers, 157
  Carer's Allowance, 60
  Carer's Benefits, 61
  costs to, 157
  Domiciliary Care Allowance, 61
  payments to, 60–1
Catholic Church, 142–3
Catholicism, 142–143, 175
Census of Mentally Handicapped, 13, 130
Census of Population, 11, 12, 55, 110, 124
Central Statistics Office, 11, 12, 46, 129, 140
Centre for Deaf Studies, 43
Centres for Independent Living, 78–9, 177
charitable model of disability, 6, 69–70, 171, 173, 177
children with disabilities,
  abuse of, 171–2
  asylum seeker and refugee, 119, 126
  deaf children, 120
  and equal opportunities, 194
  ethnic minority, 116, 119, 120, 126, 127
  National Children's Strategy, 108–9
  and social security, 162, 168
citizenship, 2, 3, 45, 139, 140, 154
Comhairle, 16, 22, 110
Commission on Social Welfare, 62, 63–4
Commission on the Status of People with Disabilities,
  and built environment, 5, 72, 74, 76, 145
  costs of disability, 63–4
  disability legislation, 22, 71, 180
  and education, 28, 36, 40, 43
  and employment, 50
  establishment of, 15
  and health, 86–7, 97
  implementation of report of, 172
  and inclusion model, 140, 154, 177, 178
  mainstreaming approach, 14
  and NDA, 15, 16, 110
  and neglect of people with disabilities, 2
  older people, 136
  and prevalence of disability, 101
  and service provision, 144
  and social exclusion, 28, 72
  and social security, 62, 63–4, 65
  and transport, 145, 146, 152

Travellers with disabilities, 121 70, 71, 72, 74, 76
communication, 22, 38, 95–6, 118, 119, 127,
community,
  based services, 92–3
  involvement, 134
  living, 137
  rating, 89
costs of disability, 5, 53, 61, 63–4, 156–7, 161–2, 168
  adaptation costs, 51, 74
Council of Europe, 24
cross-national comparisons, 32

Daly, Mary, 22
data deficiencies, 12, 62, 86, 87, 104, 115–16, 124
deaf culture, 4, 43, 56, 177
deafness,
  cochlear implants, 24
  communication with, 22, 56
  and education, 4, 28, 38
  and ethnicity, 120
  historical understanding of, 83–4
  industrial injury, 52–3
  sign language, 22, 38
  videophone, 22
  workplace adjustment, 56
decision making, 68, 81, 91, 126
defence forces, 52–53
definitions (of disability), 28, 38–9, 52, 102, 165, 172
de-institutionalisation, 33, 46, 103, 177
demography, 129–32, 138
Denmark, 34
dependency, 91, 95, 96, 168
developing countries, 155–6
difference, 86
Disabled Peoples' International, 70, 77, 178
Disability Federation of Ireland, 149, 150, 151
disability benefits,
  Blind Pension, 58–59
  Disability Allowance, 51, 57, 58, 59, 62, 63, 65, 110
  Disabled Person's Maintenance Allowance, 58, 65
  Disablement Benefit, 58, 59, 60, 62

disability benefits, *cont*
    Exceptional Needs Payments, 63
    Injury Benefit, 60
    Invalidity Pension, 57, 59–60, 62, 63, 67
    Mobility Allowance, 63
    Mobility Transport Grant, 63
    in Northern Ireland, 160–162, 166,
        169–170
    (*see also* social security)
disability movement,
    and decision making, 81
    emergence of, 69, 70, 78, 143–4
    and feminist movement, 97
    and independent living, 77
    and rights legislation, 174, 180
    social model of disability, 113, 142
disability proofing, 81
disability rights discourse, 41
disability rights legislation, 75, 169, 174, 179
Disabilities Bill, 10, 14, 21, 22, 110, 180, 199
Disability Discrimination Act (1996) (UK),
    76, 163, 164, 165
disablism, 80, 113–15, 119, 122, 129
discrimination, 22, 28, 41, 42, 113–15, 117,
    132, 140, 157, 158, 176, 195
domestic violence, 94
double discrimination, 7–8, 114, 129, 132–3
Down's Syndrome, 7
Drake, 90, 91, 139, 141, 148, 152
Drugs Payment Scheme, 89 (*see also* social
    security)

eAccess, 17–19, 26
e-design, 18–19
economic underdevelopment, 143
education,
    Back to Education scheme, 66
    and exclusion, 28, 34, 36–8, 39, 41, 43, 44
    in Europe, 32–8
    and legislation, 3, 33, 34, 38–9, 43, 180,
        194–5
    inclusive, 33, 35, 42, 43, 194–5
    and institutionalisation, 29, 33,
    mainstream, 4, 29–35
    and normalisation, 33
    and poverty, 156, 157, 166, 169
    research, 37

    segregated, 28–9, 33–4, 42, 43
    special, 28–32, 33, 34, 35, 36, 37, 41, 42,
        44, 173, 194–5
Education Act (1998), 38–9, 40, 110
education opportunities, 48
educational attainment, 4, 48, 166
educational disadvantage, 4
educational system,
    deep structure, 35–7, 44
    surface structure, 35–8, 44
e-Europe, 18
eligibility, 88–9
employers, 51, 55–6
employment, 139, 140, 143
    disincentives, 66, 161
    and education, 48, 166
    EU policies on, 103–4, 158–9
    gender and, 109
    income from, 48
    and integration, 112
    labour standards, 118
    non–discrimination and, 3, 48, 51–3, 110,
        117, 193–4
    policies and strategies, 24, 45–56, 160–5,
        169
    and poverty, 156, 157, 159
    quotas, 48–50, 52, 54
    rates, 46, 165, 167
    rehabilitative, 51
    segregated, 112
    sheltered, 24, 49, 50, 51
    supports, 66
    supported, 49, 50, 51, 150
    targets, 22, 48–50,
    and vocational training, 48
Employment Equality Act (1998), 51–3, 144
    and access, 75
    and data collection, 12, 110
    and definition of disability, 38, 52
    and discriminatory grounds, 110, 123
    and employment policy, 49
    enactment of, 19
    and enforcement of, 56
    and ILO, 55
    and nominal cost, 20, 52
    and undue hardship, 20
Employment Equality Bill (1996), 20

England, 33
epilepsy, 100 (*see* SQ)
Equal Status Act (2000), 12, 19–21, 26, 38,
    75–6, 110, 123, 144
equality, 14, 25, 26, 27, 41, 87, 139, 154
    racial, 42
    training, 85, 98
Equality Authority, 49, 52, 76, 124, 144
Equality Commission for Northern Ireland,
    164, 165, 169, 170
Equality Tribunal, 20–1, 22, 52, 56, 144
ethnic minorities, 42, 83, 95–6, 113–28
    invisibility of, 7, 121
ethnicity, 86, 95–6
    and discrimination, 8, 113–15
    and diversity, 7, 113–14
    and forms of disability, 119–20
    Ireland, 115–16, 121–4
    European context, 117
    international context, 116–19
Eurolink Age, 134
Europe, 140
    education policy in, 32–5
European Disability Forum, 70
European enlargement, 55
European Social Charter, 24
European Union,
    awareness raising, 25
    disability policy in, 24–5, 158–9
    education policy, 34, 41
    and environmental access, 71, 74–5
    equal opportunities, 25, 158
    gender equality, 99, 104
    and health insurance, 89
    and ICT, 18
    influence of, 175–6, 177, 178
    labour market statistics, 47
    legislation, 3
    mainstreaming, 24–5, 158
    multiple discrimination, 117
    non-discrimination, 25, 54–5, 81, 117, 158
    political ideologies, 140
    and poverty, 157
    rights based model, 103–4, 117, 158, 176,
        198
    training and employment, 24–5, 48,
        54–5, 103–4, 157

European Year of People with
    Disabilities, 25, 114
euthanasia, 101
expertism, 4, 37–8, 39–41, 42, 43, 84,
    177

family
    care, 99, 102, 105–6, 127, 129, 134, 135,
        138, 143
    ties, 134
    costs of providing, 157
FÁS, 16, 49, 50, 51
feminists, 97, 113–14, 143
    disabled, 97, 114
Finkelstein, V., 86
Forum of People with Disabilities, 11,
    78, 154, 177
France, 34, 54
French, 85

gay, lesbian and bisexuals, 113, 175–6
    with disabilities, 123
gender,
    and ageing, 107–8
    bias in education, 42
    and data deficiencies, 104
    and de-institutionalisation, 103
    and disability studies, 102
    and employment opportunities, 104,
        109
    and family care, 105–6
    and health, 99, 104, 107, 109
    and institutionalisation, 100
    and mental illness, 104
    and poverty, 106
    reproduction, 101
    and social model of disability, 86,
        114
genetics, 96–7
Germany, 34, 54, 140, 157
GP services,
    eligibility for, 88–9
    women with disabilities and, 93–4
Greece, 34
Green Paper on Education (1992), 35
Green Paper on Services for Disabled
    People (1984), 14

hard of hearing people (*see* deafness)
health,
    and ageing, 133–4
    education, 134
    impact of gender on, 99
    and poverty, 168
health and safety, 52
health boards, 86, 87, 92, 110
health care,
    and ethnic minorities, 95–6
    and women with disabilities, 93–4, 109
    new developments in, 7, 96–8
health expenditure, 107
health insurance, 89
Health Research Board, 14, 108, 130, 131
health services,
    community-based services, 92–3
    eligibility for, 88–9
    GP services, 88–9, 93–4, 172
    historical overview of, 83–4
    information, 125
    Irish, 86–93
    and language barriers, 95–6
    and new technology, 96
    role of voluntary sector, 90–2
    service agreements, 90, 91–2
heterogeneity, 114, 119, 121
heterosexism, 113, 115
Hong Kong, 156

IT, 17–19, 24, 156, 185
images of disability, 173–5
income maintenance (*see* social security)
independence, 77–8, 87, 96, 133, 134, 138,
    185
independent living, 68, 69–70, 77, 78, 79,
    80, 82, 93, 131, 143
independent living movement, 69, 77–9,
    150
informal care, 105–6
Institute of Design and Disability, 74
institutional disablism, 120
institutional racism, 119, 120, 124
institutionalisation, 29, 45–6, 69, 71, 100,
    172
intellectual disability (*see* learning disability)
interdependence, 80

interest groups, 22
International Classification of Functioning,
    Disability and Health (ICF), 102
International Decade of People with
    Disabilities, 25, 70, 187, 197
International Labour Organisation, 55, 104,
    118, 186
International Year of People with
    Disabilities, 25
Irish Congress of Trade Unions, 50
Irish Deaf Society, 40, 177
Irish National Teachers Organisation, 31, 43
Irish Wheelchair Association, 11, 90, 178
Italy, 34

labelling, 101, 137
    theory, 133
Labour Force Survey, 47, 55, 165
labour market,
    access, 50
    disadvantage, 46
    exclusion, 45
    non-participation in, 46
    participation in, 4, 46–7
    retention, 50
    promotion, 50
    training, 50
    advice, 50
language, 4, 22, 38, 95–6, 127
    (*see also* communication)
learning disability, 15, 78, 88, 99, 104, 105,
    107, 108, 119, 120, 122, 125, 129–30,
    132, 133, 134, 136, 137, 146
legislation, 103
    case law, 20–1, 23, 52, 54, 76
    equality, 123, 140, 179
    and gender equality, 109
    rights-based legislation, 76, 81
life expectancy, 107, 108
lifelong disability, 129, 133, 134
loss, 129, 135

mainstreaming,
    accessible environment and, 81
    approach, 3, 10, 14–17, 26, 71, 185, 179
    in practice, 17–19, 72
    and education, 29–35

employment, 109, 112
  principle of 16, 21, 26
  and EU, 25, 158
  services, 140
means-tests, 57, 58, 59, 60, 64, 66, 67, 88,
  162
media, 173–4
medical card, 88, 89
medical model of disability, 2, 6, 37–41, 43,
  52, 57–8, 76, 78, 84–6, 90, 103, 113,
  171, 172, 177
medicalisation of body, 84
medicalisation of disability, 84, 171, 172, 173
Medico-Social Research Board, 13
medieval society, 84
mental health, 78, 107, 119, 120, 121, 122, 123,
  129, 146
  services, 122
Mental Health Act (2001), 110, 177
mental health database, 14
Mental Health Ireland, 11
Mercer, 133
migrants, 115, 116, 118, 126, 127
mixed economy of welfare, 139–54
Morris, J., 91, 97, 114
multiple deprivation, 168
multiple discrimination, 114, 117, 127
multiple identities, 123–4, 127, 180

National Association of Mentally
  Handicapped in Ireland, 11
National Council for Ageing and Older
  People, 108
National Council for Curriculum and
  Assessment (NCCA), 40
National Disability Authority,
  and access to public services, 73–4
  and approaches to disability, 69, 154
  and attitudes to disability, 175
  and Barcelona Declaration, 27, 74
  and census of people with disabilities, 11
  functions of, 16–17, 21, 111, 144, 153–4
  and national standards, 140, 154
  recommendations for, 15, 16, 110
  and transport, 146, 152
National Economic and Social Council, 23,
  72, 129

National Education and Psychology Service,
  16
National Intellectual Disability Database, 6,
  13, 88, 102, 125, 130, 131–2
National Parents and Siblings Association,
  11
National Physical and Sensory Disability
  Database, 6, 14, 88, 102, 125, 131–2,
  137
National Social Service Board (*see*
  Comhairle)
National Rehabilitation Board, 14–15, 16,
  76, 110, 136
Netherlands, 119
New Targeting Social Need, 5, 159–60, 169
new technology, 96
New Zealand, 119
nominal cost, 19, 20, 26, 51, 52, 75–6
non-cash benefits, 59
normalisation, 33
Nordic countries, 103
Northern Ireland, 155, 160–70
  anti-discrimination measures, 163–5
  education, 166
  employment, 165, 167, 169
  Equality Commission for Northern
    Ireland, 164, 165, 169, 170
  income levels, 167–8
  New Targeting Social Need, 159–60, 169
  prevalence of disability, 164–6
  social inclusion policy, 159–60
  social security, 160–2, 168, 169
  welfare to work, 161–3, 169
Norway, 34
non-governmental organisations, 11, 29

occupational injuries, 52–3, 57–60, 126–7
OECD, 32, 33, 34, 43
Office of the Director of Equality
  Investigations (*see* Equality Tribunal)
older people,
  with disabilities, 107–8, 112, 162
Oliver, M., 2, 69, 70, 82, 84, 85, 113, 114, 133,
  134, 137, 172, 181
organisations of people with disabilities, 7,
  91, 117, 118, 125, 178

partnership, 88, 91, 97, 98, 118, 158–9
Partnership Agreements, 20, 21, 50, 62, 64,
    67, 73, 125, 146, 149
peer support, 68, 78
People with Disabilities in Ireland, 11, 78
personal assistance, 68, 78, 80, 93, 94, 179
personal social services, 83, 86, 87, 90
physical disability, 68, 97, 119, 122, 129, 131,
    132, 133, 134, 146, 149
political ideologies, 140
poor law, 58
positive action, 19, 48, 49, 51
poverty,
    and disability, 5, 12, 61, 62, 66, 155–6
    and education, 156, 157, 166, 169
    and employment, 156, 157, 159, 162–3,
        165, 169, 170
    gender, 106
    and health, 168
    income, 156, 157, 165, 167–8, 169,
    National Anti–Poverty Strategy, 62, 63, 125
    traps, 66
prejudice, 26

Quarterly National Household Survey, 11
Quin, S., 70, 120, 129

racism, 8, 113, 114, 115, 119–20, 122, 132, 176
    institutional, 121
reasonable accommodation, 19, 20, 52, 53,
    56, 75, 179
reasonable adjustment, 163
recognition, principle of, 7, 40, 124, 127, 171
Redmond, B., 70, 120, 135
refugees, 115, 125, 128
    with disabilities, 116, 118–19, 126, 127
rehabilitation, 24, 51, 85, 118, 127, 172, 194
Report of Constitutional Review Group, 22
representation, 36, 40, 136, 178
reproduction, 97, 101
reproductive technology, 97
residential care, 61, 65, 131, 135, 137
respect, principle of, 7, 124, 127
respite care, 93
retirement, 137, 156
right of redress, 22, 26
right to education, 194

right to work, 122–3, 194
rights, 25–6, 35, 42, 86, 87, 97, 118, 116–17,
    136, 154, 175, 177,
    human rights, 182–99
    of civil action, 21
    and gender, 103
    and independent living, 68
    socio–economic, 10, 22–4, 52
rights-based model of disability, 6, 54, 76,
    87, 103, 158, 171, 172, 174, 176, 182–99

segregation, 28–9, 33–4, 42, 43, 45–6, 50, 69,
    71, 80, 171
separation, 100, 112, 137, 140
self-determination, 77, 100, 134, 173
self-help, 78, 122
sensory disability, 68, 88, 119, 122, 130, 136,
    146, 149
service
    agreements, 90, 91-2, 110
    planning, 135–7, 138
    provision by NGOs, 139, 143, 147, 149–50,
severity of disability, 166–7
sexism, 8, 113, 114, 115, 132
Shakespeare, 94, 95, 96, 97, 114
sickle cell disorder, 120
sight impairment, 29, 56, 83, 84, 100, 133
    Blind Pension, 58–9
simultaneous oppression, 8, 114
social justice, 136
    discourse, 41–2
social model of disability, 28, 78, 79, 84–6,
    113, 141, 142, 152
social security, 57–67, 141
    Commission on Social Welfare, 4, 62,
        63–4
    complexity of system, 4, 61, 63, 64–5
    contingencies, 58, 64
    and employment, 65–6, 67
    means-testing, 57, 58, 59, 60, 64, 66, 67,
        88, 162
    and Northern Ireland, 160–2, 165, 168, 169
    payments levels, 4, 62
    payments to carers, 60–1
    social assistance, 57, 58, 64, 67
    social insurance, 57, 58, 59, 60, 61, 64, 65,
        67, 161

social insurance/social assistance mix, 57, 58, 64–5
universal benefits, 57, 64
(*see also* disability benefits, costs of disability)
social welfare (*see* social security)
Spain, 34
special education, 28–32, 33, 34, 35, 36, 37, 41, 42, 44, 173
Special Education Review Committee, 30–2, 35, 36, 38, 42
special needs approach to disability, 3, 70
SPIRASI, 116, 126
Standard Rules of Equalisation of Opportunities for Persons with Disabilities, 25, 54, 71, 104, 105, 117, 118, 143–4, 187–8, 197
statistics, 11, 13, 20,
gaps in, 12, 62, 86, 87, 104, 115–16, 124
labour market, 46–7, 55, 167
and poverty, 157–8, 168
prevalence of disability, 11, 101–2, 125, 130–2, 165, 169
prevalence of intellectual disability, 13, 130–2
maintenance of, 12
and service planning, 87–8, 125, 131–2
on special educational needs, 30
Statistics Board, 11, 12
sterilisation, 101, 171
stigma, 129, 132–3, 136, 140, 149, 157
Supplementary Welfare Allowance, 63
Sweden, 34

terminology, 11, 14, 41, 196
transnational co-operation, 24
transport,
access to, 14, 17, 27, 68, 80, 145, 146, 148
challenges for, 27
and independent living, 78
mixed economy of welfare, 6, 139, 145–52
public sector, 146, 147, 148–9, 163
private sector, 146, 147, 150–1
privatised, 146, 147, 151
NGO sector, 146, 147, 149–50
research on, 146, 154

Travellers, 7, 30, 115, 121, 124, 125, 176
with disabilities, 121, 122, 124
Treaty of Amsterdam, 3, 54, 104, 117, 158, 198
Article 3, 13, 54, 117, 158, 198
triple oppression, 8, 115
typology of models of disability, 141–2, 152

undue hardship, 20, 55
unemployment, 123, 156, 157, 159, 179
United Kingdom,
and ageing population, 129
and built environment, 73
Disability Discrimination Act (1996), 76, 163, 164, 165
disability movement in, 143, 178
Disability Rights Commission, 118
and educational attainment, 156
ethnicity, 118, 120, 126
England, 33
institutionalisation, 102
de-institutionalisation, 103
health expenditure, 107
legislation on abortion , 97
media in, 174
and prevalence of disability, 135, 166, 169
and social inclusion, 159
and welfare to work, 160
UPIAS, 28
United Nations,
and ageing population, 129
and human rights, 3, 25–6, 176, 180, 185–99
and migrant workers, 116
NGO participation, 196, 198–9
and older people, 138
and refugees, 118–19
and torture, 126
UN Roosevelt Award, 179
world conferences, 189–91
(*see also* Standard Rules)
United States,
and accessibility, 80
and ageing population, 129
Americans with Disabilities Act (1990), 54–5, 70–1
and disability rights movement, 69, 143, 180

United States, *cont.*
  and expenditure on disability, 157
  and mental health, 171
  and non-discrimination legislation, 54–5,
    70, 180
  and older people, 134, 135
  and political ideologies, 140
  poverty and disability, 106
universal design, 12, 17, 19, 22, 24, 70, 71

VHI, 89
vocational
  assessment, 24
  rehabilitation, 55
  training, 48
voluntary sector,
  asylum seekers and refugees, 128
  and disability policy, 11,
  exclusion from, 125–6
  and service provision, 29, 83, 90–3, 143,
    149–50

and information provision, 118,
  recognition and respect, 125, 127

welfare to work, 160–1, 162, 163, 169
women,
  with disabilities, 7, 8, 83, 99, 185, 187
    abuse of, 94–5, 106
    domestic violence, 94
    in ethnic minorities, 126
    and employment, 109, 112
    and health care, 93–4, 109
    and reproductive technology, 97
  role of, 142, 143, 175
workplace adjustments, 51, 56
White Paper on Education (1995), 36, 40
White Paper on Social Welfare (1986), 59
World Health Organisation, 97, 102, 104,
    107, 133, 136, 137, 165, 186
World Wide Web (*see* IT)

Zarb, G., 133, 134, 137, 167